A Literary Guide to
PROVENCE

A Literary Guide to
PROVENCE

Daniel Vitaglione

Swallow Press/Ohio University Press
Athens

To my parents, Michel and Yolande

Swallow Press/Ohio University Press, Athens, Ohio 45701
© 2001 by Swallow Press/Ohio University Press
Printed in Canada

Swallow Press/Ohio University Press books
are printed on acid-free paper ⊗ ™

09 08 07 06 05 04 03 02 01   5 4 3 2 1

Photographs are by Daniel Vitaglione unless indicated otherwise.

Frontispiece: Fontaine-de-Vaucluse
Front Cover: Sunflower Field, St-Rémy
Back Cover: Ste-Agnès: Lavender Festival

Library of Congress Cataloging-in-Publication Data

Vitaglione, Daniel, 1949–
    A literary guide to Provence / Daniel Vitaglione.
        p. cm.
    Includes bibliographical references and index.
    ISBN 0-8040-1035-8 (alk. paper) — ISBN 0-8040-1036-6 (pbk. :
 alk. paper)
    1. Provence (France)—Guidebooks. 2. Literary landmarks—France—
Provence—Guidebooks. 3. French literature—France—Provence—
History and criticism. 4. Literature, Modern—History and criticism.
I. Title.

    DC611.P958 V54 2001
    914.4'90484—dc21

                                2001016342

Contents

The High Country and Aix-en-Provence   79

From Marseille to Cannes   137

Provence

Introduction

Yesterday at sunset I was in a stony heath where some very small and twisted oaks grow, in the background a ruin on the hill and corn in the valley. It was romantic, like a Monticelli; the sun was pouring bright yellow rays upon the bushes and the ground, a perfect shower of gold, and all the lines were lovely. You would not have been a bit surprised to see knights and ladies suddenly appear coming back from hunting, or to hear the voice of some old Provençal troubadour.

—Vincent Van Gogh, letter to his brother

This guide offers a writer's view of Provence, a once independent kingdom occupying the southeast corner of France, where for centuries troubadours sang of love. The troubadours wrote in Langue d'Oc or Provençal, a language spoken throughout the entire south of France. The oldest poems to have survived are those of Guillaume d'Aquitaine (1071–1127). René Nelli has recorded 460 names and 2,700 poems of troubadours,[1] but there were certainly more. Among the most famous were Bernard de Ventadour, Peire Vidal, and Arnaut Daniel. Their poetry or *gai saber* (*Gaya Scienza*) encompassed an ethics of love, or *Fin'Amor*. Troubadours came from all social classes. Some were noble, others merchants. Of women troubadours, or *trobairitz*, the most famous is perhaps the Princesse de Die. Troubadour poems were sung to newly composed or borrowed tunes and accompanied by the viol. While some troubadours set their poems to music and sang their compositions themselves, others had "joglars" sing for them. The poetry of the troubadours included *cansos* or lyrical poems, in which the poet sang his love to his lady; *dansas* or dance songs; *planhs* (or *plang*) or funeral complaints; *sirventes* or satirical and political pieces; and *tensos* or dialogues. There were also epic poems, of which only two have survived. In Provence, historians have recorded forty-eight troubadours, including Raimbaut d'Orange, Raimbaut de Vacqueyras, Folquet de Marseille, Guillaume des Baux, and the Princesse de Die, but only a few of their poems are known.

Petrarch first saw beautiful Laura in Avignon in 1327 and settled in Fontaine-de-Vaucluse, a country retreat at the source of the Sorgue River where he wrote most of his poetry. Despite its annexation by France in 1481, Provence continued to speak Provençal. French made slow progress among the Provençal people, and for centuries it remained the language of the administration and the upper classes. In the late seventeenth century, Mme de Sévigné often made the three-week journey from Paris to visit her daughter in Grignan. At that time the Provençals continued to write plays, tales, and poems in the vernacular, but by the 1850s the French language had become a serious competitor. Joseph Roumanille and Frédéric Mistral organized a renaissance movement, the Félibrige, and encouraged other writers to compose in Provençal. Théodore Aubanel, Marie d'Arbaud, and Rose Roumanille were among the many writers who joined the félibres.

In the mid-nineteenth century Avignon was an active literary center, and the cafés of the Place de l'Horloge had become the rallying point of Provençal poets who considered themselves the true descendants of the ancient troubadours. Mistral's house in his native Maillane is a delightful visit, and Mistral, Daudet, Roumanille, and Aubanel often visited the town of Les Baux to dine and recite poetry in the ruins of its castle. It was there in 1919 that the English painter and art critic Roger Fry, following in Cézanne's footsteps, met Marie Mauron, a young schoolteacher, and that a long friendship was born. Fry introduced her to his Bloomsbury friends including Virginia Woolf, and Marie and her husband, Charles, became their official translators. It is thanks to Fry that Marie began writing novels. St-Rémy is the birthplace of

Michel de Notredame, better known as Nostradamus, the illustrious astrologer whose prophecies still fascinate and puzzle modern scholars. After traveling in Europe for a number of years he finally settled in Salon, where he practiced medicine and astrology. A tour of his house in town is a must. Daudet's famous windmill lies a couple of miles to the southeast in Fontvieille. It still stands on the top of the little hill from which you can see Arles in the distance. The scenery has not changed much. The little pathway through the pine forest leads to the castle of Montauban where he used to stay. Arles fascinated Flaubert and later Willa Cather. Van Gogh settled there. Mistral, Aubanel, Roumanille, and Alphonse Tavan often went there to eat eel stew, sit on café terraces to watch the beautiful Arlésiennes, and recline among the old sarcophagi of the Alyscamps, reciting poetry. Tarascon on the Rhône was made famous by Daudet's novel *Tartarin*, and in Beaucaire young Antoinette Rivière wrote poems in Provençal. The Camargue, a vast marshland inhabited by wildlife and *gardians*, or bull herders, attracted writers such as Folco de Baroncelli, Joseph d'Arbaud, and Henri Bosco and inspired their poems, tales, and novels.

The Luberon mountain and northern Provence contrast with the rich alluvial plain. In Lacoste lived the Marquis de Sade, who belonged to an old and noble Provençal family. Today the ruins of his castle still stand. He never actually wrote there but had plays performed in his little theater. It is near there that English writer Peter Mayle bought a house in the 1980s and began writing about his adventures and local customs. But before him, during World War II, a young Irishman and Resistance member known as Sam (Samuel Beckett) took refuge in the small village of Roussillon, famous for its ochre quarries. The Luberon and especially the village of Lourmarin fascinated Bosco and inspired several of his novels. Albert Camus came there, invited by Bosco, and bought a house. Both writers are buried in the small cemetery.

Farther east and north is the land of Jean Giono and Pierre Magnan, natives of Manosque. Giono was fascinated by the small villages of the Alps above Manosque, and Magnan described those of the valley, such as Forcalquier, Peyruis, and Digne. Sisteron was the birthplace of Paul Arène, friend of Daudet and author of several tales.

Aix is a college town where Mistral, Aubanel, Arène, and Mauron studied. Writer Louise Colet was born there, as was the Marquis of Vauvenargues. Aix was also where Emile Zola struck up a friendship with Paul Cézanne. Mont Ste-Victoire, later immortalized by Cézanne, and the little Infernet River were their favorite hunting and fishing grounds.

Marseille can boast a rich literary past. From the troubadour Folquet to Edmond Rostand and Marcel Pagnol, Marseillais have always written in Provençal or in French. Its colorful harbor fascinated many French and Provençal writers such as Daudet, Flaubert, and Bosco and also Robert Louis Stevenson. Two other notable authors are Katherine Mansfield and a young woman who taught philosophy there in 1929: Simone de Beauvoir. Cassis, celebrated by Mistral, was a favorite place of Virginia Woolf, who in the 1920s thought about buying a house there. It was in Cassis that the idea for *The Waves* was born. Mansfield also resided in Bandol, at the Hôtel Beau Rivage and the Villa Pauline. Actor Raimu had his summer residence there. Toulon was his native town as well as that of Jean Aicard, author of *Maurin des Maures*. Stevenson and Edith Wharton chose to reside in Hyères, whereas Colette preferred St-Tropez. F. Scott Fitzgerald composed *Tender Is the Night* in St-Raphaël and Juan-les-Pins. Chekhov often came to Nice, and Eze inspired Nietzsche. Nice occupied a favored place in the novels of Louis Nucéra and haunts those of Jean-Marie Le Clézio, also a native of the city. Poet Jean Cocteau loved the Mediterranean and finally settled in Villefranche and Cap Ferrat. W. B. Yeats died in Roquebrune-Cap-Martin, where he was spending the winter. Poet Marcel Firpo wrote poems in Provençal about his hometown Menton. Mansfield loved the place and settled there in 1920.

I hope this book will succeed in enticing readers to follow in the writers' footsteps and discover Provence.

Provence at a Glance

Provence at a glance

Geographic Generalities

Provence is a region located in the eastern part of the Midi or south of France. It comprises three distinct geographic areas. The Alps in the north cover half the land. Several of the peaks rise above ten thousand feet. The winters are cold and long, and temperatures of 20°F and lower are not uncommon. For centuries, communication between valleys was difficult, and the inhabitants of these regions lived in isolation. In the west and south the rich alluvial plain of the Rhône River separates Provence from Languedoc. The countryside is dotted with orchards, vineyards, fields, and market towns. The third geographic section of Provence is the rugged coast from Grau-du-Roi to Menton. The Mediterranean Sea varies in color along the coast from deep blue to emerald green. Warmer than the Atlantic and almost without tides, the Mediterranean soothes the rigor of the winters and allows the cultivation of tropical plants and fruits, including lemons, oranges, and bananas. Villages and cities on the coast lived by fishing until tourism changed their economic destiny at the end of nineteenth century.

Provençal skies are generally sunny and crystal clear, especially when the *mistral* or cold northern wind blows. The air is dry. Summer temperatures vary depending on the area. In the valleys they can reach 95°F. On the coast they are generally five to seven degrees cooler.

History in Brief

The cave of Vallonet (Roquebrune) is the most ancient archeological site in Europe. Stone tools, broken animal bones, and the vestiges of a fire show that the cave was inhabited about one million years ago. Other discoveries such as Terra Amata in Nice (400,000 years old) confirm the presence of humans in prehistoric times in Provence. The earliest peoples known to have inhabited the area were the Ligurians (900 B.C.) and then the Celts (700 B.C.). The Greeks founded Marseille in 600 B.C., and the Romans invaded the area in 125 B.C., settling there for the next five centuries. Provençal language, laws, and customs have deep roots in Latin culture.

In the fifth and the sixth centuries Provence was invaded by Visigoths and Franks. The Treaty of Verdun in 843 granted Charles the Great's grandson, Lothaire I, the kingdoms of Burgundy and Provence, which passed into the hands of his son Charles in 855. In the eighth century the Arabs had raided Provence and settled on the coast in the mountains near St-Tropez. They were finally defeated and driven out in 972.

From 1125 to 1246 Provence was the object of a fierce battle between the counts of Toulouse and the kings of Catalonia. At that time, a new religion spread in the southwest around the town of Carcassonne. Its disciples, the Cathars (from the Greek "Catharsis" or purification), preached a return to simplicity and believed in the coexistence of Good and Evil, a doctrine probably influenced by the followers of Zoroaster. In 1136, Pope Alexander III declared the Cathars heretics, and a long persecution began. French King Philippe Auguste joined forces with the pope and waged a bloody war against the entire southwest. The South was ransacked, and in 1244 the Cathars were finally defeated at Montségur. Under pressure from France, Berenger V, count of Provence, married his elder daughter, Marguerite, to King Louis IX of France in 1234 and his younger daughter, Béatrice, to Charles I of Anjou, the king's brother, who became the count of Provence. Charles III, the last descendant of the Anjou branch, bequeathed Provence to King Louis XI of France in 1481.

After the French revolution of 1789 Provence was divided into administrative units or *départements*, which today include Alpes-de-Haute-Provence (capital: Digne-les-Bains), Alpes-Maritimes (Nice), Bouches-du-Rhône (Marseille), Hautes-Alpes (Gap), Var (Tou-lon), and Vaucluse (Avignon).

Language and Culture

French is the main language of Provence, but Provençal subsists in remote villages and among the older population. Provençal is a language that evolved from Latin. In medieval times it was spoken throughout the entire South and was the language of culture and literature—the Langue d'Oc of the troubadours. It was then called Provençal, but nowadays the term Provençal refers only to the language and culture of Provence. The Southwest speaks what is now called Occitan. Provençal is not a dialect of French; it does not sound like French and is not comprehensible if you have not studied it. During the twentieth century Provençal incorporated many French words, but Catalans and Italians are still better able to understand it. There are various dialects, including Rhodanien (west), Gavot (north), and Nissart and Mentonnais (east). The farther one village is from another, the more significant are the linguistic differences. Provençal was still widely spoken before World War II, especially inland and in the rural communities. In the 1970s, it was introduced into the school system as an elective. There are few who use it as a first language, but many who understand it.

The Provençals are proud of their language, culture, and local pronunciation of French. For them the North starts a couple of miles above Orange. Traditionally they are talkative and hospitable, with a good sense of humor. There is a definite nonchalance about Southerners that is often mistaken for laziness.

Practical Information for Travelers

Best Time to Visit. Those who do not mind the crowds can travel to Provence in July and August. However, June and early September are also wonderful months for a visit, much quieter and less hot. In the winter many hotels are closed.

Tourist Information. Each town has a tourist information center that hands out free maps of the towns and brochures about hotels, restaurants, museums, special events, and other entertainment options. It is a good idea to stop by first, before visiting the town. Websites included in this guide enable you to obtain more specific details or a complete list of hotels and restaurants or the local festivals.

Hotels. For each town worth a visit, this guide suggests a few hotels. A list can be obtained through the local tourist office. Breakfast is often continental, but more and more hotels are offering it buffet style during the high season. The number of stars indicates the quality, five (very rare) being the highest category. Prices vary depending on the season and the place: high season is July and August; Cannes and St-Tropez are more expensive than Manosque or Orange. Four-star hotels start at about $200 for a double room, three-star hotels at about $75, and two-star at roughly $45. Some chain hotels such as Novotel do not charge for children, provided they stay in the same room as their parents. The lists in this guide are not exhaustive but include detailed information such as phone and fax numbers, email and Web addresses, and the availability of air conditioning (AC), pool, and parking or garage.

Restaurants. Even the smallest village has at least one restaurant. Dinner is rarely served before 7:30. Menus with prices are always posted at the entrance. The minimum for a three-course meal is about $16 without wine or alcoholic beverages. Children's menus are about $7. The tip is included in the bill.

This guide lists only gourmet restaurants or those offering local specialties. Price varies according to the number of stars. Unlike the rating scheme for hotels, one Michelin star* for a restaurant indicates very good cuisine, two stars means excellent, and three stars is the top. The lack of a star certainly does not mean that the cuisine is bad but simply that the restaurant is not one of the few that have been selected. The quality and speed of service will depend on the number of people in the restaurant and the mood of the waiter or of the cook, but on the whole, in a French restaurant, the chef is king. To get the quickest service, the rule is first come, first served—so come at 7:30. In Provence, as elsewhere in France, the doggie bag custom is totally unknown.

Most but not all restaurants have a nonsmoking section. Provence also has fast food places such as McDonald's.

Museums. Museums generally charge a fee (from $3 to $5). A discount is possible for students. Most museums close between 12:30 and 2:30, and all day on Tuesday. Some are always free, others only on Sundays. For museum enthusiasts, a pass is sometimes available, but often with a regional or time limit. Inquire at the entrance.

Telephone and Fax. From abroad dial 33 (France) and then the local number without the 0. From France dial the number without 33 but with the 0.

Transportation:

Airports. Marseille-Marignane is thirty minutes from the center. Nice is an international airport, and Delta Airlines has direct flights from New York to Nice. The airport is twenty minutes from the center.

Trains. Trains will get you most places, but a good measure of patience is necessary, for they are often late, and strikes are common. A Eurailpass is often a good deal, but it must be purchased in the United States prior to departure. Several versions are available.

Car Travel. Travel by car is the most convenient. Cars are available for rent at the airports (Marseille, Nice). Leasing a car from the United States is also a good and cheaper solution. Standard shift cars are still the rule, although more automatics are becoming available. Gasoline is more expensive than in the United States, but French cars get better gas mileage (forty to fifty miles per gallon). Diesel fuel is cheaper, and diesel cars are often an option. Contrary to what is commonly believed, driving in France presents no problem.

Roads and Tollroads. Roads are generally good. The N roads or "nationales" are larger but have more traffic. D roads or "départementales" are smaller and quieter. Freeways are tollroads and more expensive than in the United States. The speed limit on the tollway is 130 km per hour or 81 mph.

Maps. This guide includes several maps but does not replace a detailed road map of Provence, available at any service station.

Parking. Difficult in the town centers. On a street you must pay a meter. Parking lots are usually underground. When you enter, push the button, get a card, and then park. You pay at a machine before you take your car. (Insert your card and pay the required amount. Have change ready. Some machines accept a credit card payment.)

Bicycles. Western Provence is flat and ideal for biking. Bikers should use small, quiet D roads and avoid the N or national roads, where traffic is heavy.

Main Festivals

In the summer months (July and August) just about every other town has its own music, theater, or dance festival. They last from a couple of days to several weeks. However, Provençal celebrations take place over the entire year. Most include traditional dance, music, and costumes. The exact days may vary from year to year and are often chosen only a few weeks in advance. Following is a list of the most important festivals, with approximate dates:

JANUARY

Middle of the month: Festival of St-Marcel, Barjols.

FEBRUARY

First Sunday: Olive Festival, Nyons.

Middle of the month, lasting three weeks: Carnival (Mardi Gras), Nice. Lemon Festival, Menton.

Third Sunday: Corso du Mimosa (mimosa parade), Bormes, near Le Lavandou.

MARCH

End of the month: Flower Festival, Hyères.

Last Sunday: Festin des Cougourdons (small pumpkins feast), Nice-Cimiez

MAY

1: Fête des Gardians (bull herders festival), Arles.

16–18: Bravade (folk festival), St-Tropez.

23–24: Religious Festival, Stes-Maries-de-la-Mer.

Two weeks mid-May: International Film Festival, Cannes.

JUNE

Mid-June: Fête Votive (religious festival), Stes-Maries-de-la-Mer. Snail-lantern ceremony in Gorbio (near Menton) and Eze (near Nice). Medieval Festival, Manosque (three days).

Last weekend: Fête de la Tarasque, Tarascon (three days).

24 through July 2: Arles Festival—Pegoulado (night parade with traditional costumes) and bull races.

JULY

First Saturday: Venetian Festival, Martigues.

First weekend: Festival of St-Eloi, Châteaurenard. Lavender Festival, Valréas.

First week: Nostradamiques (Nostradamus Days), Salon.

6–31: Opera and classical music, Aix. Chorégies d'Orange (opera). Nuits de la Citadelle, Sisteron.

Mid-July: Jazz Festival, Juan-les-Pins (ten days).

Mid-July: Lavender Festival, Valensole. Feria (bull races, parade with costumes), Stes-Maries-de-la-Mer.

Third week: Provençal Festival, Annot.

End of the month: Medieval Festival, Eze. Giono Days,
    Manosque. Festival of Sainte-Baume, in the village.

30: Festival of the Virgin (Festo Vierginenço), Stes-Maries-
    de-la-Mer.

AUGUST

First week: Lavender Festival, Digne.

First Sunday: Grape Festival, Fréjus.

First two weeks: Theater Festival, Ramatuelle, near St-Tropez
    (ten days). Festival of St-Laurent, Eze.

15: Fishermen Festival, Bendor, near Toulon. Provençal bull races, St-Rémy.

Third weekend: Provençal Festival, Séguret. Lavender Festival, Ste-Agnès, near Menton.

SEPTEMBER

First week: Rice Festival, Arles. Diane Festival, Moustiers.

Middle of the month: Olive Festival, Mouriès, near Arles.

End of the month: Festival of St-Michel, Marseille; takes place in the 9th and 10th districts or *arrondissements.*

OCTOBER

First weekend: Olive Festival, Ollioules, near Toulon.

Middle of the month: Provençal cuisine and products, Mouriès.

23: Chestnut Festival, La Garde Freinet, near St-Tropez.

NOVEMBER

Second week: Gastronomic Days (Les Journées Gourmandes), five days including a weekend, featuring local produce and southern cuisine, Vaison-la-Romaine.

Last week: International Dance Festival, Cannes.

DECEMBER

Dance Festival, Aix.

First Sunday: Wine Festival, Bandol.

Second weekend: Shepherds Festival, Istres.

24: Provençal mass, Lucéram (near Nice), Allauch (near Marseille), Les Baux, Arles, St-Rémy, Stes-Maries-de-la-Mer, Tarascon.

Western Provence

You will see this devil of a country where the sun transforms everything and makes everything bigger than nature.

—Alphonse Daudet, *Tartarin de Tarascon*

Avignon

Around Avignon: Pont du Gard, Orange

Vaison-la-Romaine and Mont Ventoux

Valréas, Grignan

Carpentras, L'Isle-sur-la-Sorgue,
Fontaine-de-Vaucluse, Saumane

Maillane

Tarascon

St-Rémy, Salon

Les Baux

Fontvieille

Arles

The Camargue, Stes-Maries-de-la-Mer

Grignan D941

Valréas

D975

Vaison-la-Romaine

Mont Ventaux

Malaucène

Orange

D950

Carpentras

D942

Pont-du-Gard

Avignon

Isle-sur-la-Sorgue

Saumane

Fontaine-de-Vaucluse

Grand Rhône

Frigolet

Maillane

Beaucaire

D571

Cavaillon

Tarascon

St-Rémy

D99

A9

Durance

Les Baux

N570

Fontvieille

Montmajour

A54

Arles

A54

Salon

A7

Mediterranean Sea

Western Provence

Avignon

"Arriving in Avignon with a beautiful autumn sunset is a wonderful sight," noted Victor Hugo in 1839.[1] He had sailed down the Rhône from Lyons and stopped in Avignon for a couple of days. Hugo liked the city and its rich cultural past but he had trouble making himself understood with the Provençal porters who did not speak French. Fall is indeed a good season to visit Avignon, for the summer haze has cleared and you often have a very good view of Mont Ventoux in the distance and Villeneuve's castle on the other side of the river. Here, as in Florence, the highest buildings are the churches. Fortifications have survived the centuries and still surround the old town. Greeks and Romans lived there peacefully. "The nights in Avignon already contain a hint of the Greek and Italian skies," remarked Hugo, praising the warm and mild air.[2]

An old manuscript in the local archives relates the history of Avignon's Bénézet bridge, the "Pont d'Avignon" celebrated in the familiar song. In 1177, a young shepherd named Bénézet, a native of Burzet in the Ardèche region on the western bank of the Rhône, heard voices that told him to go to Avignon and build a bridge. Bénézet had never been to Avignon and knew nothing about building bridges, but the voices promised to help him. An angel disguised as a pilgrim showed him the way to Avignon. Bénézet crossed the Rhône on a boat and met with the bishop and other city officials. The men laughed at him and challenged him to lift a heavy stone, one that even thirty men could not budge. Bénézet accepted and, to everyone's surprise, managed to lift the stone and throw it into the river. The bishop promised to support

St-Bénézet Bridge

him, and Bénézet canvassed the town for money and men to help build the bridge. Construction took eight years; the bridge was completed in 1185. About nine hundred yards long, consisting of twenty-two arches, it linked Avignon to Villeneuve and was the first bridge over the Rhône. However, it was narrow and allowed only pedestrians, horses, and small carriages. Over the centuries numerous floods slowly tore it down. But the inhabitants loved their bridge and each time they restored it, until 1690 when they finally gave up. Frédéric Mistral's *Lou pouèmo dóu Rose* (The song of the Rhône, 1897) paid tribute to the mighty river. In his day (1830–1914) hundreds of ships still sailed up and down its turbulent waters and *lavandières* washed their clothes on its sun-parched banks.

Avignon has always been a hub of activity. Early in the thirteenth century the city sided with the Cathars (see "Provence at a Glance"). Louis VIII of France retaliated and laid siege to the city in 1226. After three months Avignon capitulated and had to tear down its fortifications. In 1229, King Louis IX forced Raymond VII, count of Toulouse, to sell Carpentras and some land around it to the papacy. It included about

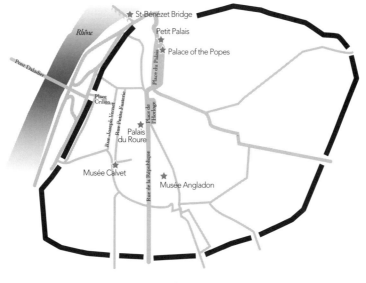

Avignon

sixty castles and the towns of Vaison and Cavaillon and became known as the Comtat Venaissin after the town of Venasque, site of the first diocese. In 1274, King Philippe IV of France, eager to reaffirm his authority over the papacy, encouraged the popes to leave Rome, where they were prey to political troubles, and to take possession of their new land. After the death of Pope Benoist XI in Perugia (1304), Philippe IV, archbishop of Bordeaux, became Pope Clément V (1305). In 1309, Pope Clément V settled in Avignon, which still belonged to Charles II of Provence, moving into the Dominican convent. His successor, Benoist XII, built the Old Palace (Palais Vieux, 1334–42) and Clément VI the New Palace (Palais Neuf, 1342–52). During the residence of the popes in Avignon, churches sprang up (St-Dider, St-Agricol, St-Pierre), and religious orders flocked to the city, which quickly grew into a large religious and cultural capital. The university, founded in 1303, originally consisted of two faculties, Arts and Canon Law. Theology was added in 1413. Art flourished. Flemish tapestry makers, French and Italian goldsmiths, cabinetmakers, sculptors, and Italian painters (among them Simone Martini) worked for the popes, cardinals, and rich

Palace of the Popes

ambassadors. The city also attracted astronomers, musicians, and poets. Conferences were held during the festivals, as well as balls, theatrical events, and banquets. The library counted over two thousand volumes and was richer than that of the king of France.

The population of the town grew from from 5,000 in 1309 to 30,000 in 1370, and the walls that surrounded the town were torn down and replaced. Over the years, the popes extended their territory, acquiring the towns Valréas (1317), Visan (1318), Richerenches (1320), and Grillon (1348) some twenty miles to the north. They reorganized the university and finally, in 1348, Clément VI bought the city of Avignon from Jeanne de Provence. In 1376, Pope Gregory XI returned to Rome and died there the following year. Urban VI was the new Italian pope, but Avignon elected another pope, Clement VII. The ensuing Great Schism divided partisans of the Avignon pope and those of Urban VI. Castille and Scotland took the side of Avignon, while England, Germany, and Scandinavia followed Rome. The schism finally came to an end after the death of Boniface IX of Avignon in 1404 and the election in Rome of Martin V in 1417. Avignon was not abandoned by the papacy, however. The pope delegated his powers to a legate there until 1791.

On April 6, 1327, in the church of Saint Claire, Francesco Petrarca (1304–1374) first set eyes on the love of his life. Her locks of beautiful golden hair flowed down her back. Her eyes with long ebony lashes were ravishing. Her face was as white as snow but without its coldness. She walked as softly as an angel and her voice sounded otherworldly, Petrarch remembered. As far as he was concerned, it was love at first sight. The identity of this woman has never been established with certainty, and some scholars even argue that she never existed. However, a long tradition holds that she was Laure de Noves, twenty years old but married to Hugues de Sade, a nobleman and ancestor of the infamous marquis. Petrarch, twenty-three years old, was Italian by birth but had lived in Provence for fifteen years. His family resided in Carpentras, the capital of the Comtat, while his father worked for the pope in Avignon. Petrarch had studied law in Montpellier and then in Bologna; after his father's death in 1326, he returned to Avignon and worked as a clerk.

The city was not only an important religious and cultural center but also a booming town. "He who has not seen Avignon at the time of the Popes has not seen anything," writes Alphonse Daudet (1840–1897) in his tale "La mule du Pape" (The pope's mule).[3] Based on what he had seen of the city during his wanderings there, Daudet readily imagined what life was like in the fourteenth century: "From morning to evening, there were processions, pilgrimages, the streets were covered with flowers . . . cardinals arrived on the Rhône . . . and the Pope's soldiers sang in Latin in the marketplaces." Clerks, cobblers, weavers, seamstresses, sculptors, musicians, and many other artists, craftspeople, and manual laborers worked in the entourage of the pope; festivals were numerous in Avignon for, as Daudet justly remarks, "in our country when the people are happy they must dance, and since in those days the streets of the town were too narrow for the farandole, fifes and tambourines were played on the bridge in the cool breeze of the Rhône and day and night there was dancing, dancing . . . Oh happy times! Happy town!" Mistral's *Nerto* takes place in Avignon during the troubled times in 1388 when partisans of the Roman pope besieged the palace. Nerto is a beautiful blond-haired woman from Châteaurenard whose father sold her soul to the devil for a few ounces of gold to pay his gambling debts.

During the Revolution of 1789 Avignon took the side of the king and was then divided between partisans of the papacy and those who advocated return to France. On September 14, 1791, France annexed the city. Life in Avignon proceeded at a slow pace, quite unperturbed. Like elsewhere in Provence, the people still spoke Provençal but, by the 1850s, French had made inroads, especially among members of the upper class. Mistral attended school there, first at the Pensionnat Millet (1841–45), then at the Pensionnat Dupuy. He came from the small village of Maillane, a few miles south, where Provençal was still the vernacular, and was shocked to learn that in the schools students were forbidden to communicate in his beloved language, even during recess. Fortunately, at the Pensionnat Dupuy Mistral befriended the young tutor Joseph Roumanille. Although Roumanille (1818–1891) was twelve years older than Mistral, they felt a deep affinity. Roumanille was born in St-Rémy, four miles from Maillane, and his family knew the Mistrals. Roumanille shared Mistral's love of Provençal and introduced him to the works of authors such as Jacques Boé (1798–1864), known as Jasmin, who had written poems and songs (*Françouneto*, 1840) and had been received in Parisian salons. In Nyons, a small town in upper Provence where he had taught for two years, Roumanille had actively participated in the literary meetings of Provençalists Camille Reybaud, Eugène Lisbonne, and Barthélemy Chalvet. He had published poems written in Provençal in *Lou tambourinaire et le ménestrel* (The drummer and the minstrel, March–November 1841), a Provençal and French weekly review edited in Marseille by Pierre Bellot and Louis Méry. He also contributed to Joseph Désenat's *Lou bouil-abaïsso* (The bouilla-baisse, 1841–46), edited in Marseille but written only in Provençal and in verse. "Touti dous abrasa dóu desir de sourgi lou parla de nosti maire, estudieran ensèn li viéi libre prouvençau, e 'm'aco nous diguerian de restaura la lengo segound si tradicioun e entresigne naciounau" (Burning with the desire to rehabilitate our mother tongue, we studied the old Provençal books together and decided to restore the language according to its traditions and national characteristics), says Mistral in

Joseph Roumanille, photo: Palais du Roure, Avignon

Lis Isclo d'Or (The Golden Isles, 1876).[4] Anselme Mathieu (1828–1896), a classmate from Châteauneuf-du-Pape, joined Mistral and Roumanille in their efforts. Roumanille later published some of Mathieu's poems in *Li Prouvençalo* (1852).

In 1847, Mistral left Avignon to study law in Aix, but he kept in touch with Roumanille and Mathieu. In 1853, Jean-Baptiste Gaut published a collection of poems in Provençal entitled *Roumavagi deis Troubaires* (The troubadours' pilgrimage). Mistral was one of the contributors. In his preface, Gaut proudly declared: "Provençal is not dead; the Troubadours live on."[5]

Roumanille worked in Avignon as a proofreader for the publisher Seguin and continued to write poems, which appeared in collections

Frédéric Mistral, photo: Palais du Roure, Avignon

such as *Li margarideto* (The daisies, 1847) and *Li Prouvençalo*. He also met Théodore Aubanel (1829–1886). Born in Avignon to an illustrious family of publishers, Aubanel studied law in Aix and then returned home to work in the family business. Like Roumanille, he spoke Provençal fluently. Aubanel, Roumanille, and Mistral regularly met at the home of Paul and Jules Giéra, rue de la Banasterie, or in their summer residence of Font-Ségugne on the road to L'Isle-sur-la-Sorgue. Also present at these meetings were Alphonse Tavan (1833–1905), Jean Brunet (1822–1894), Antoine Crousillat (1814–1899) from Salon, and Eugène Garcin (1831–1901). The group called themselves *félibres* (or *felibres*, in the Provençal spelling), a term that Mistral had heard used by Marthe Vare, an elderly Provençal woman of Maillane, when she told tales of the past to other women during the olive harvest. The story was in Provençal and in verse. All women seemed to know it. Vare used it in reference to a vision of Saint Anselm in which the Virgin Mary explained to her son the seven pains that she had suffered for him, the fourth being when he went to the temple to talk to "li sèt felibre de la Lèi." Mistral did not know what the term "felibre" meant and interpreted the phrase as "doctors of the Law." In his Provençal dictionary, *Lou tresor dóu Félibrige* (1886), Mistral confirms the mysterious origin of the term and mentions seven etymological attempts to explain its origin by scholars who linked the term to the Germanic, Gaelic, Greek, or Hebrew languages. Mistral favored a Latin derivation (*fellebris:* nursling). According to him, the poet is the one who is nursed by the Muse. The *felibre*, or *felibresso* if a woman, is a modern troubadour. The Provençal tongue became identified with the mother who fed the felibres, her children. This is probably the true origin of the term, although it is by no means accepted by all Provençal scholars.

In his memoirs, *Memòri e raconte* (1906), written at the age of seventy-six, Mistral says that the historic meeting took place in Font-Ségugne on a beautiful Sunday, May 21, 1854. According to the account in his memoirs, the original founding members were seven: Théodore Aubanel, Jean Brunet, Paul Giéra, Anselme Mathieu, Joseph Roumanille, Alphonse Tavan, and himself. But Provençal scholars contest this number and argue that it too strangely coincides with the number of the Virgin Mary's sufferings in the legend. Claude Mauron, professor at the University of Provence, has shown that Mathieu and Brunet were not present and believes that they were added later to the core group consisting of Mistral, Roumanille, Aubanel, Giéra, and Tavan.[6] Santo Estello, whose saint's day is celebrated on May 21, became the félibres' patron saint, and a seven-point star was chosen as their sign. The goal of the *Félibrige* movement was to defend Provençal language and traditions.

Mistral codified the Provençal language on the basis of his Rhodanien dialect. Other areas such as Marseille, Nice, and Menton have different spellings adapted to their own pronunciation. In 1855, Mistral and Aubanel launched a yearly review, *L'armana prouvençau* (The Provençal almanac), written only in Provençal. The first three reviews

Théodore Aubanel, photo: Editions Aubanel, Avignon

were published by Aubanel, but after some disagreements, Roumanille, who had opened his own publishing house in rue St-Agricol in 1855, took over. In 1858 the almanac sold about two thousand copies. Following the immense success of Mistral's poem *Mirèio* (1859), published in Avignon by Roumanille, the movement developed rapidly, and many other talented poets rallied to its cause, including several women such as Reine Garde, Rose-Anaïs Roumanille (the poet's wife), Marie d'Arbaud, Hortense Rolland, Antoinette Rivière from Beaucaire, and Lazarine Nègre from Manosque. As the number of participants grew, the félibres organized themselves with a chief or *capoulié*. Later, in 1885, Mistral founded *La revue félibréenne*, edited by Paul Mariéton, and in 1891, *L'aiòli*.

Rose-Anaïs
Roumanille,
photo: Delgado,
Museon Arlaten

Marie d'Arbaud,
photo: Delgado,
Museon Arlaten

It was during one of the early meetings at the Giéras' that Aubanel met and fell in love with Jeanne-Marie Manivet, otherwise known as Zani. She was four years older and a good friend of Josephine Giéra. With her large brown eyes and dark hair, beautiful Zani won the hearts of many a poet, including Roumanille, for whom she was the "fairy who transformed the troubadours' hearts." The bright red dress she wore the day Aubanel met her in 1850 inspired his famous poem "La mióugrano entre-duberto" (The half-open pomegranate, 1860). The intense, obvious sensuality of the poem scandalized the Catholic press. However, in 1854 Zani joined a convent and, in 1861, Aubanel married Josephine Marzen. Aubanel wrote poems (*Li fiho d'Avignoun*, The girls of Avignon) and plays such as *Lou pan dóu pecat* (The bread of sin). Roumanille became a publisher in his turn, and his bookshop in rue St-Agricol became one of the rallying points of the group. He continued to write poems, including *Lis oubreto* (Small works, 1859), and *Li conte prouvençau* (Provençal tales, 1893). The félibres, despite their shared love of Provençal and the poetry of the troubadours, were not always in agreement on the goal and methods of their movement. Roumanille wrote only in Provençal and did not care to be read or praised by the French press, unlike Mistral and Aubanel, who preferred to add French translations to their poems.

In 1859 an Irish traveler by the name of William Bonaparte-Wyse was wandering the streets of Avignon and entered Roumanille's bookshop. Browsing its shelves, he discovered Mistral's *Mirèio* and other Provençal authors and was enthralled. He asked to meet Mistral. Wyse was thirty-five years old and his maternal grandfather was Lucien Bonaparte, the French emperor's brother. He and Mistral struck up a friendship. Over the years, Wyse came to be accepted as a félibre, for he learned Provençal and even managed to write poems such as *Li parpaioun blu* (The blue butterflies, 1868) and *Li piado de la Princesso* (The Princess's footsteps, 1882). Wyse participated in the poets' meetings and festivals. He died in Cannes in 1892.

Among Avignon's famous literary visitors were Prosper Mérimée (1803–1870), who often came to see his friend, the naturalist Esprit Requien, and symbolist poet Stéphane Mallarmé (1842–1898), who first came in July 1864 and met Aubanel and Mistral. Mallarmé then taught at the lycée from 1868 to 1871 and renewed his contact with the félibres. John Stuart Mill died in Avignon in 1873 in a small cottage on the route du Pont-des-Deux-Eaux.

Folco de Baroncelli-Javon (1869–1943) was born in Aix-en-Provence but grew up in the family home in Avignon, the Hôtel du Roure. The Baroncellis descended from a Florentine family who had settled in Avignon in the sixteenth century. Baroncelli was educated in Avignon and then attended the Lycée in Nîmes, where his mother was from. He was a good student and enjoyed reading the classics, especially Homer and Virgil. Like his classmates, Baroncelli found the corrida and bulls fascinating. During the summer holidays he lived on his grandmother's estate of Bellecote near Nîmes and learned to speak Provençal from her. After graduation Baroncelli returned to Avignon and worked for the tax administration. But Baroncelli loved poetry and befriended the félibres who were frequent guests of his parents. In 1891, the Hôtel du Roure became the headquarters of *L'aïoli*, the Provençal review launched that year by Mistral and edited by Baroncelli. Like its predecessor, the *Bouil-abaïsso*, the new review was named after a Provençal dish in which *aï*, or garlic, is the salient ingredient. Baroncelli wrote short stories (*Babali*, 1889) and poems such as *Blad de luno* (Moon wheat, 1910). His cousin, writer Joseph d'Arbaud, attended the Saint Joseph school in Avignon from 1884 to 1893. Later, he and Baroncelli frequented the Café de Paris, one of the félibres' favorite meeting places. The Hôtel du Roure is now the Palais du Roure, a museum of Provençal culture.

Avignon is also the city where Henri Bosco was born in 1888, at 3 rue Carreterie. His father, a tenor, had moved there from Marseille and taught at the Music Conservatory. However, because of Henri's fragile health, when he was three, his parents moved to Le Mas du Gage in the country, a couple of miles south. "You could see meadows with very thick grass, thick hawthorn hedges, a few farms and, in the summer, golden stacks. Beautiful tender-wood poplars divided the meadows and a wall of very old cypresses often protected a field or a house from the wind," he recalls in *Antonin* (1952).[7] At the age of ten,

Bosco became a boarder at the Ecole des Ortolans in Avignon and then in the lycée. At the same time he studied the violin at the conservatory. He later attended the University of Grenoble, graduated in Italian, the language of his ancestors, and became a teacher. In 1912, he obtained a position in Avignon. Mistral, who lived only a few miles south of his house, had a decisive influence on him. "At the age of fifteen I already admired Mistral as the equal of Homer, and I continue to do so," he was proud to admit.[8] His classics teacher would often take his small class out under the olive trees near Maillane or the Abbey of Frigolet and, after studying the Odyssey or Theocritus, he would point in the direction of the poet's hometown and recite passages from *Mirèio*. As a young man, Bosco went to Maillane and met the famous poet. "I immediately succumbed to his charm. He looked imposing yet friendly. Tall, handsome and serene, a natural joviality made him accessible," he remembered.[9] Other than *Antonin*, Bosco did not set any stories in Avignon. The land there was "too flat" for his taste; he preferred the Luberon mountains in the east.

Among the local writers of Avignon one must also cite Félix Gras (1844–1901) *capoulié* of Félibrige (1891–1901, following Roumanille) and author of Provençal poems and novels such as *Li Papalino* (The pope's partisans, 1891) and *Li Rouge dóu Miejour* (The Reds of the South, 1896). Max-Philippe Delavouët (1920–1990), author of *Lou camin de la crous* (Stations of the cross, 1965) and *Pouèmo* (1983), and Marius Jouveau (1878–1949), *capoulié* (1922–41), historian of the movement, and author of poems such as *En Camargo* (1909) and *La flour au casco* (A flower on the helmet, 1919). Avignon also inspired Henriette Dibon (1902–1989), whose poems include *Li mirage* (1923) and *Li lambusco* (The wild vines, 1934), and Marcelle Drutel (1897–1985), whose sensual poems *Li desiranço* (The desires, 1933) caused some scandal in her day. Finally, music and the theater occupy an important place in the artistic life of Avignon, and its summer festival, created in 1947 by Jean Vilar, attracts a larger audience every year.

Tourist information. 41 cours Jean Jaurès. Tel: 04 32 74 32 74. Fax: 04 90 82 95 03. Email: <information@ot-avignon.fr>.

What to see. Strolling through the old town, the visitor will discover dozens of small boutiques and souvenir shops and local cafés and small ethnic restaurants. The must see is of course the *Palais des Papes:* 25 unfurnished rooms, hallways, bedrooms, kitchens, chapels, and papal apartments; guided tours or audio tours in English are available (Tel: 04 90 85 62 25). Next to the Palace, *Le Petit Palais* contains a remarkable collection of medieval paintings including works of the Avignon School (Tel: 04 90 86 44 58). In the town center, the *Place de l'Horloge* with its cafés and restaurants is the ideal stop for a drink. Nearby is the *Palais du Roure*, 3 rue du Collège du Roure, which displays an important collection of Provençal costumes and furniture; guided visits on Tuesdays at 3:00 and by appointment only (Tel: 04 90 80 80 88). The *Musée Aubanel*, 7 place St-Pierre, is closed for repairs as of this writing. The *Musée Calvet*, 65 rue Joseph Vernet, contains a rich collection of paintings and sculptures from the fifteenth to the twentieth century (Tel: 04 90 85 75 38). The *Musée Angladon*, 5 rue Laboureur, houses an impressive collection of Degas, Cézanne, Picasso, Modigliani, and other renowned painters (Tel: 04 90 82 29 03).

Where to stay. ****: *Mirande*, 4 place de l'Amirande. AC, garage. Tel: 04 90 85 93 93. Fax: 04 90 86 26 85. *Europe*, 12 place Crillon. AC, garage. Tel: 04 90 14 76 76. Fax: 04 90 14 76 71. *Cloître St-Louis*, 20 rue Portail Boquier. Pool, parking. Tel: 04 90 27 55 55. Fax: 04 90 82 24 01. ***: *Mercure Cité des Papes*, 1 rue Vilar, near the palace. Tel: 04 90 86 22 45. Fax: 04 90 27 39 21. *Primotel Horloge*, 1 rue Félicien David. AC. Tel: 04 90 16 42 00. Fax: 04 90 82 17 32. *Novotel*, Nord et Sud. Nord: Tel: 04 90 03 85 00. Sud: Tel: 04 90 87 62 36. AC, pool, parking. **: *Hôtel Blauvac*, 11 rue de la Bancasse. Tel: 04 90 86 34 11. Fax: 04 90 86 27 41. *Danieli*, 11 rue de la République. Tel: 04 90 86 46 82. Fax: 04 90 27 09 24. *Hôtel d'Angleterre*, 29 blvd Raspail. Parking. Tel: 04 90 86 34 31. Fax: 04 90 86 86 74. *Ibis*, 12 blvd St-Dominique. AC. Tel: 04 90 82 00 00. Fax: 04 90 85 67 16.

Where to eat. Hôtel de l'Europe.* Hôtel Mirande.* Isle Sonnante,* 7 rue Racine. *Christian Etienne*, 10 rue de Mons. *Hiély-Lucullus*, 5 rue de la République. *Brunel*, 46 rue de la Balance.

Around Avignon: Pont du Gard, Orange

From Avignon several day trips are possible. You should not miss the Pont du Gard, a Roman aqueduct built in the first century A.D. Take N100 west to Remoulins and then follow the sign for the Pont du Gard. The drive takes about thirty minutes. Orange, in the north, is only thirty minutes from Avignon by freeway. Its Arch of Triumph, built by the Romans around 20 B.C., is well preserved. The town is famous for its summer music festival, Les Chorégies, held in the Roman theater *(plate 1)*, with wonderful acoustics that have remained intact over the centuries. This festival, created in 1869 and dedicated to opera and classical music, takes place in the summer (late June, early July) and lasts from three to four weeks. Orange was the home of Raimbaut, one of the most famous Provençal troubadours, prince of Orange and owner of lands throughout Provence. He was clever, well educated, brave, and wellspoken. "E fos bons trobaires de vers e de chansons; mas mout s'entendeit en far caras rimas e clusas" (He was a good troubadour who wrote poems and songs but especially excelled in rich and obscure rhymes), says the chronicler of the *Vida*.[10] According to tradition, he fell in love with Mary of Verfeuil and then with the countess of Urgel. He left his kingdom to his daughters and grandsons Uc and Guillaume des Baux. When Avignon and the Comtat passed into the hands of the popes, Orange remained independent and represented thus a little enclave in the papal territory. In the sixteenth century, the principality was inherited by William of Naussau, founder of the Netherlands. His successor, Maurice of Nassau, fortified his castle with stones from the extensive Roman ruins, and Orange became a Protestant stronghold. Later, Louis XIV occupied Orange and, with the Treaty of Utrecht (1713), the town returned to France.

Tourist information. Cours Aristide Briand. Tel: 04 90 34 70 88. Opera: (Reservations) Tel: 04 90 51 83 83. Fax. 04 90 11 04 04. Website: <www.choregies.asso.fr>.

What to see. *Théâtre Antique* and *Musée* right across from it. Same ticket. *Arc de Triomphe.*

Where to stay. ***: *Mercure*, route de Caderousse. AC, pool, parking. Tel: 04 90 34 24 10. Fax: 04 90 34 85 48. *Hôtel Arène*, place de Langes, near the Roman theater. AC, garage. Tel: 04 90 11 40 40. Fax: 04 90 11 40 45. **: *Ibis*, route de Caderousse. AC, pool, parking. Tel: 04 90 34 35 35. Fax: 04 90 34 96 47. *St-Florent*, 4 rue Mazeau, near the theater. Tel: 04 90 34 18 53. Fax: 04 90 51 17 25. *: *Arcotel*, 4 place aux Herbes. Tel: 04 90 34 09 23. Fax: 04 90 51 61 12. Email: <jor8525@aol.com>. B&Bs: *Domaine La Violette*, chemin de Lauriol. Pool, parking. Tel: 04 90 51 57 09. Fax: 04 9034 86 15. Email: <herming@avignon-pacwan.net>. *La Barque aux Romarins*, route de Roquemaure. Parking. Tel & fax: 04 90 34 55 96. *Villa de l'Arc*, 13 rond-point de l'Arc de Triomphe. Tel: 04 90 11 78 61.

Where to eat. Chez Daniel. Le Parvi. La Roselière.

Vaison-la-Romaine and Mont Ventoux

Heading northeast to Vaison-la-Romaine, D 975 passes through hundreds of acres of vineyards that produce the famous Côtes du Rhône. The drive is peaceful, straight, and almost inebriating. After thirty minutes you arrive in Vaison-la-Romaine, one of the best-preserved Roman sites in Provence *(plate 2)*. It extends for about forty acres and includes a small theater and a museum. A Roman bridge across the Ouvèze still stands even after the 1992 flood that caused serious damage to the town and killed thirty-seven people. It is in this little town that Théodore Aubanel wrote his poem *La Vénus d'Arles*. A ten-minute drive south on D 938 from Vaison-la-Romaine will take you to Malaucène at the foot of Mont Ventoux, six thousand feet high *(plate 3)*. In April 1336, Petrarch and his younger brother climbed to the top despite the warnings of a local shepherd. Very few people had made it to the top in those days, and there was no pathway. The hike was indeed exhausting, but the view over the Rhône and its green valley was rewarding. Today a little road climbs to the top in about thirty minutes.

Tourist information. Place du Chanoine Sautel. Tel: 04 90 36 02 11. Fax: 04 90 28 76 04. Email: <ot-vaison@axit.fr>. Website: www. vaison-la-romaine.com>.

What to see. Roman ruins and museum.

Where to stay. ***: *Hostellerie le Beffroi,* upper town. Pool, garage. Tel: 04 90 36 04 71. Fax: 04 90 36 24 78. **: *Le Logis du Château,* Les Hauts de Vaison. Pool, parking. Tel: 04 90 36 09 98. Fax: 04 90 36 10 95. B&Bs: *Château de Taulignan,* fifteenth-century castle. Pool, parking. Tel: 04 90 28 71 16. Fax: 04 90 28 75 04. Website: <www. chateau-provence.com>. Mme Delesse. 1 mile from the center. Pool, parking. Tel: 04 90 36 38 38. Mme Verdier. Pool, parking. Tel: 04 90 36 13 46. Fax: 04 90 36 32 43.

Where to eat. *Le Moulin à Huile, Le Brin d'Olivier, L'Auberge de la Bartavelle.*

Valréas, Grignan

Valréas, thirty minutes to the north of Vaison, was part of the Comtat Venaissin and home of Marcel Pagnol's ancestors, who worked there as cardboard makers and stonemasons. A few miles west is the small village of Grignan and its castle where the marquise de Sévigné's daughter Françoise lived after her marriage to the count of Grignan, governor of Provence, in 1669. Mme de Sévigné (1626–1696) is mainly known as the author of a voluminous correspondence. The marquise came to Grignan in 1672 and 1690 and each time stayed for about one year— travel from Paris took about three weeks at the time. She dearly loved her daughter, took great care of her grandchildren, and enjoyed the Provençal lifestyle. Sévigné's last visit was in 1694. She stayed there until her death in April 1696. She was buried in the castle's small graveyard. The marquise loved Provence and the castle. "Their castle is very beautiful and wonderful. It is impressive. Food is excellent and there are a thousand people to meet," she wrote her cousin Bussy-Rabutin.[11] In another letter to Madame de Guitaut, she remarked that, in the area, poverty and illness were unknown and that the castle was literally "enchanté." Dinners were royal feasts of dishes such as partridges, quails fed with thyme and marjoram and roasted to perfection, and for dessert melons, grapes, or figs, according to the season. "My dear cousin, what a life!" she exclaimed.[12] Madame de Sévigné also liked the surrounding countryside and especially the Grotte de Rochecourbière, a cave where she often went to relax and daydream. The castle is open to visitors (Tel: 04 75 46 51 56).

Tourist information. Grande-rue. Tel: 04 75 46 56 75. Website: <www.guideweb.com/grignan>.

Carpentras, L'Isle-sur-la-Sorgue, Fontaine-de-Vaucluse, Saumane

Thirteen miles northeast of Avignon lies Carpentras, former capital of the Comtat. This is truffle country. The fungus looks like a black potato and grows a few inches underground, usually near the roots of oak trees. It can be found only by trained pigs or dogs. Its market price varies but can reach five hundred dollars a pound. The area also produces a good Côtes du Ventoux. A couple of miles east is the Vacqueyras home of troubadour Raimbaut, son of a poor Provençal knight who, according to the *Vida*, had lost his mind. Raimbaut worked at the courts of Raimbaut d'Orange and Guillaume des Baux. He sang well and composed many *sirventes* and songs. The prince of Orange appreciated Raimbaut's talents and recommended him to his friends.

Twenty minutes farther south is the charming little town of L'Isle-sur-la-Sorgue, a former weaving center and now the antiques capital of Provence. It is also the birthplace of poet René Char (1897–1988). Char was the youngest of four children. His father owned a plaster factory and was also the town's mayor. Char attended the lycée in Avignon and then the Ecole de Commerce in Marseille before beginning to work in the family factory. However, Char's real interest was poetry. Under the influence of surrealism and especially of Paul Eluard, Char wrote and published collections of poems such as *Cloches sur le coeur* (Bells on the heart, 1928) and *Le tombeau des secrets* (The tomb of secrets, 1930). Char moved then to Paris, where he participated in the meetings of the surrealists with Dali and Breton. In 1932, he married Georgette Goldstein. After 1935, Char distanced himself from surrealism and during World War II he joined the Resistance. In the 1950s, he divided his time between Paris and his summer residence in L'Isle-sur-la-Sorgue. It is there that he wrote *La parole en archipel* (Words in archipelago, 1962) and *Les chants de la Balandrane* (Songs of Balandrane, 1977). He also entertained numerous guests including his friend Albert Camus and German philosopher Martin Heidegger. Char had met Heidegger in Paris in 1955. Both had a keen interest in the pre-Socratic philosophers and especially Heraclitus. Heidegger came to Isle and from 1966 to 1969 he gave summer seminars in nearby Le Thor. Char wrote many poems about the Sorgue, his hometown, and Les Dentelles de Montmirail, an interesting geological rock formation near Carpentras. Char died on February 19, 1988, at the age of eighty, shortly after remarrying. He is buried in the town's cemetery. His second wife, Marie-Claude, still lives at their house in the Busclats.

> Rivière trop tôt partie d'une traite, sans compagnon
> Donne aux enfants de mon pays le visage de ta passion
> Rivière où l'éclair finit et où commence ma maison,
> Qui roule aux marches d'oubli la rocaille de ma raison
> Rivière, en toi terre est frisson, soleil anxiété.
> Que chaque pauvre dans sa nuit fasse son pain de ta moisson.
> Rivière souvent punie, rivière à l'abandon;
> Rivière des apprentis à la calleuse condition,
> Il n'est vent qui ne fléchisse à la crête de tes sillons.

René Char,
photo: Roger-Viollet

River leaving too suddenly, alone
Give the children of my country the traits of your passion
River where the lightning ends and my home begins
That runs over the steps of oblivion the rocks of my reason
River, in you the earth is a shiver, the sun anxiety.
May each pauper in his night make his bread from your harvest.
River often punished, abandoned river;
River of the apprentices with a callous condition
There is no wind that will not bend at the crest of your furrows.

(René Char, from "La Sorgue: Chanson pour Yvonne")[13]

A few miles east of L'Isle-sur-la-Sorgue, past cherry orchards
and vineyards, is the famous Fontaine-de-Vaucluse, the source of the
Sorgue River *(plate 4)*. Situated at the foot of a low mountain dotted
with pine trees and caves, the small village attracts several thousand
tourists every year.

Bluio Sorgo que varaies
E cascaies
Au mitan di roucassoun,
As retengu si cansoun,

Bluio Sorgo, dins sa barco,
Amourous coume n'i' a plus,
L'as pourta dins soun trelus,
Toun Petrarco

Blue Sorgue you who meander
and flow
amidst the rocks,
you have remembered his songs,

Blue Sorgue, in his boat
a lover like him no longer exists,
you carried in all his beauty
your Petrarch

(Théodore Aubanel, from "Li fiho d'Avignoun")[14]

Petrarch discovered the place with his father at the age of ten. Later he took every opportunity to visit his friend Philippe de Cabassole, bishop of Cavaillon, owner of the castle the ruins of which still exist today. In 1337 Petrarch bought a cottage and stayed there until 1341, after which time he returned to Italy. But he loved the Vaucluse more than any other place in the world and he returned there to live from 1346 to 1347 and one last time from 1351 to 1353. He had a small house, a dog, and two servants. "A wild mountain battered by winds and surrounded by clouds thrusts its peak into the air; at its foot are fountains, kingdoms of the nymphs. There lies the source of the Sorgue. The soft rushing and coolness of its waters are very pleasant. Watching it flow over the green emeralds is an enchanting spectacle."[15] In this secluded village, far from the crowds and noise of Avignon, Petrarch read his favorite troubadours, Arnaut Daniel, "gran maestro d'amor," but also Peire Vidal, Pierre Rugier, Raimbaut d'Auvergne, Raimbaut de Vac-

Petrarch: Musée Pétrarque, Fontaine-de-Vaucluse

queyras, Joffroy Rudel, and Folquet de Marseille. He knew their poems
by heart. When he was not reading, Petrarch strolled along the river-
banks, hiked up the mountain, and explored the caves and forest. He
understood and spoke Provençal and got along well with the local inhabitants. He lived frugally, picked figs and almonds, and fished; his
servants tilled his two gardens, one near the house and one just above
the source of the Sorgue. Here he found the peace and serenity he
longed for:

> Qui non palazzi, non teatro, o loggia,
> Ma'n lor vece un'abete, un faggio, un pino

Tra l'erba verde, e 'l bel monte vicino
Onde si scende poetando, e poggia

Here are neither palaces, theaters, nor elegant terraces,
But firs, beeches, and pines
Among the green grass, and the beautiful neighboring mountain
Where I climb, write poetry, and rest

(Petrarch, from Sonnetti)[16]

It is in the Vaucluse that Petrarch wrote most of his important works. "Almost all of the poems that my pen produced . . . were composed there or inspired by the place," he explains in his correspondence.[17] Even after his beloved Laura died in 1348, during a plague epidemic, Petrarch always returned to the Vaucluse. The small village had become home. "I love this place more than any other in the world. It suits my studies best. There I slowly spent the best years and the happiest moments of my life. It is there that I intend to live in my old age and there that I wish to die," he confided to a friend.[18] Destiny decided otherwise, and Petrarch died in Italy in 1374. In 1804, the village erected a column in his memory. It still stands today. A small museum, said to be built where Petrarch's house once stood, contains lithographs, manuscripts, and old editions of his books.

Two miles from the Fontaine-de-Vaucluse, on a little winding road (north on D 25 and right on D 57) is Saumane. It is very small but is one of the most beautifully restored villages of Provence. It is perched atop a hill and on a clear day you can see Avignon in the distance. About seventy people live there year-round. There are neither shops nor hotels, just a charming restaurant. A *borie*, or ancient stone hut, sits intact in the middle of the pine forest on the hill. Next to it is the entrance to a medieval castle. Walls and a fence surround it and a sign says Private Property. The castle seems to be in good condition and buildings have been added on the lawns. It cannot be visited but is apparently for sale. Few people know that it belonged to the Marquis de Sade. It is there that the young marquis spent his childhood, raised by his uncle, Father Jacques de Sade, a Petrarch scholar. Sade loved to play in the mysterious underground galleries and in the surrounding hills with the village boys. It is there that he learned to speak Provençal. Sade also recalled that his uncle was a man of loose morals who had many affairs with local women.

What to see. The source of the Sorgue can be reached on the pathway in twenty minutes. Walking shoes are recommended. *Musée Pétrarque.* Tel: 04 90 20 37 20.

Where to stay. **: *Hôtel Restaurant du Parc.* Tel: 04 90 20 31 57. Fax: 04 90 20 31 57. *Les Sources.* Tel: 04 90 20 31 89. *Le Château.* Tel: 04 90 20 31 54. B&B: M. Robert Beaumet, chemin de la Tapy, in Saumane. Pool, parking. Tel: 04 90 20 32 97.

Where to eat. Philip, at the foot of the spring. *Les Sources.*

Maillane

Ten miles south of Avignon is the small town of Maillane, home of Frédéric Mistral (1830–1914), Provence's most important poet and winner of the Nobel Prize in literature (1904). Mistral was born on the Mas du Juge, a large farm just outside town. Its current residents are distant cousins. Curiously enough, Adelaïde, Mistral's mother, wanted to name her son Nostradamus, after the famous Provençal doctor and astrologer (see St-Rémy), as if she had foreseen his destiny, but the local authorities refused and she chose Frédéric instead. In those days, Maillane numbered about 1,500 people, most of them farmers, and there, as in many other neighboring villages, Provençal was the main vernacular. Mistral grew up on his parents' farm. "Moun enfanço proumiero se passé dounc au mas, en coumpagno di bouié, di segaire e di pastre" (I spent my childhood on the farm in the company of plowmen, reapers, and shepherds), he remembers in *Lis Isclo d'Or.*[19] He attended the small elementary school there and then, a couple of miles farther west in St-Michel-de-Frigolet, he studied at a former abbey recently made into a boarding school. Alphonse Daudet chose it as the setting for his tale "L'Elixir du Père Gauchet" in *Lettres de mon moulin* (Letters from my mill). There, in a little rundown chapel at the end of the gardens, Gauchet had installed a distillery where behind closed doors he secretly concocted his beverage from a recipe a witch had given him. Nobody else was allowed inside, but the other monks helped by collecting plants and herbs in the surrounding hills. Gauchet's elixir rapidly became famous and the money from the sale was used to restore the abbey. Unfortunately, Gauchet began to develop a taste for the elixir, which, as a matter of fact, contained a large quantity of alcohol, and became a drunk, effectively putting an end to the business.

There may have been some truth to the story for, in 1841, the school in St-Michel-de-Frigolet closed down because of mismanagement and Mistral went to Avignon. He later attended college in Aix with his friend Anselme Mathieu and graduated in law in 1851. Mistral then returned home and helped his aging father manage the farm. But he had not given up his literary ambitions. He collected the local legends, attended all the festivals, and began writing an epic poem. After several years of hard work, in February 1859, the twelve cantos of *Mirèio* were published by Roumanille in Avignon. To reach a larger audience Mistral had added a French translation and then went to Paris to seek the help of a famous author. First he thought of George Sand, for after her early provocative novels with rebellious female protagonists, in the 1840s Sand turned over a new leaf and embarked on a series of simple country tales to show the rich cultural heritage of her native Berry. She encouraged a truly popular literature and helped young writers in this direction. But, unfortunately, Sand was not in Paris and Mistral went to see the great poet Alphonse de Lamartine instead. The latter was immediately enthralled by Mistral's poem, and the praise Lamartine subsequently gave it in the press was partially responsible for its success. It was during his trip to Paris that Mistral met Daudet for the first time. Daudet, also an apprentice writer, invited Mistral for dinner at his place and a long friendship began. Daudet never missed an opportunity to travel to Provence to visit Mistral and, along with the other Félibres, they traveled to the Camargue, Les Baux, Arles, and Cassis, enjoying *bouillabaisse, aïoli*, and the local red wines.

Happy and encouraged by Lamartine's enthusiasm and the promise of success, Mistral went back to Maillane and resumed his literary activities. After his father's death in 1858, Mistral's older half-brother inherited the Mas du Juge, and Mistral and his mother were forced to move out. They bought a smaller house in Maillane, which Daudet called La Maison du Lézard (The Lizard's House) because on its walls there was a small sculpture representing a lizard. "The poet's house is situated at the end of the village; it is the last house on the left on the way to St-Rémy—a small two-story house with a yard in front," Daudet wrote in *Lettres de mon moulin*.[20] The house still stands, but after serving as the town's small library, it is now undergoing a complete restoration. Originally, on the first floor there were the kitchen and dining room "with a light wallpaper . . . a yellow-checked couch and two armchairs," according to Daudet. There were also two statues and a photograph of him by Hébert. Upstairs were two small bedrooms. Mistral's was "a modest peasant room with two beds." The walls were bare and Daudet recalled that Mistral refused to use the money from the prize he had been awarded for *Mirèio* to buy wallpaper, as his mother suggested, because, he argued, that money was "for the poets." Almost directly across from his house was an old café where he often stopped by to see his friends and play a game of cards. Today, it is the town's only restaurant, and its elegant Provençal cuisine is worth a detour.

After the success of *Mirèio*, Mistral worked on a second epic called *Calendau*. It came out of Roumanille's press in 1867, and like *Mirèio* was accompanied by a French translation. The story takes place in the eighteenth century and tells of the love between Calendau, a young fisherman from Cassis, and Esterello, unhappily married to Count Sévéran of Les Baux. After many adventures that take him all over Provence, Calendau finally confronts Severan, kills him, and wins Esterello's heart. It was the occasion for Mistral to celebrate local folklore and especially this time the world of fishermen. Unfortunately, the poem did not fare as well as *Mirèio*, but Mistral's writing continued unabated. *Lis Isclo d'Or* (1876) is a collection of poems including *cansoun, sirventes, plang,* and *pantaï* (dreams) dedicated to the islands facing Hyères.

Mistral's house in Maillane

*Mistral's desk, permission
Musée Frédéric Mistral*

Western Provence

The living room, permission Musée Frédéric Mistral

The kitchen, permission Musée Frédéric Mistral

In 1876, after a long bachelor life, Mistral finally married. "Es meiour d'èstre ama que d'èstre renouma" (It is better to be loved than to be famous), wrote Aubanel in his poem "Le noço de Mistrau" (Mistral's wedding).[21] The bride was young Marie Rivière, the daughter of Burgundian friends. Mistral had a new two-story house built in his one-acre front yard and he moved in with his wife. They had no children. His mother lived in the Maison du Lézard until her death in 1883.

Besides *Nerto* (1884), mentioned in the chapter on Avignon, Mistral wrote another tragic poem, *La Rèino Jano* (1890). Jeanne of Anjou, queen of Naples and countess of Provence, had a very unhappy married life and fought to keep her throne before being thrown in jail and suffocated to death. Mistral also dedicated a poem, *Lou pouèmo dóu Rose* (The song of the Rhône, 1891), to the mighty Rhône, at the bottom of which lived a mysterious beast or Drac. From 1861 on, Mistral worked on a Provençal dictionary, *Lou tresor dóu Félibrige*, a scholarly and monumental work first published in sixty small leaflets (1879) and then in two volumes (1882, 1886). He lectured extensively throughout Provence, attended festivals, and contributed poems to the *Armana*. He was also *capoulié* or head of Félibrige until 1888 and, in 1891, created another review, *L'aiòli*.

Around 1895, Mistral conceived the project of opening a Provençal museum in Arles. He became a member of the National Society of Ethnography and the following year established contact with officials in Arles, obtaining six rooms in the tribunal of justice on the rue de la République. For years he worked hard collecting regional costumes, furniture, pictures, postcards, paintings, and other artifacts representing Provençal life. In 1906, with the money from his Nobel Prize and from his memoirs, *Memòri e raconte*, he moved his museum to its present location in the Palais Laval. His Nobel Prize, awarded in 1904, earned him the visits of many important literary and political figures such as Presidents Raymond Poincaré and Theodore Roosevelt. In his later years, Mistral worked on a Provençal translation of Genesis (1910). An entire generation of young Provençal writers followed in his footsteps. He died at home in Maillane on March 24, 1914, and was buried in the local cemetery. His wife stayed on and led a quiet life on the property until her death in 1943. Today Maillane's population is about 1,700 people. The older villagers still speak Provençal and every year they celebrate Mistral's birthday and the anniversary of his death.

D'engaugna Paris en tout
Cadun s'acoumodo
E lou mounde vèn pertout
Esclau de la modo:
Nàutri, li bon Prouvençau,
Chivalié dóu Sant Grasau,
Faguen-nous félibre
E restaren libre.

To imitate Paris in everything
Everyone attempts
And everywhere people become
Slaves of fashion:
We, the good Provençals,
Knights of the Grail,
Let us become *félibres*
And we will remain free.

(Frédéric Mistral, from "Li bon prouvençau"
[The good Provençals])[22]

What to see. Mistral's house and museum are delightful to visit. The house is intact and a guided tour shows the richly decorated parlor with contemporary paintings, photographs, and sculptures. Across from the parlor is Mistral's library with several editions of his works, his favorite books, and an important collection of manuscripts and letters. In the back and facing the Maison du Lézard is a Provençal kitchen, and upstairs the bedrooms. It is open to the public every day except on Mondays. The tour takes about forty minutes and is in French, but a leaflet is available in English. Tel: 04 90 95 74 06. Fax: 04 90 90 52 84.

Where to stay. There is a B&B in town with pool and parking. Tel: 04 90 95 80 12.

Where to eat. L'Oustalet Maianen, directly across from Mistral's home, serves excellent local dishes in a warm and friendly atmosphere. Tel: 04 90 95 74 60. Fax: 04 90 95 76 17.

Tarascon

A fifteen-minute drive west of Maillane is Tarascon. Its poet Ricau was "bons cavalier fo e bons trobaire e bons servire. E fes bons sirventes e bona cansos," says the author of the *Vida* of the troubadours (he was a good, generous knight and a talented troubadour. He wrote good sirventes and fine songs).[23] But Tarascon is perhaps best known as the hometown of Daudet's famous protagonist and lion-hunter Tartarin. A house has been converted into a small museum dedicated to this character. It contains posters of press articles and theater and movie adaptations of the series of Tartarin novels as well as some paraphernalia. *Tartarin de Tarascon* was published in 1872 and slowly became a success. Daudet describes Tarascon as a little town where hunting is men's primary pastime. But since the days when they used to kill the *tarasco*, or local dragon that lived in the Rhône and terrorized the population, game has been scarce. Animals hide and, on their way to the Camargue, wild ducks make a detour to avoid the dangerous town, because the men there, and especially Tartarin, have the reputation of being good hunters.

Since there are no wild animals to hunt, every Sunday the men shoot their hats, after which they sit under an olive tree and feast on *daube* (beef stew), salami, anchovies, and raw onions. Their giant picnic feast is naturally accompanied by "one of those nice wines of the Rhône valley, that make people laugh and sing."[24] The inhabitants of Daudet's Tarascon are not rich, except the milliner, of course, but they are happy. In his little town, Tartarin occupies a position of honor. He has always been considered something of a hero, but no one knows exactly why—perhaps because of his talent for hat hunting but perhaps also because he has read a lot and can tell exciting stories about faraway places such as those described by James Fenimore Cooper and the explorers of Africa, India, and the Far East. He owns a collection of daggers, knives, poisoned arrows, spears, and guns that indeed commands respect. However, except for a day trip to Beaucaire, right across the Rhône, he has never been away from Tarascon.

Tartarin is a middle-aged man, "forty to forty-five years old, short, fat, squat, with a ruddy complexion."[25] He wears a short beard and his sparkling eyes betray a natural joviality. Like any other well-respected hunter, he smokes a pipe. Daudet describes him as a combination of Don Quixote and Sancho Panza, which to some extent represented the Southern temperament, with its unattainable dreams, nonchalance, and sensuality. One day, as a circus with lions passed through town, Tartarin seized the opportunity to show off. He took his guns and stood in front of the lion's cage despite his ferocious roaring. Such bravery was enough to reinforce his status in the eyes of the townspeople, but now they demanded more of their idol, arguing that his place was in Africa, lion hunting. After weeks of hesitation, Tartarin finally left town. Tartarin spent a few months in Algeria, then a French colony, but his trip was disastrous. As far as hunting is concerned, he killed only a donkey and a tamed, blind lion whose skin he nevertheless sent to Tarascon. He also was robbed of his money, and a camel followed him all the way home. When he returned to Tarascon everyone had admired the lion skin he had sent and received him with the honor befitting a hero. The camel was for a moment mistaken for the *tarasco*.

Daudet wrote the novel to entertain and amuse its readers. Provençals, however, and especially the Tarasconnais, did not always enjoy the way he had portrayed them and, for many years, Daudet recalled, he could not go there, for "they" were waiting for him, he maintained, with loaded guns. In any case, the novel eventually became a success and so Daudet wrote two sequels: *Tartarin sur les Alpes* (1885), in the same style but with less flavor; and *Port-Tarascon* (1890), translated into English by Henry James.

Modern Tarascon seems to have kept its perennial serenity. It is quiet and small. Its thirteenth-century castle is one of the best preserved in the region and was the favorite residence of the counts of

Tarascon's castle

Provence. But Tarascon is especially known for its Fête de la Tarasque at the end of June *(plates 5, 6)*. The origin of this festival dates to the fifteenth century. The *tarasco* was evil and ate sailors, washerwomen, and children who crossed the river or lingered on its banks at night. For centuries the population lived in fear until, one day, Sainte Marthe tamed it by a simple sign of the cross. During the festival six men dressed in medieval costumes run a large plastic replica of the dragon-like creature through the streets. Recently, the character of Tartarin has joined the celebrations, as well as musicians from all over Provence. The festival lasts four days and includes a ceremony of homage to King René and an *abrivado* or bull race in the streets.

Next to the Rhône is a statue dedicated to the town's most famous writer, Alexandrine Brémond (1858–1898), known as Bremoundo de Tarascoun (Bremonde de Tarascon) and author of collections of poems such as *Velo blanco* (White veil, 1870) and *Li blavet de Mount-Majour* (The cornflowers of Montmajour, 1882). Facing the town, on the other side of the river, is Beaucaire, site of a famous fair during the Middle Ages. Beaucaire was also the hometown of Antoinette Rivière (1840–1865) or Antouniéto de Beu-caire (Antoinette de Beaucaire). Louis

Bremonde de Tarascon

Antoinette de Beaucaire,
photo: Delgado, Museon
Arlaten

Roumieux, whose daughter Paul Arène courted, encouraged Antou-niéto to write. Her poems were promising, but she died of tuberculo-sis at the age of twenty-four. After her death, Roumieux collected her poems and had them published in a book titled *Li belugo* (The sparks, 1865).

Vierge, as ben fa de mouri jouino,
Car noun as vist la rouino
De ti pantai d'amour;
As ben fa de segui la negro Segnouresso,
Avans que noste mounde, o tèndro felibresso,
Treboulèsse tocant de sa laido rumour.

Virgin, you chose well to die young,
For you did not see the ruin
Of your dreams of love;
You chose well to follow the black Sovereign
Before our world, sweet poetess,
Disturbed your songs with its ugly clamor.

(Frédéric Mistral, from "Pèr la Felibresso" [For the poetess])[26]

Tourist information. 59 rue des Halles. Tel: 04 90 91 03 52.

What to see. Castle, Tel: 04 90 91 01 93.

Where to stay. ***: *Les Echevins,* 26 blvd Itam. AC, garage. Tel: 04 90 91 01 70. Fax: 04 90 43 50 44.

St-Rémy, Salon

Four miles southeast of Maillane is St-Rémy *(plate 7)*. With a popula-tion of about nine thousand, the town is larger than Maillane. It devel-oped in the fourth century under the protection of the Abbey of Saint

Rémy in Rheims, from which it borrowed its name. One mile south is Glanum, site of a Celtic sanctuary, where in the second century B.C. the Greeks founded Glanon near a spring. When the Romans settled there two centuries later, the town became Glanum. Since digging at this site first began in 1921, archeologists have uncovered a village about three hundred yards long, once home to perhaps five thousand people. It comprised individual houses, a forum, several temples, and baths. At the entrance are a well-preserved mausoleum and municipal arch. Glanum was abandoned after Germanic tribes sacked it in 270. St-Rémy is now a picturesque small town facing the Alpilles (small Alps) in the south that inspired Van Gogh, Mistral, and Daudet. Joseph Roumanille was born there on the Mas des Pommiers (The Apple Farm). His parents were poor gardeners and Joseph was the eldest of seven siblings. Roumanille's mother, like Mistral's, did not speak French, which, as he often said, influenced his decision to write in Provençal. He attended school in Maillane and after graduation obtained a teaching position in Nyons. Roumanille lived and worked most of his life in Avignon. He died there in 1891 but was buried in St-Rémy.

St-Rémy is also the birthplace of Marie Mauron (1896–1986). Her maiden name was Roumanille and she was a distant cousin of the félibre. She grew up on a farm and spoke Provençal before French. As a child she participated in all the farm activities such as the *olivades* or the gathering of olives in the winter and *vendanges* or grape picking in the fall and attended the traditional *veillées* with storytelling. She went to school in town and then in Beaucaire and Marseille where her teacher, Mme Colombelle, was Marcel Pagnol's aunt. Encouraged by her father who had a high respect for education, Mauron studied in Aix and upon graduation became an elementary school teacher. Her career took her to Marseille, Les Baux, Gignac, and Mas Blanc. In 1919 she married Charles Mauron, a childhood friend. When she was working and living in Les Baux, Marie met the English painter Roger Fry, who was traveling through Provence, and introduced him to her husband and Charloun Rieu (1846–1924) of Le Paradou, author of poems such as *Li cant dóu terraire* (Songs of the land, 1897) and a friend of Mistral. Fry's enthusiasm about Cézanne, literature, and Provence surprised and fascinated the Maurons and a long-lasting friendship was born. Charles Mauron and Fry shared an interest in Mallarmé and Paul Valéry. Fry came back to St-Rémy the following summer and he and the Maurons toured Mont Ventoux, the Luberon, and the Camargue on their bicycles. Fry had brought a new book to Marie: Marcel Proust's *A l'ombre des jeunes filles en fleurs.*

On another occasion Fry came to St-Rémy with Peter Lucas, a professor of literature at Cambridge, and E. M. Forster, whose *Passage to India* had just been published by Virginia and Leonard Woolf's Hogarth Press. The book was a success and, on Fry's initiative, the Maurons began translating it into French. Translations of many other works followed, including Woolf's *Flush* and *Orlando* and T. E. Lawrence's *Seven Pillars of Wisdom.* Marie would read the novels to Charles, who was slowly losing his eyesight. Then they would translate and she would type, as she recalls in *Le printemps de la Saint-Martin* (1978). But Fry also recognized Marie's literary talent and encouraged her to write her own novels. When she finally completed her first Provençal story *Mont Paon*, only to have it rejected by the major French publishers, Lucas took the manuscript with him to England and arranged for Cambridge University Press to publish it in English as *Mount Peacock* (1934). Marie's major literary influence was Rieu, who recited his Provençal poems to her when she was still a child. It was he who inspired her to write about Provence. Fry invited the Maurons to London and introduced them to the Woolfs and other Bloomsbury intellectuals. Contact with the Bloomsbury group continued up to World War II despite Fry's accidental death in 1934. Later, Charles wrote literary criticism and studied the relationship between psychoanalysis and literature. Marie became a successful writer and poured forth novels about Provence such as *Le Quartier Mortisson* (The Mortisson neighborhood, 1941), *Le sel des pierres* (The salt of stones, 1942), and *Le royaume errant* (The roaming kingdom, 1953). She also wrote popular books about Provençal customs and tales and actively participated in the defense of the Provençal language. She died in St-Rémy at the age of ninety and was buried in the small graveyard.

St-Rémy is also proud to be the birthplace of the famous astrol-

Marie Mauron, photo: Editions Laffont (private collection)

oger Michel de Notredame, better known as Nostradamus (1503–1566), whose prophecies still puzzle modern scholars and scientists. Nostradamus came from an old Provençal family. His paternal grandfather was a Jew who converted to Catholicism and changed his name (Ben Guesson) to Notre Dame. His maternal grandfather was St-Rémy's treasurer. Nostradamus and his four siblings grew up in town. His grandparents taught him the rudiments of astrology and shared with him their knowledge of medicinal plants. In 1520, Nostradamus went to Montpellier to study medicine. His diploma in hand in 1530, he traveled in the Southwest to Toulouse and Agen where he met the Italian doctor Julio Scaligero and married Anne de Cabrejas. Nostradamus devoted his time to fighting the plague that killed his wife and two children in 1533. For the next five years, the prophet traveled extensively in Belgium, Germany, and Italy. In 1545, he came back to Provence and settled in Salon, where one of his brothers lived. He married Anne Ponsard, a widow, and had six children.

In Salon, Nostradamus lived in a modest house on rue Farreigoux, where he practiced medicine. However, he never abandoned his interest in astrology, and prepared almanacs and predicted the future, making sure to explain to the authorities that he was not a sorcerer and not involved in magic. Nostradamus also wrote a treatise on the art of making jams, but he is best known for his *Prophéties* published in 1555 in Lyons. They consisted of rhymed quatrains written in French. The book was a success and was published in a new edition in 1558. People came from all over France to consult him; his clientele included the Duke of Savoy, the Count of Tende, and Catherine of Medici, wife of King Henry II. Nostradamus has his disciples but also his detractors, for his prophecies are cryptic and can be interpreted in various ways. He died in 1566 and was buried in the Cordeliers Church in Salon. His brother Jean wrote *Vie des plus célèbres et anciens poètes Provençaux* (Lives of the most famous and ancient Provençal poets, 1575) and his son César *Poésies* (1606) and *Histoire et chronique de Provence* (History and chronicle of Provence, 1614).

It was to the hospital of St-Paul-de-Mausole, a former Augustinian monastery, in St-Rémy, that Van Gogh admitted himself in May 1889. He stayed one year. Between his bouts of depression he was allowed to take walks outside and paint. He produced over 150 paintings and drawings, including *Starry Night*.

St-Rémy:

Tourist information. Place Jean Jaurès. Tel: 04 90 92 05 22. Website: <www.saintremy-de-provence.com>.

What to see. Roman ruins of *Glanum:* Tel: 04 90 92 23 79. *St-Paul-de-Mausole*, near Glanum. Tel: 04 90 92 67 00.

Where to stay. ****: *Hostellerie du Vallon de Valrugues*, chemin Canto Cigalo. AC, pool, parking. Tel: 04 90 92 04 40. Fax: 04 90 92 44 01. *Château des Alpilles*, one mile on D 31 west. AC, pool, parking. Tel: 04 90 92 03 33. Fax: 04 90 92 45 17. ***: *Les Ateliers de l'Image*, 5 avenue Pasteur. AC. Tel: 04 90 92 51 50. Fax: 04 90 92 43 52. *Les Antiques*, 15 avenue Pasteur. Pool, parking. Tel: 04 90 92 03 02. Fax: 04 90 92 50 40. *Mas des Carassins*, 1 chemin Gaulois. Parking. Tel: 04 90 92 15 48. Fax: 04 90 92 63 47. **: *La Reine Jeanne*, 12 rue Mirabeau. Tel: 04 90 92 15 33. *Cheval Blanc*, 6 avenue Fauconnet. Garage. Tel: 04 90 92 09 28. Fax: 04 9092 69 05. B&Bs: *Mas Clair de*

Lune. Pool, parking. Tel: 04 90 92 02 63. Fax: 04 90 92 15 65. Mme Brun, route de Noves. Parking. Tel: 04 90 92 09 94.

Where to eat. Maison Jaune, 15 avenue Carnot. *Orangerie Chabert,* 16 blvd Hugo. *Les Saveurs Singulières,* 12 chemin de Bigau.

Salon:

Tourist information. 56 cours Gimon. Tel: 04 90 56 27 60. Fax: 04 90 56 77 09. Website: <www.visitprovence.com>.

What to see. Château Musée de l'Empéri displays a fine collection of military uniforms, flags, and ancient weapons. Tel: 04 90 56 22 36. *Nostradamus's House.* Ten rooms with ancient furniture and wax figures. Tel: 04 90 56 64 31.

Where to stay. ****: *Mas du Soleil,* 38 chemin St-Côme. AC, pool, parking. Tel: 04 90 56 06 53. **: *Hôtel d'Angleterre,* 98 cours Carnot. Tel: 04 90 56 01 10. Fax: 04 90 56 71 75. *Ibis,* route d'Aix Pelissanne. Pool, parking. Tel: 04 90 42 23 57. Fax: 04 90 42 10 57.

Where to eat. La salle à manger. 6 rue Joffre. *Craponne,* 146 allées Craponne.

Les Baux

Perched high on a bluff, six miles south of St-Rémy (on D 5), is the ancient village of Les Baux. "Païs que ressènt lou ferun, rèn que de colo demasiado, tou laboura pèr d'ensarriado" (Wild country, only abandoned hills, strewn with ravines), says Mistral in *Calendau*.[27] During the Middle Ages it was the home of powerful lords whose domain extended to the valley and included several other towns in Provence. Les Baux was famous for its festivals attended by rich knights and ladies and troubadours such as Raimbaut d'Orange. Its princes successfully defended their stronghold against the Catalans and the Arabs. Legend has it that during his retreat Abd-al-Raman hid his treasure in one of the caves in the valley where, to this day, the Cabro d'Or (Golden

Goat) watches over it. In 1426, at the death of Alix, its last princess, the small kingdom became part of Provence. In 1483 the town rebelled one last time against the king of France, but in vain. The king besieged the town and burned the castle. The castle was later rebuilt, but Richelieu finally destroyed it in 1632. Les Baux was also the home of Countess Esterello, the unhappy wife of Count Sévéran, characters in Mistral's *Calendau*. It is there that Calendau was thrown into the dungeon. Fortunately, he managed to escape and killed Sévéran in a duel.

Over the years, the numerous wars against the Catalans, the Moors, and the kings of France took their toll, and by the time Daudet visited the village toward the end of the nineteenth century, Les Baux was a little more than "a dusty hillock of ruins, wild rocks, old castles with coats of arms, crumbling, shaking in the wind like an eagle's nest."[28] But the place had an excellent inn, and Mistral, Daudet, and their friends rarely missed the chance to feast on its delicious cuisine. After Chef Cornille had served them a hearty meal and several bottles of local wine, the group would wander about the narrow winding streets singing songs and reciting poems until dawn. Marie Mauron taught in the little school for five years (1917–21). In the summer of 1959, Jean Cocteau and his team, including Jean Marais and Yul Brynner, came to shoot a few scenes of his film *Le testament d'Orphée*.

Tourist information. Ilot Post Ténébras. Tel: 04 90 54 34 39. Fax: 04 90 54 51 15. Website: <www.lesbauxdeprovence.com>. Email: <tourisme@lesbauxdeprovence.com>.

What to see. Parking is available just outside the village for a stroll through the narrow cobbled streets and shopping in the souvenir stands. The small *Chapelle des Penitents* is beautifully decorated by painter Yves Brayer. *Castle* and *Museum*. Tel: 04 90 54 55 56. *Musée Yves Brayer:* 04 90 54 36 99.

Where to stay. Hotels and the major restaurants are situated at the foot of the village, in the valley. ****: *Oustaù de Baumanière.* AC, pool, parking. Tel: 04 90 54 33 07. Fax: 04 90 54 40 46. *La Cabro d'Or.* AC, pool, parking. Tel: 04 90 54 33 21. Fax: 04 90 54 45 98. ***: *Auberge de la Benvengudo.* AC, pool, parking. Tel: 04 90 54 32 54.

Fax: 04 90 54 42 58. *Mas de l'Oulivié*. AC, pool, parking. Tel: 04 90 5435 78. Fax: 04 90 54 44 31. B&B: *Le Mas de l'Esparou*, route de St-Rémy. Pool, parking. Tel: 04 90 54 41 32.

Where to eat. Baumanière. ** Riboto de Taven.* * *Cabro d'Or.* *

Fontvieille

A couple of miles south on D 78 and D 17 is Fontvieille, the heart of Alphonse Daudet's country. Daudet was actually born in Nîmes, where his father owned a silk manufacture. However, his parents wanted him to grow up a healthy boy and so sent him to live with a family of farmers in the village of Bezouce, on the outskirts of town. It is there that he learned to speak Provençal. He then returned to Nîmes to attend school, but in 1849 a crisis in the silk business forced the Daudets to move to Lyons, where they stayed until 1857. Life there was so gloomy that Daudet often skipped school to go boating on the Rhône. He missed the South terribly. Fortunately, one day, he discovered a copy of Mistral's magazine *Armana prouvençau* and immediately began to write verse. Daudet worked for a while as an assistant in a boarding school in Alès (Cévennes) and finally moved to Paris to live with his older brother Ernest.

Daudet continued to write, and his first collection of poems, *Les amoureuses* (1858), although largely ignored by the press, attracted the attention of Empress Eugénie, who hired him as clerk to the Duke of Morny. Daudet was elated. He enjoyed his job and had enough time left to write. He also frequented the avant-garde cafés and clubs where he met Paul Arène, a native of Sisteron with whom he wrote the *Lettres de mon moulin*. It is also in Paris that he met Mistral when he came to promote *Mirèio* in 1859. In 1865, Daudet married Julia Allard, a young Parisian novelist. But success came very slowly for Daudet, and *Le petit chose* (1868) and *Lettres de mon moulin* (1869) did not fare well at first.

Daudet's permanent home was in Paris, but his heart had remained

Alphonse Daudet, photo:
Musée Daudet, Fontvieille

in Provence, where he went as often as he could. Fontvieille's castle of
Montauban was Daudet's first Provençal home *(plate 8)*. It belonged
to his aunt Mme Ambroy, a widow who lived there with her four sons.
Daudet first came there when he was twenty years old and was thereafter a frequent guest. "Wonderful people, blessed home! . . . How
many times, in winter, did I come here, to breathe the healthy airs of
our small Provençal hills, return to nature, and cure myself of Paris
and its fevers. I'd arrive without notice, sure of their welcome, an-
nounced by the fanfare of peacocks and hunting dogs."[29] Daudet was
always warmly received. He loved the country atmosphere of the
place, its gardens, and its animals and sheep pen. There were "no lawns,
no flower beds, or anything that recalled a garden, or an enclosed property; only a small pine forest among the gray rocks, a nature and wilder-
ness preserve with bushy paths all slippery with dry pine needles."[30]
All around the castle were olive groves, mulberry trees, wheat fields,
and vineyards.

"An ancient Provençal family lived there twenty years ago, as original and beautiful as their house," Daudet remembered with nostalgia.[31] Mme Ambroy was a simple and very sociable woman and she loved him as one of her sons. She would often entertain him with stories of her past that delighted his vivid imagination. Daudet also loved to hang around the kitchen and sit by the fireplace, chatting in Provençal with the cook, and to talk about the stars with Bagasse the shepherd. Sometimes Daudet would eat roasted chestnuts and listen to Pistolet, the warden with a white beard and facetious eyes, tell tales of yore. The visits to his aunt's left an indelible imprint on his artistic sensitivity. "Every sentence I write echoes the shade of your pines and the murmur of the mistral and our casual conversations," he later wrote to Timoleon, the youngest cousin.[32]

About one mile outside the village, perched on little fragrant hill, is Daudet's famous *moulin* or windmill *(plate 9)*. "That mill was in ruins. A pile of stones, iron, and old boards that had not been aired out in years that lay, with its limbs broken, useless like a poet," Daudet says as he immediately fell in love with it.[33] The place was romantic and inspiring: "I loved it for its pitiful condition, its footpath hidden by the grass, that small, gray and fragrant mountain grass that Father Gaucher used in his elixir."[34] Built in 1814, the old mill never actually belonged to Daudet and, despite what he said in his *Lettres de mon moulin*, was still operational at the turn of the century. His mill was of course only the symbol of his attachment to Provence. There among the pines, in "un petit coin parfumé et chaud" (a little niche, warm and fragrant), a small twig of thyme in his mouth and the cicadas for companions, "a thousand leagues from the newspapers, stagecoaches, and fog," he came to relax and dream. The magic of the place provided him with a mine of emotions and images that, once back in Paris, he wove into stories. Fontvieille and the mill were his *Pamperi-gousto* or Imaginary Land. At night, as he took possession of his rundown mill, the poet tells us "twenty rabbits were sitting in a circle on the front porch basking in the moonlight." Upstairs resided an old gloomy owl who stared at visitors. All around the mill was "a beautiful forest of pines radiating with light." The bucolic peace was disrupted only by the sound of a fife, a curlew hiding in the lavenders, or the bells of mules. "All this beautiful Provençal scenery feeds only on light," he remarked before Van Gogh.[35]

The mill is at the center of the beautiful, melancholy tale entitled "Master Cornille's Secret." At a time when most farmers took their wheat to the factories to be ground, villagers were surprised to see that Cornille could still do business with his old mill. "In the evening one could see the old miller walking along the footpaths urging on his donkey laden with big sacks of flour in front of him."[36] But the origin of this flour remained mysterious since everyone now brought their wheat to the newly installed flour milling works on the road to Tarascon. One day, they discovered that the heavy sacks he was seen carrying contained, in fact, nothing but dirt and pebbles. Cornille was too proud to show that he was indeed out of business. The villagers took pity on him and, shameful, brought their wheat back to Cornille.

On sunny days, Daudet would have an early breakfast, pick up his myrtle stick and Montaigne's *Essais*, and leave Fontvieille on foot to pay Mistral a visit. After a couple of hours' walk he would reach Maillane. The welcome was warm as usual. The poet's mother had set the table: leg of lamb, goat cheese, fig jam, grapes, and a good old bottle of Châteauneuf-du-Pape. After the meal Mistral would read him excerpts from his latest poem. Often, the two would travel to Avignon and visit Roumanille and Aubanel. "In those days Félibrige had not become an academic discipline. We were in the first days of *the Church*, full of enthusiasm and naivety, without schisms or rivalry," Daudet remembered.[37] He and his joyous companions with apostle-like beards visited the Camargue and Les Baux and never missed a festival. Going back to Paris must have been hard. In 1872, inspired by a tragic event involving Mistral's nephew, Daudet wrote a successful drama, *L'Arlésienne*.

Besides Fontvieille, Daudet also stayed in Orgon, near Cavaillon. He often went there in the 1880s as a guest of the Parrocels at their castle of Sainte-Estève. It is there that he began writing *Numa Roumestan* (1881), a novel in which he elaborates at length on the differences between France's southern and northern cultures. By this time, Daudet had joined Flaubert's group of friends that included Zola and Edmond de Goncourt and, under their influence, wrote excellent novels such as *Sapho* (1884), a story of the love between Marie Rieu and Jean Gaussin, a Southern man. Brought to the stage the following year, the play triumphed. By then Daudet was famous. His *Fromont Jeune* (1874), a Parisian novel in the fashion of the day, *Lettres de mon moulin*, and *Tartarin* only confirmed his talent. Daudet always considered himself a Provençal and at the beginning of his career a félibre. He encouraged the publication of reviews in Provençal and even wrote several poems in Provençal for the *Armana*. "Yes, I am a Southerner. I truly am. All my childhood sensitivity, all my inspiration comes from the South," he proudly claimed.[38]

A couple of miles south of Fontvieille on D 17 is the Montmajour monastery. Built in the tenth century by Benedictine monks, it was a center of spiritual life until, like the others, it fell victim to the revolutionary rage in 1789. When Daudet visited, it was in a bad state of disrepair. He saw, he relates, sea eagles "fluttering their wings in its ruins." Today the monastery belongs to the state and is being restored. It is open to the public (Tel: 04 90 69 84 74).

Tourist information. 5 rue Marcel Honorat. Tel: 04 90 54 67 49. Fax: 04 90 54 69 82.

What to see. Daudet's Mill. Tel: 04 90 54 60 78. A fifteen-minute walk from the center of town. The visit to the mill takes only ten minutes but under it is a small museum with photographs of Daudet, postcards, and souvenirs. From the mill one has a good view of the valley and the monastery of Montmajour. A small path in the pine forest leads downhill to Montauban, ten minutes away on foot. The mansion is still in good condition but only two rooms are open to tourists. They include photographs of Daudet and his friends as well as historical information about the area.

Where to stay. ****: *Regalido*, rue Mistral. AC, parking. Tel: 04 90 54 60 22. Fax: 04 90 54 64 29. ***: *Hostellerie Saint Victor*, chemin des Fourques. AC, pool, parking. Tel: 04 9 0 54 66 00. Fax: 04 90 54 67 88. *Le Val Majour*, route d'Arles. Pool, parking. Tel: 04 90 54 62 33. Fax: 04 90 54 61 67. **: *Daudet*, route d'Arles. Pool, parking. Tel: 04

90 54 76 06. Fax: 04 90 54 76 95. *La Ripaille*, one mile in the direction of Les Baux. Pool, parking. Tel: 04 90 54 73 15. Fax: 04 90 54 60 69. *Auberge des Balastres*, route de Tarascon. Pool, parking. Tel: 04 90 54 67 27. Fax: 04 90 54 72 21. *: *Chez Bernard*, 6 cours Bellon, in the town center. Tel: 04 90 54 70 35. Fax: 04 90 54 68 59. *Le Laetitia*, rue du Lion. Parking. Tel: 04 90 54 72 14. Fax: 04 90 54 81 75. B&B: *La Tanière*, route du Moulin. Pool, parking. Tel: 04 90 54 61 40.

Where to eat. Regalido.* Le Patio, 117 route du Nord. *La Cuisine au Planet*, place du Planet. *La Table du Meunier*, cours Bellon. *Le Moulin de Grasiho*, cours Bellon.

Arles

"I wish I could have stayed longer and fully enjoyed all the remarkable details of the cloister of Saint-Trophîme," wrote Gustave Flaubert, passing through Arles in 1840.[39] Flaubert was just twenty-one years old and was traveling with Dr. Cloquet, his sister Lise, and Father Stephany, all family friends. The group had toured the Southwest and was now en route to Corsica. They stopped in Arles for a couple of days, strolled through the town, and visited the arenas. "These Roman monuments are like a skeleton whose bones stick out here and there through the ground," Flaubert noted.[40] The theater reminded him of plays of Plautus and Terence he had read in school. Flaubert also watched the Provençals and especially the women of Arles, famous for their looks: "The Arlésiennes are beautiful . . . They are of the so-called Greco-Roman type; their waists are large but svelte like a marble barrel. Their exquisite profile is wrapped in a large scarf of red velvet over their head and tied under their necks, which enhances the blackness of their hair and contrasts with the luster of their skin, warmed up by the reflection of the sun."[41] Having visited the town and satisfied their curiosity, Flaubert and his group then left for Marseille.

One of the most famous artistic figures of Arles was painter Vincent Van Gogh, who arrived in town for the first time in February 1888.

Western Provence

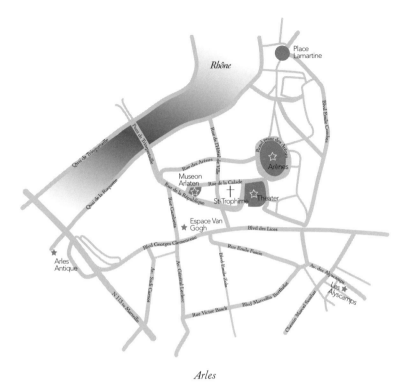

Arles

The letters he wrote his brother Theo contain interesting descriptions and insights about Provence. Van Gogh was then unknown and struggling with financial and health problems. His doctor had recommended the south of France, which finally gave him the opportunity to see Cézanne but also Zola and Daudet's country. "Before getting to Tarascon. I noticed a magnificent area of huge rocks piled up in the strangest and stateliest forms . . . but here in Arles the countryside seems flat," he wrote to his brother Theo.[42] Van Gogh had in mind the creation of an artist colony and hoped to carry out his project in Provence. Upon his arrival, he took a room at the hotel-restaurant Carrel, a small pension in rue Cavalerie. The first time he attempted painting outside the weather was cold and the wind so strong that he was unable to work: "The sky is a hard blue, with a great bright sun which has melted almost all the snow, but the wind is cold, and so dry that it gives you

Arlésienne

Mistral and Daudet, photo: Musée Daudet, Fontvieille.

goose-bumps." So, temporarily unable to paint, he reread Daudet and wandered about town, fascinated by the Provençal colors and forms. "The women here are beautiful, no humbug about that," he noted, adding in passing that they reminded him of paintings by Renoir or Fragonard.

The South struck him as a different country altogether. He noticed that, unlike in the north of France, the people of Provence were "more artistic in their own persons and in their manners," as he watched "the adorable little Arlésiennes going to their first communion." The priest in his surplice looked like "a dangerous rhinoceros," and the men drinking absinthe in the cafés seemed to him like "creatures of another world." The style of Provençal dress, the way the Provençals harmonized the colors of their clothes, reminded Van Gogh of the art of Goya and Velasquez: "They will pin a touch of pink on a black frock, or devise a garment of white, yellow, and pink, or else green and pink, or else blue and yellow, in which there is nothing to be altered from an artistic point of view."

Arles: The Arenas

Provence suited Van Gogh. "The air here certainly does me good," he wrote. The colors of spring and the bright light fascinated him. "Nature here is so *extraordinarily* beautiful. Everywhere and over all the vault of the sky is marvelous blue, the sun sheds a radiance of pale sulphur that is soft and lovely. What a country! I cannot paint it as lovely, but it absorbs me so much that I let myself go, never thinking of a single rule; I have no doubts, no hesitation in attacking things; I am beginning to feel that I am quite a different creature from the one I was when I came here." In the summer, Van Gogh complained about the nagging mosquitoes and the deafening summer chirp of the cicadas that "sang as loud as the frogs," but these were trivialities and on the whole he thoroughly enjoyed himself. He knew he had found inspiration there: "I have no fear that I shall always love this countryside. I am convinced that nature down here is exactly what one needs to give one color." The Provençal summer with its gold and copper tones and "the green azure of the sky blanched with heat" reminded him of Cézanne, the master whose deft hand and subtle use of colors managed to catch "the harsh side of Provence," according to Van Gogh. The Mistral also played its role in Van Gogh's brush stroke: "I have already

Arlésienne

told you that I have always to fight against the mistral, which makes it absolutely impossible to be master of my stroke."

When he was not painting, Van Gogh immersed himself in Zola and Daudet, and their literary landscapes influenced him as much as the real ones. Provence was the land of light and vivid colors but also that of the detailed descriptions of Zola and wonderful poetic prose and humor of Daudet. When his apartment was finally ready to receive Gauguin, Van Gogh wrote to his brother: "Last night I slept in the house, and though there are some things still to be done, I feel very happy in it. At present it reminds me of the interiors of Bosboom. Its surroundings, the public garden, the night cafés, and the grocer's are not Millet, but short of that they are Daumier, absolute Zola. And that's quite enough to supply one with ideas, isn't it?" Van Gogh had read

L'oeuvre with great interest and agreed with Zola that, for an artist, success was a heavy burden.

Van Gogh had also been to Fontvieille where, in Daudet's footsteps, he climbed the little hill above the village where the famous mill sat. He knew *Lettres de mon moulin* almost by heart, and Daudet's images, characters, and descriptions of the scenery haunted him. Provence was not just the south of France for him; it was the land of Daudet, the poet whose magic prose lured him south. "Here's the country of good old Tartarin; I enjoy myself in it more and more, and it is going to be our second Father land," he wrote to Theo. The Provençales, the sunflowers, and the cafés—Van Gogh had already seen them in Daudet. "Do you remember that wonderful page in Tartarin, the complaint of the old Tarascon diligence? Well, I have just painted that red and green vehicle in the courtyard of the inn. You shall see it; a simple foreground of gray gravel, a background very, very simple too; the two carriages brightly colored, green and red, the wheels—yellow, black, blue, and orange," he remarked.

Happy, healthy, but lonely, Van Gogh was elated when his best friend Paul Gauguin finally arrived in October. The two painters rented rooms in "la Maison Jaune" (the yellow house). Van Gogh admired and respected Gauguin, five years older. On the other hand, Gauguin found Van Gogh's technique too "romantique." Their relationship rapidly deteriorated and when, on December 23, Van Gogh cut off part of his ear and offered it as a present to a prostitute, Gauguin packed his bags. He left the next day. On December 24, the police took Van Gogh to the hospital in town. From then on Van Gogh spent his time in the hospital of Arles and St-Paul-de-Mausole (in St-Rémy), where he stayed for a year. When his spirits were good, he was allowed to go out and paint. It is there that he produced some of his best paintings. In May 1890, Van Gogh left Provence for Auvers-sur-Oise, near Paris. On July 27, he shot himself.

When in Arles, and without knowing it, Van Gogh may have crossed paths with Mistral or the other Provençal poets who regularly came there to wander about town, have drinks, and watch the young ladies saunter by. In his *Lettres de mon moulin*, Daudet describes Arles as "a marvelous little town, one of the most picturesque in France, with its round, sculpted balconies, its old black houses with small Moorish doors, oval and low."[43] He and Mistral would go to the Place des Hommes to meet their friends Roumanille and Aubanel, who had come from Avignon. Then, the small group would go to the Alyscamps cemetery where, as Daudet recalled, they lay in the grass among the ancient sarcophagi and listened to Aubanel recite his latest poems. The happy companions would also carouse in the cafés or cross the Rhône to Trinquetaille to eat eel stew and mingle with the *gardians* or bull herders of the Camargue. Often, their day ended with a stroll down the boulevard des Lices and a last drink on a terrace to watch once more the beautiful and proud women of Arles.

Willa Cather loved Daudet's stories. Traveling through Provence with her friend Izabel McClung, Cather arrived in Arles on September 16, 1902. Finally, after the glamour of the Riviera, she had reached the heart of Provence! "It is with something of relief that one quits the oppressive splendor of Monte Carlo to retrace one's steps back into Daudet's country. . . . It is a high, windy, dusty country, just anchored on the banks of the turbulent Rhône, where the mistral continually threatens to dislodge it and blow it away."[44] The town smelled of olives and grapes, and the leaves of the sycamore trees had turned a beautiful reddish gold. Cather was elated. "Who could be gloomy on a September morning at Arles?" she wondered. She and Izabel strolled about town, visited the arenas and the Alyscamps, and observed the celebrated Arlésiennes. With "clear-cut features, olive skin, oval face, and fine full eyes set off by their costumes of velvet and lace . . . and ribbon caps on their blue-black hair," the women of Arles definitely represented an original type to her eyes, a harmonious blend of Moorish and Roman blood, and their beauty, Cather added, was certainly at the origin of "the songful bent of their country."[45] Cather regretted not being able to see a bullfight, but bullfights were held only on Sundays, and she and her friend had to leave.

Finally, it is difficult to speak about Arles without mentioning Yvan Audouard (1914–), a journalist and author of tales such as *Contes de Provence* (1986) and *Les lions d'Arles* (1988).

Lou jour trais si darrié belu;
Alin s'espandis un fum blu,
Dirias que li mountagno tubon;
Dins lou grand flume negre e siau
Vesès courre d'uiau
Lou fio di fanau que s'atubon,

De-long doù Rose e dis adoub,
s'entènd un cant de pescadou
O lou siblet d'un capitàni;
Cansoun e brut atravali
A cha pau se soun esvali,
Arle sèmbo un païs de nàni.

Plus res camino sus li pont,
Tout se fai mut; la vilo a som,
Es lasso, vou dourmi tranquilo;
Lis oustau se soun pestela
E de soun mantèu estela
La niue agouloupo la vilo.

The day casts its last lights;
Far away a blue smoke rises,
It seems as if the mountains smoke;
In the great, black and quiet river
One sees, flashing like lightning,
The fires of the lanterns being lit,

Along the Rhône and the docks
One can hear a fisherman's song
Or the captain's whistle;
Song and noise from labor
Have slowly disappeared;
Arles looks like a country of dreams.

No one walks on the bridges anymore,
All is quiet; the town is sleepy,

It is weary and wants to sleep in peace;
The houses are locked
And night with its starry cape
Closes in upon the town.

(Aubanel, from "Vesprado a Trenco-Taio"
[Evening in Trinquetaille])⁴⁶

Tourist information. 35 place de la République. Tel: 04 90 18 41 20. Fax: 04 90 18 41 29. Email: <ot-arles@visitprovence.com>. Website: <www.ville-arles.fr>.

What to see. All the following places can be visited on foot and in one day. *Arènes & théâtre.* Tel: 04 90 18 41 22. *St-Trophîme.* Tel: 04 90 49 38 34. *Fondation Van Gogh.* Tel: 04 90 49 94 04. *Museon Arlaten,* 29 rue de la République Tel: 04 90 93 58 11. This museum contains a rich collection of Provençal furniture, costumes, and paintings, including Mistral's cradle and photographs of the major Provençal writers. If one has the time, the cemetery of *Alyscamps* is just a ten-minute walk from the center. Tel: 04 90 49 38 34. The *Musée d'Arles Antique* is on the bank of the Rhône and is definitely worth a visit. Tel: 04 90 18 88 88.

Where to stay. ****: *Jules César,* blvd des Lices. AC, pool, garage. Tel: 04 90 93 20. Fax: 04 90 93 33 47. *Nord Pinus,* place du Forum. AC, pool, garage. Tel: 04 90 93 44 44. Fax: 04 90 93 34 00. ***: *D'Arlatan,* 26 rue du Sauvage. Tel: 04 90 93 56 66. Fax: 04 90 49 68 45. *New Hotel,* 45 avenue Sadi Carnot. AC, pool, garage. Tel: 04 90 99 40 40. Fax: 04 90 93 32 50. **: *Calendal,* 22 place Dr Pomme. AC. Tel: 04 90 96 11 89. Fax: 04 90 96 05 84. *Amphithéâtre,* 5 rue Diderot. AC. Tel: 04 90 96 10 30. Fax: 04 90 93 98 69. B&B: Mme Poirier Ferrand, La Ravetière, route de Fontvieille, four miles from Arles, in Raphèle-les-Arles. Tel: 04 90 98 04 71. Pool, parking.

Where to eat. L'Olivier, 1 bis rue Réattu. *Le Jardin de Manon,* 14 avenue des Alyscamps.

The Camargue, Stes-Maries-de-la-Mer

South of Arles lies the Camargue, a vast and desolate marshland stretching between two branches of the Rhône, for years the refuge of hermits and exotic birds *(plate 10)*. Take D 570 south in the direction of Les Saintes-Maries-de-la-Mer (twenty-one miles) and stop at the Musée Camarguais, six miles south of Arles. The ticket can include a visit on a pathway through the marshland (one and a half hours). Bring a pair of binoculars for bird watching and some mosquito repellent if you are traveling in the spring or fall. For centuries these mosquito-infested marshes, battered by strong winds, were inhospitable. Those who ventured there were brave and solitary men. "Like the sea, unified despite its waves, this plain exudes a feeling of aloneness and boundlessness, and the Mistral's powerful breath blowing permanently, without obstacle, seems to flatten and enlarge the scenery," noted Daudet.[47] Years later, Simone de Beauvoir was fascinated by the region. "I love the Camargue's barrenness," she writes in her autobiography.[48] In 1970, the French government made most of it a wildlife sanctuary and national park. Biologists have counted over four hundred species of birds such as pink flamingoes, egrets, ibis, herons, and cormorants. The area is also rich in other wildlife (foxes, wild boars, bobcats, etc.); an abundance of eels and carp attract fishermen.

"The clusters of tamarisks and bulrushes seem like small islands on a calm sea," writes Daudet.[49] Salt mining was, for a long time, the only commercial activity for the few people who worked there, facing cold winter winds and the hot summer sun. The crossing on foot of the Camargue cost Frédéric Mistral's Mirèio her life—she died in Stes-Maries-de-la-Mer, on its western shores. Monks had ventured there and began draining the area. Then the *gardians* or bull raisers moved in *(plate 11)*. They are still there, living on farms or *manado* and raising horses of the Carmaguais type—white, short, stocky, but gentle. The gardians, dressed in colorful costumes (which they do not wear only for tourists), are generally reserved men who spend most of their time on horseback. They are not talkative but they are friendly. Many of them

The Camargue

welcome visitors on their premises and are happy to share their way of
life with them.

The small town of Les Saintes-Maries-de-la-Mer was originally
situated one mile inland from the Mediterranean shoreline, but over
the centuries the sea has gained ground, and the town is now danger-
ously close to the shore. The historian Strabon mentions that the
Greeks once built a temple of Artemis there and, in the fourth century
B.C., Festius Avenius recorded the existence of an old city. But the
town owes its unusual name to a medieval legend, according to which,
around A.D. 48, a group including Mary Magdalene, Lazarus, Mary
Jacobe (the Virgin Mary's sister), Mary Salome (mother of the apostle
John), and their servant Sara left Jerusalem in a small boat without sail
or oars and miraculously landed on these Provençal shores. Mary

Jacobe, Mary Salome, and Sara stayed in the region to preach the gospel. A small oratory and later, in the twelfth century, a church were built in the name of the two Marys. In 1448, at the instigation of King René of Provence, digging under the church uncovered the bones of the two Marys. René decided that every year pilgrimages should be made in their memory. The gypsies, who probably arrived in the region around that time, began their own pilgrimage to honor Sara who, they believe, did not arrive with the others from Jerusalem but was already living in the Camargue before the two Marys came ashore and helped them survive. Today, the traditional festivities in honor of the saints continue to attract several thousand visitors, including gypsies from all over France and neighboring countries. On May 24 the gypsies decorate the statue of Sara in the church, carry it to the shore, and douse it with water. Then they dance and sing until dawn. On the next day (Mary Jacobe's birthday), the statues of the two Marys are placed in a small boat and carried to the shore, where they are sanctified by the bishop. On the Sunday nearest October 22 (Mary Salome's birthday), a similar festival takes place.

The wide-open spaces and the feeling of solitude that emanates from the Camargue exerted a powerful fascination on the minds of a few Provençal writers. Folco de Baroncelli, after his marriage to Henriette Constantin in 1895, moved to Stes-Maries to lead the life of a gardian. He bought several horses and bulls and restored an old mas, L'Amarée. He lived there year-round with his wife and three girls, Nerto, Maguelone, and Frédérique (who married Henri Aubanel, the poet's nephew). Baroncelli campaigned to preserve the Camargue area and its wildlife from greedy developers who planned to drain its marshes. He was also a friend of the gypsies, sympathized with the struggle of Native Americans, organized the gardians into a proud community, and brought new vigor to their traditions and festivals. In 1914 he left to fight in the trenches of northern France. Upon his return in 1918 he resumed his work on the mas. But then things began to turn sour. His wife was ill and returned to Avignon, taking their daughters with her. Baroncelli also faced financial difficulty and was finally evicted from L'Amarée. Fortunately, the gardians helped him out, collecting funds and building

Folco de Baroncelli, photo: Musée Baroncelli,
Stes-Maries-de-la-Mer

him another mas, *Le Simbeu* (The Tamer). Baroncelli died in Avignon
and was buried in Stes-Maries.

In 1897, Joseph d'Arbaud (1874–1950), Baroncelli's cousin and
friend, followed in his footsteps to the Camargue. D'Arbaud was born
in Meyrargues, a few miles north of Aix, into a family where Provençal values and language were very much alive. His mother, Marie
d'Arbaud, taught him Provençal and wrote poems (*Li mouro de ribas*,
The blackberries of the hills, 1863), like her own father, Valère Martin.
D'Arbaud studied in Avignon and then read law in Aix and, in both

places, he met with the félibres. Like his cousin Baroncelli, he rented a mas in the Camargue and learned the art of bull riding. He also wrote poems such as *Lou lausié d'Arle* (The laurel of Arles), with a preface by Mistral. Tuberculosis forced him to live in Switzerland for a while. After World War II he returned to Aix, married, and succeeded Emile Sicard as editor of *Le feu*. D'Arbaud's masterpiece is *La bèstio dóu Vacarés* (The beast of Vacarés, 1926) written in Provençal with a French translation. The tale takes place in the fifteenth century in the southernmost tip of the Camargue, where one day the gardian Jacques Roubaud, mounted on his horse Clair-de-lune, met a strange beast, half man, half goat. The creature could speak and introduced himself, saying that he was a demigod but that his end was near. The beast helped Roubaud tame his wild horse Castor and then disappeared in the marshes. Roubaud was dumfounded and spent most of the following days trying to find the demigod again, but in vain. When he finally caught a glimpse of him, he was emaciated and dying. By the time Roubaud went home to fetch food, the beast had vanished into thin air again. D'Arbaud was also the author of many tales and poems such as *Li cant palustre* (Songs of the marsh), published after his death.

This story of the beast of Vacarés had a major influence on Bosco, who was one of d'Arbaud's best friends. His novel *Malicroix* (1948) tells the story of Martial Mégrémut's solitary life in the Camargue, where Mégrémut settled after inheriting a house from his uncle, Cornelius Malicroix. The latter had come to the Camargue to retire after a life spent sailing around the world. He lived there with his dog and Balandran, his dutiful servant. The experience of solitude presents a considerable challenge for Mégrémut, because his family is above all sociable and rarely ventured out of their village. But after a few weeks, he falls in love with this forlorn country where "the wind is drunken" and "words, noises, silences and even objects speak an idiom of their own." Water and the wild open spaces of the Camargue are two elements that attracted Bosco to the Camargue and inspired his imagination. Nature around him made him feel as if he were in a dream: "I was in the low lands, completely surrounded with water whose presence I felt under the soil of this flat island, a mere band of silt attached by the plants that

Joseph d'Arbaud, photo: Editions Grasset

mist and rain had soaked and made flexible. The clay soil yielded under my steps and I knew that the roots of the tall willows drank in the very heart of the river under that earth rotten with humidity. Hedges of trees and bushes prevented me from seeing the shore but through their grayish wall a faint whisper and the great murmur of the powerful fleeting waters."[50]

The Camargue and Stes-Maries-de-la-Mer reminded Van Gogh of Holland: "One night I went for a walk by the sea along the empty shore. It was not gay, but neither was it sad; it was—beautiful. The deep blue sky was flicked with clouds of a blue deeper than the fundamental blue of intense cobalt, and others of a clearer blue, like the blue whiteness of the Milky Way. On the blue depth the stars were sparkling, greenish, yellow, white, rose, brighter, flashing more like jewels than they do even in Paris. The sea was a very deep ultramarine." The vastness of the Mediterranean and its myriad colors imparted to Van Gogh a profound feeling of freedom and completely reassured him that coming south was the best decision he had made. "Now that I have seen the sea here I am absolutely convinced of the importance of staying in the Midi, and of piling up on, exaggerating the color. Africa is not far away. I have the conviction that simply by dint of staying on here I shall set my individuality free."[51]

Tourist information. 5 avenue Van Gogh, on the boardwalk. Tel: 04 90 97 82 55. Fax: 04 90 97 71 15. Website: <www.saintesmariesde lamer. com>.

What to see. Camarguais Museum. Tel: 04 90 97 10 82. Small museum created in a former cattle and sheep ranch. *Baroncelli Museum.* A very small museum located near the church and dedicated to Baroncelli and the Camargue, Tel: 04 90 97 87 60. *Church.* Place de l'Eglise. Twelfth-century fortified church. Cycling, fishing, horseback riding available as well as boat rides on the Rhône, a good way to catch a glimpse of the wildlife.

Where to stay. A few miles north of Stes-Maries on D 570: ****: *L'Auberge Cavalière.* AC, pool, parking. Tel: 04 90 97 88 88. Fax: 04 90 97 84 07. Email: <auberge.cavaliere@wanadoo.fr>. *Le Mas du Tadorne.* AC, pool, parking. Tel: 04 90 97 93 11. Fax: 04 90 97 71 04. ***: *Mas des Roseaux.* Pool, parking. Tel: 04 90 97 86 12. Fax: 04 90 97 70 84. *L'Etrier Camarguais.* AC, pool, parking. Tel: 04 90 97 81 14. Fax: 04 90 97 88 11. Website: <www.letrier.com>.

In Stes-Maries: ***: *Galoubet.* AC, pool, parking. Tel: 04 90 97 82 17. Fax: 04 90 97 71 20. *Mas des Rièges,* route Cacharel. Pool, parking. Tel: 04 90 97 85 07. Fax: 04 90 97 72 26. **: *Lou Marques,* rue Vibre. Tel: 04 90 97 82 89. Fax: 04 90 97 72 24. Email: <hotelloumarques @netcourrier.com>.

The High Country and Aix-en-Provence

The horizon was a distant serpentine line of hills gently sprinkled with blue.

—Jean Giono, *Le hussard sur le toit*

The Luberon, Gordes

Roussillon

Goult, Ménerbes, Oppède-le-Vieux

Lacoste

Bonnieux and Environs

Lourmarin and Environs

Manosque

North of Manosque: Jean Giono's Provence

Farther North: Serres, Mens, Gap

Sisteron

Digne

Aix-en-Provence and Environs

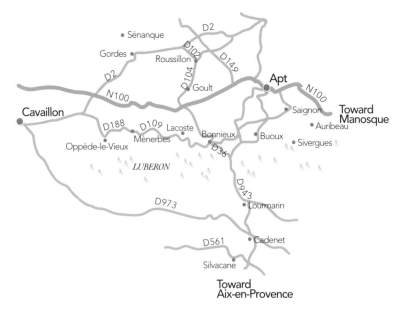

The Luberon

The Luberon, Gordes

Northern Provence is a country of mountains. East of the little town of Cavaillon is the Luberon, a low mountain (3,690 feet at Mourre Nègre) that extends about forty miles. It is covered with a dense forest of pine, beech, oak, and cedar trees, and in 1977 the government made it a national park. People have lived on this mountain since prehistoric times. Ligurians and Romans settled there. In the Middle Ages, the Luberon became a refuge for the Waldenses, disciples of the twelfth-century religious leader Peter Waldo (Valdes), who opposed the hierarchy and dogmas of the Catholic Church and preached a return to apostolic simplicity. In the sixteenth century, many Waldenses joined the Protestants in waging bloody wars against the Catholics. In the spring of 1545, the Baron of Oppède launched a fierce battle against the Protestants and Waldenses. Many were killed or sent to the galleys. The rest fled. To this day, many Protestants come here in pilgrimage, and the story of the persecution is still alive in local memories.

The Luberon is also the place with the highest concentration of *bories* in Provence. These are ancient round stone huts that one can see in the middle of fields. There are approximately three thousand of them all over Provence. Shepherds have used them for centuries but their origin remains mysterious. Archeologists believe that in certain places, such as in the settlement near Gordes, they were used as permanent homes. The stone dwellings have been restored, and the village of bories is well worth a visit *(plate 12)*. Gordes (D 2 from Cavaillon) itself is a beautiful Provençal village on the southern slope of a steep hill and with a Renaissance castle at its center *(plate 13)*. A few colorful shops, cafés, and restaurants make it an ideal stopover for lunch. A couple of miles north on D 117 lies the monastery of Sénanque, surrounded by lavender fields *(plate 14)*. Built in the twelfth century, it was the home of Cistercian monks until the middle of the sixteenth century when the Waldenses ransacked it. Abandoned and then restored, the monastery is now the residence of a small community of six monks. It is open to visitors except on Sunday morning and religious holidays.

Tourist information. Place du Château. Tel: 04 90 72 02 75.

What to see. Bories. Tel: 04 90 72 03 48. *Castle.* Tel: 04 90 72 02 75. *Abbey of Sénanque.* Tel: 04 90 72 05 72.

Where to stay. ****: *Les Bories,* route de Sénanque. AC, pool, parking. Tel: 04 90 72 00 51. Fax: 04 90 72 01 22. *La Bastide de Gordes,* rue de la Combe. AC, pool, parking. Tel: 04 90 72 12 12. Fax: 04 90 72 05 20. ***: *Le Gordos,* route de Cavaillon. Pool, parking. Tel: 04 90 72 00 75. Fax: 04 90 72 07 00. *La Gacholle,* route de Murs. Pool, parking. Tel: 04 90 72 01 36. Fax: 04 90 72 01 81. B&Bs: *La Badelle.* Pool, parking. Tel: 04 90 72 33 19. Fax: 04 90 72 48 74. M. and Mme Mifsud. Pool, parking. Tel & Fax: 04 90 72 08 13. *Mme Governale.* Pool, parking. Tel: 04 90 72 41 43.

Where to eat. Les Bories. * *L'Estellan. Mas Tourteron,* route des Imberts.

Roussillon

A fifteen-minute drive east on D 2 between vineyards is the small village of Roussillon, famous for its ochre quarries *(plates 15–17)*. This industry has now stopped but the beautiful quarries have been turned into a small park. Some older residents still remember that on a cold November afternoon in 1942 a tall and lanky man with green eyes and round glasses arrived in the village, exhausted. He and his companion

Suzanne Deschevaux-Dumesnil had walked almost all the way from Lyons. Like many other members of the French Resistance, they had fled Paris, occupied by the Germans, and barely escaped arrest by the Gestapo. Provence was in the *zone libre* at that time and still unoccupied by enemy troops. The man, who went by the name of Sam, spoke French but with an accent. Irishman Samuel Beckett (1906–1989) was thirty-six years old and had been living for the past four years in Paris, where he befriended his compatriot James Joyce. Beckett was relatively unknown then. He was the author of *More Pricks Than Kicks*, banned in Ireland, and *Murphy*, a novel, but neither had brought him money or fame. Strangely enough, an editor had approached him for an English translation of the Marquis de Sade's *Cent-vingt jours de Sodome* (120 days of Sodom). Beckett could certainly have used the money and even liked Sade's "visions of love and physical ecstasy," according to biographer Deirdre Bair.[1] But he was afraid of linking his name to that of Sade and refused to jeopardize his literary career. Did Beckett know that one of Sade's Provençal residences was the castle of Lacoste, a couple of miles south of Roussillon?

Beckett and his companion lodged in Roussillon's only inn, the Hôtel de la Poste run by Mme Escoffier, widow of the famous chef. The hotel no longer exists, but the restaurant David occupies the site. During World War II the Hôtel de la Poste was crowded with refugees. At first, Sam and Suzanne kept to themselves and spent their time visiting the beautiful countryside, hoping like everyone else that the war would soon end. But in November 1942, the Germans finally occupied all of France including Provence, shattering all hopes. At the hotel, Beckett made the acquaintance of painter Henri Hayden and his wife Josette, and befriended Miss Beamish, an English lady who lived in a small house at the edge of the village. In the evenings, he would listen to the radio or play chess with Hayden. But the routine soon became unbearable and the hotel too small and boring. Depression set in. So, early in 1943, he and Suzanne moved into a larger house right at the end of town, on the road to Apt. Its owner, M. Rousset, was a notary in Cavaillon. The house was about six hundred square feet and sat on three acres of land. It was secluded and peaceful and suited Beckett

Samuel Beckett,
photo: Roger-Viollet

Beckett's house in Roussillon

The High Country and Aix-en-Provence

Plate 1. Orange: The Theater

Plate 2. Vaison-la-Romaine

Plate 3. Mont Ventoux

Plate 4.
Fontaine-de-Vaucluse

Plate 5. Tartarin de Tarascon

*Plate 6.
Tarasque Festival*

*Plate 7.
Sunflower Field,
St-Rémy*

Plate 8.
Montauban
Castle

Plate 9.
Daudet's Mill

Plate 10. The Camargue

Plate 11. A Gardian

Plate 12.
Village des Bories

Plate 13. Gordes

Plate 14. Sénanque Abbey

Plate 15.
Vineyards in
the Luberon

Plate 16.
Roussillon

Plate 17.
Roussillon: Ochre quarry

Plate 18. Vaugines church

Plate 19.
The Durance
River near
Manosque

Plate 20.
The Valensole
Plateau in the fall

Plate 21. On the road to Banon

and Deschevaux-Dumesnil. They lived there for two years. Beckett read, wrote *Watt*, and resumed his activities in the Resistance. In April 1945, he left for Ireland. Roussillon has not forgotten its former guests; the cultural center regularly organizes readings and plays by Beckett. M. Rousset's daughter has put the house up for sale. Built at the beginning of the twenty-first century, it is now in need of repairs. The town hall is interested in purchasing it, and Associate Mayor Henri Marcou and Annie Joly, a former journalist, are planning to turn *La Maison de Beckett* into a center for writers.

In August 1950, Professor Laurence Wylie arrived in Roussillon to live for one year. Wylie was on sabbatical from Haverford College in Philadelphia, where he taught French civilization. His project was to research the social life of a southern rural community. After a week of traveling in the Luberon he selected Roussillon as a good village for sociological study, rented a house, and moved in with his wife and their two young sons. The inhabitants were friendly, and the Wylies were rapidly accepted into the community. To understand conversations between locals, Wylie began to learn Provençal, which at the time was still widely used. Wylie took notes on every aspect of social life, from school to amorous traditions, weddings, work, and funerals, and took hundreds of photographs of the village and its inhabitants. His research was published as the successful book *Village in the Vaucluse* (1957), in which, for the sake of discretion, Roussillon is called Peyrane. During the year he spent in Roussillon, Wylie never heard the name of Beckett. However, when Wylie read *En attendant Godot* (Waiting for Godot, 1952) in the original French a few years later, he was surprised to find that in Act 2 the character Vladimir mentions living in the Vaucluse, remembers the ochre quarries ("là-bas tout est rouge!"), and recalls picking grapes for a man by the name of Bonnely.[2] In his English translation, Beckett replaced Vaucluse with Macon and deleted the names of Bonnely and Roussillon. Vladimir says: "Picking grapes for a man called . . . I can't think of the name of the man, at a place called . . . can't think of the name of the place." But the original French version provides evidence that Roussillon was still in Beckett's mind when he wrote his play. The origin of the name Godot has piqued curiosity.

Beckett never fully explained himself on this subject. Did he borrow the name Godot from Provençal (*Godo:* a lazy man)? Beckett, permanently settled in Paris, never returned to Roussillon, although he did send postcards to a few friends there.

Tourist information. Place de la Poste. Tel: 04 90 05 60 25. Fax: 04 90 05 60 25. Email: <ot-roussillon@axit.fr>.

What to see. The former quarry: starting from the tourist office, the visit takes about forty-five minutes on foot (round-trip). Good walking shoes are recommended. Closed on rainy days. Beckett's house is a ten-minute walk on the road to Apt, to the left of the black metal cross.

Where to stay. ***: *Mas de Garrigon,* two miles north on D 2. Pool, parking. Tel: 04 90 05 63 22. Fax: 04 90 05 70 01. *Les Sables d'Ocre,* route d'Apt. AC, pool, parking. Tel: 04 90 05 55 55. Fax: 04 90 05 55 50. B&Bs: *Les Passiflores.* Pool, parking. Tel: 04 90 05 69 61. Fax: 04 90 05 69 61. *Les Gaillanes.* Pool, parking. Tel: 04 90 05 75 63. *Les Sablières.* Pool, parking. Tel: 04 90 05 66 02. Fax: 04 90 05 73 18.

Where to eat. David, place de la Poste.

Goult, Ménerbes, Oppède-le-Vieux

From Roussillon drive down to Goult (D 104) and Ménerbes (D 218), a picturesque village on a small hilltop near where English writer Peter Mayle and his wife bought a house in the 1980s. Mayle's account of his experience of life in the Luberon, as reported in *A Year in Provence* (1989), is a very good introduction to the area and contains faithful and amusing descriptions of the local way of life and customs. Following its success Mayle wrote a sequel, *Toujours Provence,* the novel *Hotel Pastis,* and several other books. Although his wife and he have now left the area, *les Anglais,* as they were known locally, have made Ménerbes famous. With a good dose of humor, Mayle communicates to the reader both his enthusiasm for Provence and his bewilderment at local customs. Always curious and eager to meet the locals, Mayle is a model traveler. His adventures in the Luberon are true to life and entertaining, and, at times, reminiscent of Daudet.

Three miles to the west (D 188), among the vineyards, is Oppède-le-Vieux, perhaps the Luberon's best-preserved medieval village. During the Middle Ages it was part of the Comtat Venaissin and belonged to the popes. It developed into a prosperous walled town, a Catholic stronghold with a castle and a church. In the fifteenth century its population reached two thousand. After Oppède gained its independence from the pope, it passed into the hands of powerful barons determined to eliminate the heretics. Later the town spread outside the enclosing walls into the more fertile valley. Gradually the castle was deserted and, after the 1731 earthquake, finally abandoned. Its ruins still stand, and a handful of residents (thirty-seven by a recent count) still cling to their village. There are two café-restaurants. Parking is available outside the village and is guarded in the summer.

> *Where to stay.* B&Bs: *Mas Marican*, Goult. Pool, parking. Tel & Fax: 04 90 72 28 09. *Les Peirelles*, Ménerbes. Pool, parking. Tel: 04 90 72 23 42. Fax: 04 90 72 23 56. *Mas du Guillaumet*, Oppède-le-Vieux. Pool, parking. Tel: 04 90 76 82 47. *Le Moulin à Vent*, Oppède-le-Vieux. Pool, parking. Tel: 04 90 76 90 60.

Lacoste

Back on D 109, a short drive away from Ménerbes on the right is the tiny Abbey of St-Hilaire. It is located just before the village of Lacoste, at the end of a short dirt road, a quarter of a mile away from D 109. The abbey was built in 1254 by White Friars (Carmelites). The Carmelite monks lived there until 1779 when, their number declining, it was closed down. Bought by the monks of Sénanque, it then passed into the hands of successive farmers. Today it is privately owned but also a classified historical monument. The visit is free. The village of Lacoste, a mile away on D 109, overlooks the valley and faces Bonnieux in the east. Lacoste is one of the few Luberon villages whose population (about four hundred) has remained constant since the Middle Ages. Its houses have been maintained and restored. On top of it sit the ruins of an old castle. Few people knew the history of the castle as well as did its late owner, M. Bouer. Its origins are indeed ancient, for it was built on the site of a Roman fortress. The earliest known lord was Baron Eldebert in the eleventh century. It then became the property of the Barthélemys of Simiane who enlarged and remodeled it, adding an extra story. In 1649 Gaspard de Sade bought the place, and his descendant, the infamous Marquis de Sade (1740–1814), received it as a wedding present from his father.

At the time the castle comprised forty-two rooms, including twenty-two bedrooms, several boudoirs, a chapel, and underground galleries. It was three stories high and surrounded by gardens planted with olive and almond trees. Like his predecessors, Sade transformed the place, adapting it to the fashion of the time and, being especially fond of the theater, having a small stage built on the second floor. The theater could accommodate 120 spectators (half seated, half standing) and was approximately 30 feet square. Local notables were often invited to the performances. Sade adapted the contemporary plays of Voltaire, Diderot, and Regnard, but he also wrote his own, such as *Le mariage du siècle* (The wedding of the century). He regularly acted, as did his wife and some of the villagers and staff. He even hired professional actors and had at one time a troupe of a dozen men and women who would perform for him and his guests.

Sade was a libertine whose amorous adventures defied the existing moral order and especially offended his mother-in-law, who used every means in her power to see that he be punished. She was successful: altogether, Sade spent thirty-five years in jail. It is there that he wrote most of his literary works. Before psychologists and doctors adopted his name as a modern label for deviant sexual practices, for centuries it had represented Provençal respectability and honor. The Sades had been notables since the twelfth century, living in Avignon and including among their members governors, lawyers, consuls, and ambassadors who worked with the popes. They were wealthy and owned property including the castles of Mazan, Saumane, and Lacoste. Beautiful Laure de Noves, reputedly the Laura with whom Petrarch fell in love, was married to Hugues de Sade.

Louis Alphonse Donatien, Marquis de Sade, was born in Paris to Count Jean-François de Sade, a general in the royal army, and his wife Marie Elénore Maillé de Carman, a distant cousin of the royal family who served as lady-in-waiting to the Princesse de Condé. Except for his father, Sade's paternal relatives never left Provence. His uncle Jacques de Sade was a priest and the author of a three-volume biography of Petrarch, *Mémoires pour la vie de François Pétrarque* (1764–67), an invaluable work, even for modern scholars. Four of Sade's aunts were nuns in Avignon and Cavaillon. At the age of four, Sade was sent to Avignon to be educated. There, he lived with his grandmother and then with his uncle Jacques in the Saumane Castle. Sade and his uncle would also often visit Lacoste. Sade grew up a healthy boy and learned Provençal from his grandparents and the village boys with whom he played. Little is known about his childhood. Like any other boy his age, he seems to have been fascinated by the castle's numerous underground galleries and by the amorous adventures of his uncle who, despite being a priest, had numerous mistresses.

Unfortunately, Sade's Provençal days came to an end at the age of ten when his father decided he should return to Paris to receive the education proper to his class. Sade was enrolled as a boarder in the Collège Clermont (now Lycée Louis le Grand), where he spent the next four years. After graduation, in 1755, he was made an officer and began his career in the king's army. Sade fought in Prussia, achieving the rank of captain at the end of the Seven Years' War, in 1763. That year, he married Renée de Montreuil. His father arranged the marriage, but at first the marquis refused, for he was in love with a beautiful Provençale named Laure de Lauris. However, accepting his father's bribe of the castles of Saumane and Lacoste, he finally acquiesced.

Sade resided in Lacoste only temporarily, usually in the spring or summer. Often he came with his wife and three children, but on other occasions he instead brought his mistresses, which caused a scandal among the staff and relatives. The rest of the year Sade and his family lived in Normandy at the Montreuil family castle of Echauffaur.

Physically the marquis was rather handsome, of average height for his time (five feet, two inches) and well proportioned. With blond hair, a fair complexion, and light blue eyes, he looked more like a Northerner than a Provençal, but Provence remained dear to him.

Sade's immoral behavior, gambling, and sexual perversions apparently began during his adolescence or even earlier, if we believe his biographers' claim that he may have spied on some of his uncle Jacques's sexual encounters. (In 1762, Jacques was arrested in a brothel.) Marriage did not put an end to the marquis's immoral conduct: six months after his wedding, he was jailed fifteen days for whipping a prostitute. But prison was not a solution for Sade and he never learned his lesson. In 1772, several prostitutes in Marseille accused him of forcing them to eat a great quantity of aphrodisiac candies, after which they became violently ill. Sade and his valet Latour were found guilty of poisoning and sodomy, the Parliament of Aix condemned them to death. Alerted, the two men left Lacoste and found temporary refuge in the kingdom of Savoy. Informed of their presence, the Duke of Savoy had the two men arrested and imprisoned in the fortress of Miolans. Five months later Sade and Latour escaped and left for Italy. In 1777, Sade returned to Paris. He was immediately arrested and jailed in Vincennes. In his little cell, Sade corresponded with his wife; sometimes his children visited him. He was not allowed to read Jean Jacques Rousseau but found consolation in Petrarch. "I read him voraciously and with immense pleasure," he wrote to his wife in 1779.[3] Transferred to the insane asylum at Charenton and freed in 1790, he was arrested again four years later, this time by the revolutionaries, and barely escaped the guillotine. Sentenced again in 1801, he was sent back to Charenton, where he died in 1814. Except for *Justine* (1791), it was in his cell that he wrote the majority of his licentious works such as *Les cent-vingt jours de Sodome* or *La philosophie dans le boudoir* (1795). His writings had great influence on authors such as Lautréamont, Maupassant, and Apollinaire. Provence does not occupy a major place in Sade's works except perhaps in *La marquise de Gange* where he describes Avignon, Cadenet, Aix, and Tarascon.

In 1796, Sade, heavily indebted, sold Lacoste to Stanislas de Rovère. Later it passed into the hands of M. Gothon, husband of Sade's servant. It became then the property of Cyprien Jean, a local mason. When the late M. Bouer, a local English teacher descended from Sade's friend Thomas Paulet, purchased it in 1944, only a pile of rubble remained. But Bouer was a man with a dream. After years of thorough research in the archives, Bouer began the immense task of restoring the castle with the help of volunteers. The castle is now state property. The owner of the Café de Sade in town tells the story of a foreign visitor who encountered Bouer working near the castle. Bouer, in the French manner, introduced himself to her only as "the owner of the castle," which both surprised and fascinated the foreigner. He answered her questions about the progress of the restoration and then returned to his work. Very excited, the visitor then walked down to the café for a drink and told the owners that she had just talked to the marquis. She explained that he had been very courteous and argued that the stories about his sexual obsessions were probably exaggerated.

Where to stay. B&Bs: *Ferme l'Avellan.* Pool, parking. Tel: 04 90 75 85 10. Fax: 04 90 75 85 40. *Bonne Terre.* Pool, parking. Tel: 04 90 75 85 53. Fax: 04 90 75 85 53.

> Passant,
> Agenouille-toi pour prier
> Près du plus malheureux des hommes.
> Il naquit au siècle dernier
> Et mourut au siècle où nous sommes.
>
> Passerby,
> Kneel and pray
> Near the unhappiest man.
> He was born during the last century
> And died in the century in which we live.
>
> (From the Marquis de Sade's epitaph)

Bonnieux and Environs

From Lacoste you can drive down to picturesque Bonnieux, which Roumanille chose for the setting of his tale *Mademoiselle d'Inguimberti*. In the eighteenth century, Roumanille relates, Mlle d'Inguimberti, a local notable, had become rather pious in her old age and often went to church to pray in front of a painting of St. Anthony. When the church was empty she would talk to the saint and one day she even invited him over for dinner. To her great surprise, one day Anthony answered that he accepted. Mlle Inguimberti was elated and immediately went home to tell her maid to prepare a good dinner for the next day, as she was expecting company. When Anthony arrived the following evening, the maid recognized Luquet, the beadle disguised as the saint, and after he had feasted and drunk several glasses of wine, she went to get the vicar. The latter came disguised as St. Peter, scaring Luquet, and kicked him out of the house, telling Mlle Inguimberti that he had escaped from Paradise. You can stop over to visit the small but interesting bread museum (Musée de la Boulangerie, Tel: 04 90 75 88 34) and have lunch at the Fournil.

A couple of miles north of Bonnieux, on D 149, is the old Roman bridge, Pont Julien, built in the third century B.C. over the Coulon River on the road from Italy to Spain. Ten minutes east of Bonnieux on D 113 is the interesting archeological site of Buoux, occupied by the Ligurians and then the Romans. In the fourteenth and fifteenth centuries a veritable fortress stood there. Farther east are the small villages of Saignon, Auribeau, and Sivergues that Bosco chose as the setting for his melancholy novel *L'habitant de Sivergues* (1935), in which the protagonist discovers hidden in the church an old diary that registered the atrocities of the religious wars between the Waldenses and the Catholics.

Where to stay. ****: *La Bastide de Capelongue*, route de Lourmarin. AC, pool, parking. Tel: 04 90 75 89 78. Fax: 04 90 75 93 03. ***: *Hostellerie du Prieuré*. Tel: 04 90 75 80 78. Fax: 04 90 75 96 00. *Auberge de l'Aigle Brun*, three miles on D 36. Pool, parking. Tel: 04

90 04 47 00. Fax: 04 90 04 47 00. B&Bs: *Les Terrasses du Luberon.*
Pool, parking. Tel & fax: 04 9075 87 40. *Le Clos du Buis.* Pool, parking. Tel: 04 90 75 88 48. Fax: 04 90 75 88 57. Website: <luberonnews.com>. *Les Trois Sources.* Pool, parking. Tel: 04 90 75 95 58. Fax: 04 9075 89 95. Website: <luberon-news.com/les-troissources>.

Lourmarin and Environs

Ten minutes south of Bonnieux is Lourmarin, where Henri Bosco and Albert Camus (1913–1960) rest in peace. Bosco revered the Luberon as a magic mountain that inspired his imagination. Bosco discovered Lourmarin in the early 1920s when a friend of his, Robert Laurent-Vibert, bought the fifteenth-century castle on the western end of the village. Peaceful and romantic, the castle was surrounded with pines, lavender, rosemary, and olive trees. Bosco and his wife Madeleine spent many summers there and helped catalogue books for the library. At the death of Laurent-Vibert in a car accident in 1925, the castle became the property of the Academy of Aix, but Bosco continued to play a major part in its administration. In 1940, he and Madeleine bought a small cottage in the vineyards near the village as their vacation home. It was only "two bedrooms, a front porch, a little bit of water and a lot of sun" but large enough to entertain his friends. Marseillais poets Gabriel Audisio and Louis Brauquier often came to visit.

Bosco loved the atmosphere of serenity and peace that ruled the countryside. To his eyes the Roman past was everywhere present. His first novel, *Pierre Lampedouze* (1924), tells the story of an aspiring Parisian poet who inherits a small property in the village of Cucuron not far from Lourmarin and comes to settle there permanently. *Le sanglier* (The wild boar, 1932) also takes place in the Luberon. It is a mysterious tale of gypsies and secretive villagers hunting an elusive wild boar. Imagination, myths, and death are woven together and take the reader on an inner voyage. *Le Trestoulas* (1934), on the other hand, tells

Henri Bosco, photo: Fond Bosco, University of Nice

of the villagers' more utilitarian concerns, their taciturn character, their ancestral attachment to the land, and their traditional village feuds. The notary, who in France is also the real estate lawyer, plays an essential part in Bosco's novels and represents the link between life and the afterlife. Like Bosco himself, most of his characters, such as Constantin Gloriot in *L'âne Culotte* (Culotte the donkey, 1937) or Frédéric Meyrel in *Un rameau de la nuit* (A night bough, 1950), are dreamers who slowly become bewitched by the discreet magic of the mountain. No one before Bosco had so persistently tried to discover the Luberon's ancient secrets and so successfully described its hidden beauties. Most of the places Bosco mentions, including Sivergues, Cucuron, and Vau-

Lourmarin

gines, are real. Some others, however, such as Geneval, Sancergues, and Cabridelle, are figments of his imagination.

Albert Camus first came to visit Lourmarin in 1946 with journalist friends invited by Bosco. The two had met in Paris. Undoubtedly, the solitude and silence of the place reminded Camus of his native Algeria. His first days spent in Lourmarin left a vivid impression: "I lived in an old restored castle with enormous rooms, whitewashed, and furnished with ancient and rare pieces of furniture, and all day long I walked through a country of hills, olive trees, and cypresses. The days glittered with sun, the evenings were mild, and the nights bright with stars," he wrote to Patricia Blake.[4] Camus was then thirty-three years old. He was the editor of *Combat* and the successful author of *L'étranger* (1942) and *Caligula* (1945). Since the war he had lived in Paris but often came to Provence to visit his friend René Char at Isle-sur-la-Sorgue. The dry air and sunshine gave him new energy, and his discussions with the poet delighted him.

Camus grew fonder of the South every year and, in 1958, with the money from his recent Nobel Prize, he and his wife Francine bought a

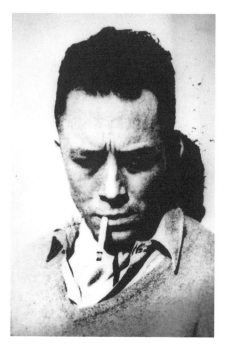

Albert Camus,
photo: Roger-Viollet

house in Lourmarin, on the rue de l'Eglise (now rue Albert Camus). It was a modest house with a small yard planted with olive trees. Downstairs, a kitchen, dining room, and two bedrooms. On the second floor, two more rooms and a bath. Camus had an office built in the attic, for he intended to live there permanently. But Francine and their children were attached to Paris and came to Lourmarin only during the school vacation. Camus often ate at Ogier's in town but was constantly bothered by tourists and journalists, so he finally retreated to his house and asked his maid to cook for him.

Camus spent most of his day writing in his office or on the terrace in the Provençal sun. He worked on *Le premier homme* (The first man). He allowed himself long pauses to walk through the hills and vineyards. Sociable and unpretentious, he maintained good relationships with the locals who always welcomed him in their cafés and homes. As far as anyone can tell, he and Bosco did not see each other. The two men were going to be closer in death, though. Suffering from health problems due to tuberculosis contracted at an early age, Camus had chosen Lourmarin as the place he would be buried, but he certainly did not foresee his death on January 3, 1960, in a car accident near Sens in Burgundy. Following his wish, Camus was buried in Lourmarin's cemetery, a half-mile south of the village. Francine lies next to him. Bosco followed him there in 1976.

Lourmarin Refuge

Si je mourais dans une ville
Emportez bien vite ma cendre
Ce n'est pas là qu'il faut m'étendre
Mais ailleurs dans un champ d'argile.
En Provence, il est des collines
De calcaire frais, pleines d'antres.
Mettez-y mon âme, elle y entre.
Il suffit qu'on incline . . .
Le Luberon et les Alpilles
Abritent ces refuges
Deux vieux cyprès, l'ombre du Juge
Et quatre mots pour la famille
Rien de plus. Pas une prière
Quatre mots clairs en apparence
Où l'on dise: "Il est dans la terre"
Et puis le Silence.

Lourmarin Refuge

If I were to die in a city
Quickly take away my ashes
It is not there that I should lie
But elsewhere in a field of clay.
In Provence, there are hills
Of fresh limestone, full of dens.
Place my soul there, it will fit.

Simply tilt it . . .
The Luberon and the Alpilles
Hide such refuges
Two old cypress trees, the shadow of the Judge
And four words for the family
Nothing more. No prayer
Four words clear in appearance
Where it will be said: "He is in the ground."
And then Silence.

(Bosco)[5]

Tourist information. 8 avenue de Girard. Tel: 04 90 68 10 77. Website: <www.lourmarin.com>.

What to see. Le Château. Tel: 04 90 68 15 23.

Where to stay. ***: *Le Moulin,* rue du Temple. AC, garage. Tel: 04 90 68 06 69. Fax: 04 90 68 31 76. *Hôtel de Guilles,* route de Vaugines. Pool, parking. Tel: 04 90 68 30 55. Fax: 04 90 68 37 41. **: *Le Paradou.* Tel: 04 90 68 04 05. B&Bs: *Villa St-Louis.* Parking. Tel: 04 90 68 39 18. *La Luberonne.* Pool, parking. Tel: 04 90 08 58 63. *La Lombarde.* Pool, parking. Tel: 04 90 08 40 60. Fax: 04 90 08 40 64.

Where to eat. Le Moulin.** *Auberge de la Fenière.** *L'Antiquaire. Maison Ollier.*

South of Lourmarin, near La Roque d'Anthéron, famous for its summer piano music festival, lies the twelfth-century Cistercian abbey of Silvacane. Unlike Sénanque, it was already abandoned at the end of the eighteenth century. Since then it has been completely restored and is open to the public. From Lourmarin you can also go east to Vaugines and its picturesque church *(plate 18)* and drive through Cucuron, "gallant vilajoun prouvençau quiha sus un mamèu dou Leberoun coume un passeroun sus uno coucourdo" (charming little village that sits on a hill in the Luberon like a sparrow on a pumpkin), according to Roumanille.[6]

Where to stay. In Vaugines. **: *Hostellerie du Luberon.* Tel: 04 90 77
27 19. Fax: 04 90 77 13 08. B&B: *Les Grandes Garrigues.* Pool, parking. Tel: 04 90 77 10 71.

In Cucuron. **: *Hôtel de l'Etang.* Tel: 04 90 77 21 25. Fax: 04 90
77 10 98. *: *L'Arbre de Mai.* Tel & Fax: 04 90 77 25 10.

Manosque

At the eastern end of the Luberon lies the Durance valley *(plate 19)*
with market towns such as Manosque and Sisteron. The traveler is now
in the Southern Alps and, venturing farther north through Embrun and
Briançon, will encounter distinctive Alpine characteristics in the architecture, language, and traditions. For a long time, northern Provence
was considered to be a backcountry, a place of lone shepherds and
taciturn farmers. Roads were few and, except in the valley, communication between villages difficult. Many inhabitants of the region abandoned their homes, attracted by the promise of work and an easier life
in the southern cities. Those who stayed behind were deeply attached
to their land. Novelists Jean Giono and Pierre Magnan have, each in
his own way, successfully described the beautiful nature of this high
country and the race of rugged people who inhabit it.

Northern Provence has always produced scholars, poets, and
writers. In the Middle Ages troubadours went from castle to castle
all the way to Embrun, and sang of love and beauty or criticized war
and political decisions. Centuries later literature continued to flourish.
In Manosque, Jean Toussain Avril (1775–1841) published a French-
Provençal dictionary (1839) to help the local population learn French.
In the second half of the nineteenth century, the peaceful little town
rallied with enthusiasm to the ideal of the félibres, and Mistral was
acclaimed there as a hero. Elémir Bourges (1852–1925), a young and
promising writer, was born there but, unfortunately for Manosque, he
left at the age of twenty-two and settled permanently in Paris. There,

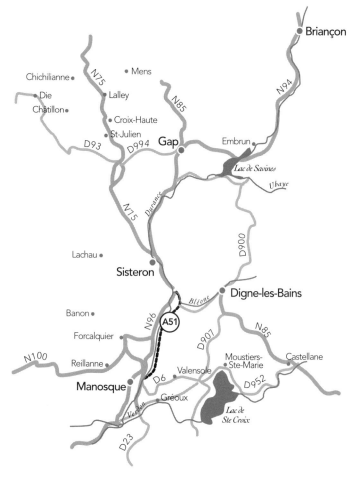

The High Country

Bourges worked as a journalist, befriended Mallarmé, and attempted to become symbolism's main novelist. His most famous novel is perhaps *Le crépuscule des dieux* (Twilight of the gods, 1884). On the whole, his work bears little trace of Provence.

In contrast, the story of Lazarine Nègre, Manosque's famed poetess, is deeply imbedded in the cultural and literary revival of Provence, a movement in which, as the chapter on western Provence has shown, women's contributions were welcomed and encouraged. The life of Lazarine Nègre is a good example of the collegial atmosphere that existed between Provençal writers, both men and women. Nègre (1848–1899) was the eldest of four children. Her parents were simple farmers who spoke only *Gavot*, one of Provençal's northern dialects. In those days, Manosque was an active market town with a population of about five thousand. Its economy was based on the production of wheat, wine, oil, and vegetables and the manufacture of silk. Lazarine learned to speak, write, and read French at school. She helped with the usual household tasks and took care of her three siblings. Like many young girls of the time, she was married at the age of fifteen. Her husband, Antoine Eugène Pourcin, was, as it happened, Jean Giono's great-uncle. But Nègre's married life was not a happy one and after she lost her only son at an early age, her marital problems grew worse. Taking advantage of the reinstatement of divorce (1884), she left her husband, thus becoming Manosque's first divorced woman! She moved to Marseille and, near the famous Canebière, the city's main street, she and her sister opened a poultry shop.

But Nègre also had literary ambitions. Like every Provençal, she had read *Mirèio* and dreamed of writing in her turn. Whenever she had the time, she jotted down poems in French, the language she was taught in school; but one day, after listening to Father Xavier de Fourvières preach in Provençal in St-Laurent Church, she decided she should write in the language she knew best. She got hold of books and learned on her own and with the help of Paul Arène and of *Moussu Mistral*, to whom she sent her first poems. She introduced herself as "uno pauro manosquino, gros enfantas mai pas couquino" (a poor woman from Manosque, a big child but not mischievous).[7] Mistral, imposing but always fraternal, was happy to see a woman of the people express herself in his beloved language. He corresponded with her, gave her advice, and encouraged her to write. One day, Nègre and her mother even made the long trip to Maillane to meet the Master, taking along a tureen of homemade *bouillabaisse*.

Whenever he was in Marseille, Mistral without fail would pay her a visit. Nègre took an active part in the meetings of the Marseillais

Laʒarine Nègre
(private collection)

félibres of the *Escolo de la Mar* (School of the sea) and of the review *La sartan* (The frying pan), published in Provençal (Marseillais dialect) by editor and bookseller Paul Ruat (1862–1940). In the backyard of their home on the boulevard Buisson, she and her sister had built a little *cabanon* or patio with kitchen and table, baptized Magali after the song in *Mirèio,* where they entertained their poet friends. Nègre's Provençal is a mixture of *Gavot* and Marseillais. Her poems in French appeared in *Le journal de Forcalquier* and those in Provençal in such reviews as *L'aiòli* or *L'armana.* She had not abandoned Manosque, and whenever she felt homesick she went there to visit her parents and siblings. She died in Marseille at the age of fifty-one. Four years later, her sister collected her poems and published them in book form as *Li remembranço* (Memoirs, 1903). Manosque named a street after her.

> Lei blad roussejon coumo d'or,
> Lou vent gingoulo dins lei pibo,

Lei prat soun plen de bouton d'or,
Lou mentastre embaumo lei ribo.
Soulet, soulet, moun paure cor
Bèlo la mort!

Quand tu cantes, bèu roussignòu,
Ieu toumbe de grosse lagremo,
Dóu bouenur fau pourta lou dòu.
Qu'es dur, moun Diéu, d'èstre fremo!
Ah! que sariè dous lou linçòu
Que fai tant pòu!

The wheat turns golden,
The wind blows in the poplars,
The fields are full of buttercups,
Mint perfumes the slopes.
Lonely, lonely, my poor heart
Cries for death!

When you sing, beautiful nightingale,
Big tears fall from my eyes,
I mourn my happiness.
It is hard to be a woman!
How soft the frightening shroud
Seems!

(Lazarine Nègre, from "Couer matrassa"
[Wounded heart])[8]

Manosque is still a little town but its contribution to literature is immense, since it also produced a literary genius in Jean Giono, Provence's greatest novelist. Giono (1895–1970) was born at 14 rue Grande, in the old town, on the same street as Lazarine Nègre. His grandfather came from the Piedmont region in Italy, and his father, after years of wandering, finally settled in Manosque where, in 1892, he married Pauline Pourcin, a local girl. He was a shoemaker, and after school, Jean, his only child, sat next to him and watched his deft hands work. The place felt cozy. It was small but full of baskets, needles, nails, thread, hammers of all sorts, shoelaces, old heels, and worn-out boots, and the strong smell of leather wafted through the air. Amid this jumble, five cages full of nightingales—one of them baptized Garibaldi—managed to live and sing. The workshop's only window opened onto a backyard where occasionally a shepherd would leave his flock of sheep for the night. Giono had a great admiration for his father who, along with being an excellent artisan, was also very kind to others and used his knowledge of medicinal plants and ointments to help relieve their pains. His influence was formative.

Giono's mother worked on the first floor ironing clothes for the townspeople with the help of Louisa and Antonine. "My mother's workshop was wonderful. She and her helpers sang. Antonine smelled like plums and the first Louisa vanilla. The second Louisa ate Berlingots [hard candies]," he writes in *Jean le Bleu*.[9] In rue Grande everybody knew one another. Giono met a little girl who smelled of musk, an acrobat, and a mysterious man in black with whom he read the *Iliad* in the fields. There was also Francesco Odripano, who taught him that, next to the two most important things in life—poetry and the art of healing—"man's happiness lies in small valleys."[10] Le Tonneau (The Barrel) was the local café owned by a Mexican, or rather the son of a French *gendarme* who was hanged in Mexico. After selling his perfume shop in a small village near Guadalajara, the Mexican came to Manosque. In his luggage was a large chest that contained stones, herbs, and, wrapped in a newspaper, his father's head, reduced to the size of a fist by an Indian shaman.

Every Saturday, Manosque held its cattle fair, and the smells of sheep, pigs, and horses blended together and flowed down the narrow streets, forcing people to seek refuge in a local café. The stench was so bad, says Giono, that "all the winter birds were frightened and flew up into the hills crying sadly as if it were the end of the world."[11]

Giono loved literature and, since the age of fourteen, he had read every novel he could lay his hands on. In 1911, Giono left school and got a job in a local bank. Three years later, the Maurin family moved into the rue Grande. M. Maurin was a barber who thought that he

Jean Giono, photograph: Les Amis de Giono, Manosque

would have more customers on this busy street than on the outskirts of town where they had been living. Seventeen-year-old Elise Maurin was finishing high school in Aix but came home for the weekends. Jean and Elise met, found that they shared a passion for literature and poetry, and a long love story began. It was interrupted by the outbreak of World War I; at the end of 1914, Giono was drafted and, like many of his contemporaries, he spent four long years fighting in the trenches of northern France. Shellshocked but happy to be alive, he returned to his hometown in 1918 and resumed his work in the bank. The war had plowed deep furrows in his sensitivity, and he became a pacifist. In 1920, he married Elise, with whom he had two daughters, Aline and Sylvie.

Giono's first-floor office, courtesy Sylvie Giono

Giono's work in the bank left him ample time to dream and invent tales. His first novel, *Colline* (English translation as *Hill of Destiny*, 1929), a simple story of village life in the surrounding hills, met with immediate success. Within a couple of years Giono produced two other successful novels in the same genre: *Un de Baumugnes* (1929; translated into English as *Lovers Are Never Losers*) and *Regain* (Harvest, 1930). Giono then decided to write full-time and gave up his position at the bank. He bought Lou Paraïs (Paradise), a modest house on the slope of the Mont d'Or, and settled there with his family and mother.

Giono lived in Lou Paraïs all of his life. A five-minute walk up a short but steep slope named Les Vraies Richesses, after one of his books, is a small pathway on the right that cuts across vegetable and flower gardens and leads straight to the house. Lou Paraïs faces south and commands a good view of the town and Durance valley. When Giono moved in it comprised a kitchen and dining room downstairs and two bedrooms upstairs, but after Giono's mother-in-law moved in with them, in 1934, Giono elevated the attic and divided it into two rooms. One of them became his office. He also had tried to acquire the small

Bust of Giono, in Giono's garden

cottage and plot next to Lou Paraïs, but the owners persistently refused
to sell until their nephew Henri Fluchère, one of Giono's friends, inherited it in 1968. Fluchère finally sold it to him and Giono was happy
to have the extra space. The garden has a beautiful fountain and two
huge chestnut trees, a few palm trees, and small cedars.

   In his attic with a view over Manosque's roofs, Giono would light
his pipe, dip his quill pen into his homemade ink mixture, and write his
stories. He remained an avid reader, and his library includes hundreds
of volumes, among them the complete works of Stendhal, the memoirs of Casanova, and books by Walter Scott, Machiavelli, Balzac,
Whitman, Faulkner, and Melville, whose *Moby-Dick* he translated into

French with Joan Smith and Lucien Jacques. The translation occupied him for years, and Giono's attraction to Melville is puzzling. "I saw whales sleeping in the foam of the hills," Giono said, looking back to these happy years.[12] He knew little of Melville's life except what he read in a small biography but thought he had a direct intuition into his inner being: "Above all I loved the shy tenderness of his frantic heart."[13] Giono's taste in literature was eclectic. He was fond of detective stories and also attracted to Buddhism and Taoism. Every month his publisher Gallimard would send him the firm's latest detective story, a custom that, judging by the number of books of this genre in his upstairs library, must have lasted for quite a few years. On one wall in the downstairs library is a painting of Mogul horses and on the mantelpiece is a stone head representing an Asian man. This statue is undoubtedly ancient but its origin still eludes specialists. It had apparently decorated the porch of a peasant's home in the Alps. Giono was fascinated and bought it from him. The walls and stairways are decorated with paintings by Bernard Buffet (then a poor apprentice who lived for two years rent-free in a small cottage that belonged to Giono), Yves Brayer, and Marseillais Pierre Ambrogiani.

That Manosque was dear to Giono there is no doubt. He loved its fountains, its small shops, and the warm atmosphere of the Café Grand Glacier where he regularly met his friends to chat. Parts of *Le hussard sur le toit* (The horseman on the roof, 1951) are set there. But in his opinion, Manosque was, on the whole, too materialistic. Its people were obsessed with sales and figures. "Its heart is a multiplication table. It wakes up in the middle of the night and in a low voice, counts its trucks one more time," he writes in *Manosque des plateaux*.[14] According to him, the small Provençal town constantly kept "its fingers pointed at the prices" and peered over the valley and the neighboring hills "with a purchasing and selling eye."[15] It was, he said, "an overcooked loaf of bread: all crust and no crumb."[16] However, he never left town save for a trip or two. He died there of heart problems on October 9, 1970, and was buried in Manosque's small cemetery. His wife survived him by many years. She passed away in 1999 at the age of one hundred.

Tourist information. Place du Dr Joubert. Tel: 04 92 72 16 00. Fax: 04 92 72 58 98. Website: <www.ville-manosque.fr>.

What to see. *Giono's house* is a ten-minute walk from the center. Visit by appointment only, on Fridays at 3:00. The visit is free and guided (in French). With a little luck his daughter Sylvie will be there. Tel: 04 92 87 73 03. The visit lasts about one hour and includes Giono's library and office with desk, memorabilia, photographs, sculptures, pens, quills, and souvenirs of all sorts. *Centre Jean Giono,* 1 rue Elémir Bourges, in the town center. Tel: 04 92 72 76 10. It contains a library with manuscripts, rare editions, and translations of his works, critical studies, films, etc. A walk through the old town is a must, and on 14 rue Grande a plaque has been put up.

Where to stay. ****: *Hostellerie de la Fuste,* three miles from the town center, pass the bridge over the Durance, in the direction of the freeway (A 51), continue in the direction of Valensole, veer left on D 4 immediately after the bridge over the Durance. Tel: 04 90 72 05 95. Fax: 04 92 72 92 93. **: *Campanile.* Tel: 04 92 71 73 50. Fax: 04 92 71 73 89. B&Bs: *Les Cigales,* Montée des Vraies Richesses. Tel & Fax: 04 92 72 11 25. Mme Dossetto, 346 avenue des Savels. Tel: 04 92 72 07 49. Fax: 04 92 72 07 49.

Where to eat. La Fuste. * *Dominique Bucaille,* 43 blvd des Tilleuls, in the center.

North of Manosque: Jean Giono's Provence

What fascinated Giono and sparked his imagination were the high plateaus north of Manosque *(plate 20)* and their isolated villages, where a handful of individuals still clung to their land. He had traveled there on foot as a child and the sight of these impoverished people, determined to resist the exodus, marked him for life. Giono was not interested in Mistral and the Provençal renaissance per se. His ideal, which he developed in his early works, was to love and respect life in all its forms. Giono was a poet with an aesthetic and moral message international in scope. However, he understood and spoke Provençal and loved his region: "I have spent all my life on this generous land. The lessons I received from its vast undulating hills, its wide open valley, its boundless plateaus, and its sky—so deeply arched that one cannot ignore its roundness—are lessons that all the peasants of this land have received," he writes in *Noé*.[17] Sometimes the geography of his novels is correct; Giono speaks about actual villages such as Banon, Reillane, or Lachau. At other times, like Daudet, Arène, and Bosco, he invented names for villages such as Les Bastides Blanches in *Colline* or Aubignane in *Regain*. "I want it known that I am not on a train, a streetcar, or the boulevards of Marseille with a notebook in hand, copying reality and that all this while, on the contrary, I have had my hands in my pockets. In fact, what I write—even when I try to be very near reality—is not what I see but what I recall," Giono says, leaving some room for the selective process of memory.[18]

Giono's novels take us north. It is there, somewhere near Reillane and Vachères, that he set *Colline*, his first story. Les Bastides Blanches is "a hamlet in ruins, halfway between the valley and its roaring steam harvesting machines and the big lavender desert. It is the country of wind, situated in the cold shadow of the Lure mountains."[19] A dozen people still live there and remember the glorious days when its population reached over one hundred. Now life is almost at a standstill. Men play *boules* and the women wash the clothes in an old Roman sarcophagus. But one day, old Janet, the *sourcier* or spring finder and also prophet, becomes ill, and at the same time water stops running from the spring. Little Mary falls sick after drinking water from the stable, Janet hallucinates, and because of the drought, a forest fire breaks out. When Janet eventually dies the water mysteriously flows again and Mary is cured.

Banon *(plate 21)* is on the Albion Plateau, a half-hour west of Forcalquier (D 950). In *Le hussard sur le toit* Giono described it as "an ash-color town camouflaged among the rocks and dwarf forests of gray oaks."[20] Angelo Pardi, the protagonist (a colonel in the army of Piedmont-Sardinia, the twenty-five-year-old illegitimate son of Duchess Ezzia Pardi), arrived there in 1838. It was eight o'clock in the evening and the sun still shone on the horizon. The air was dry and hot. Pardi had ridden on horseback all day, headed north in the valley beyond to the castle of Fer, near Noyers. Pardi, exhausted by his travels, took a room at the only inn. He ordered two bottles of Burgundy, some sugar, and pepper, mixed them all together in a large bowl, and drank. Afterward he smoked a cigar, lay down on the bed, and fell asleep with his boots on. The next day he resumed his route north, riding through the forest of beech trees "scattered here and there on very poor grazing grounds, brown like a fox, and stretching as far as the eye could see on waves of lavender and small rocks."[21]

The small path led through a hamlet called Redortiers, once a real village where Giono's wife, Elise, had taught in 1915. "Stuck to the abrupt slope of the plateau like a little wasp's nest," the village was probably also the model for Aubignane in *Regain*.[22] In this novel, Panturle, a sturdy middle-aged man, and old Mamèche are the only residents left. Mamèche's husband died shortly after his arrival when the well that he was digging collapsed on him, an episode that Pagnol reproduced in his *Jean de Florette*. Then, Mamèche's toddler accidentally ate some hemlock and died. However, she was determined to stay and subsisted by making baskets. She promises Panturle that she will bring him a wife, which she eventually does, and life begins anew.

Angelo Pardi also passed through the hamlet of Contadour a couple of miles farther north on D 5, where from 1934 to 1939 Giono and some of his friends and followers lived during the Easter vacation and the summer months, thus anticipating the communes of the 1960s. The group of about one hundred lived in tents or in old farms that they bought in common and restored. Many of Giono's followers were intellectuals and teachers who had read his books and considered Giono their guru. They came from all over France and also from abroad. They were all pacifists and some of them communists. They cooked together and in the evenings discussed literature. When inspired, Giono read excerpts from his translation of *Moby-Dick*. They would hike together and walk to Revest-du-Bion to visit a painter friend of his. Today a few farms and part of the mill still stand. There is only one café-restaurant. You can also leave your vehicle, walk around, and have a picnic. About three thousand feet in altitude, Contadour commands a magnificent view of the Luberon and Mont Ventoux. The air is pure and dry and, in early summer, the smell of lavender is invigorating.

Giono's Pardi, our guide for Provence's northern frontier, continues his route north, over the pass and down to the hamlet of Les Omergues. There he discovers that the residents have all mysteriously died. A young doctor arrives on the scene and explains that there is an epidemic of cholera and that all of Provence is affected, a historical fact. Pardi eventually reaches his destination in the Jabron Valley. To reach this valley the modern traveler has to go to Revest-du-Bion and take D 18 to Séderon or D 950 and D 518 to Montbrun. The scenery is wild and deserted. The little village of Lachau on the right bank of the Méouge, past Séderon on D 542, is the setting for *Deux cavaliers de l'orage* (Two riders of the storm, 1965). The protagonist Marceau, a giant, and his younger brother Ange often came to Lachau for the market and the peacock fair in the fall. They lived in the Hautes-Collines, a farm in the mountains nearby, where they raised mules. Lachau was then a lively town with hotels, a doctor, and cafés. Farmers, woodcutters, and shepherds came to dance and drink on Saturday nights. The small peacock fair held every fall was the occasion for the people of the valley to get together, and the goal was not to so much to buy poultry as to be happy, wrote Giono. All the buyers came from Hautes-Collines, a place of dark forests and cold winds, but the sellers were from St-Hilaire, "a country of sunny slopes, a place of tenderness, full of flowers."[23] It was during this fair that Marceau killed with his fist a horse that had been spooked, a feat that made him famous and started his wrestling career. Unfortunately, his fame made his younger brother jealous and eventually led to a brutal fight and fratricide.

Where to stay and eat. In Banon. **: *Les Voyageurs*, place de la République. Tel: 04 92 73 21 02. The only hotel in town. Its chef prepares local dishes, according to season (hare, wild boar, venison, or escargots, and "pieds-paquets"(sheep's trotters), all at a moderate price). B&Bs: *Bas-Chalus*, near Forcalquier. Pool. Tel: 04 92 75 05 67. Fax: 04 92 75 39 20. Email: <Amis.@ wanadoo.fr>. *La Beaudine*, in Forcalquier. Pool. Tel: 04 92 75 01 52.

Farther North: Serres, Mens, Gap

Giono's country extends farther north. N 75 will take you to Serres and Aspres-sur-Buëch. A little farther north is the small town of St-Julien-en-Beauchêne where Giono used to spend his vacation and the village of Baumugne that inspired the novel mentioned earlier. In the dark ages, Giono tells us, the inhabitants of this peaceful community were declared heretics and got their tongues cut off. Thereafter, they began to communicate using harmonicas.

On the western slopes of the Lus-la-Croix-Haute is the Plateau de Grimone where Bobi, the poet-vagabond in *Que ma joie demeure* (translated into English as *Joy of Man's Desiring*, 1934) arrives on a moonless night. There Bobi meets Jourdan, his wife Marthe, and a handful of courageous farmers. Bobi teaches them new "ecological" ideas such as the preservation of forest and bushes to encourage the return of wildlife such as deer and wild boar, and the planting of daisies and hawthorn to attract birds. Bobi's ideas bring new meaning to the lives of these mountain farmers. The novel is undoubtedly the best of Giono's early period and the one in which he develops his philosophy.

Farther west is Châtillon-en-Diois, the setting of *Les âmes fortes* (Strong souls, 1950), a later novel in which he set aside his poetic-idealism and used techniques anticipating the Nouveau Roman of Alain Robbe-Grillet and Michel Butor. Châtillon is "a peaceful little town between two mountain slopes, without noise. The word that one hears the most is: sun. We're going out in the sun. We'll go out in the sun. Come and enjoy the sun. He went out to enjoy the sun. It is not sunny. It will be sunny. I can't wait for the sun to come out. Here is the sun. I'm going to go out in the sun. And so on. It is the biggest noise."[24] There, as in many other small towns of these high Provençal valleys, time seems to have stopped. "By the time a shopkeeper turns around you can kill a donkey with figs. The lollipops melt in the windows,"[25] Giono claims in the manner of Pagnol. Fifteen minutes north on the Drôme River is Die, where in the twelfth century a famous *trobairitz* or female troubadour known only as Comtessa de Dia or Princesse de Die, lived and wrote poetry. She is sometimes called Beatrice although, according to scholars, there is no record of her name. She was in love with Raimbaut d'Orange, but the *Vida* says she was the wife of Guillaume of Poitiers and that she was "bella domna e bona" (a beautiful and good lady). Only five songs have survived, from which the following passage is taken:

> Valer mi deu pretz e mos paratges
> E ma beutatz e plus mos fins coratges;
> Per qu'eu vos man lai on es vostr' estatges
> Esta chanson, que sia messatges,
> E voill saber, lo meus bels amics gens,
> Per que vos m'etz tant fers ni tant salvatges
> No sai si s'es orgoills o mals talens.

> My name of high descent should help me,
> And my beauty, and the purity of my heart most of all;
> Therefore I send this song to you down there,
> To your dwelling, let it be my messenger,
> And I wish to know, my fair gentle friend,
> Why are you so barbarous and cruel to me,
> Is it pride, or wishing ill?[26]

A couple of miles down the road, turn right on D 66 toward Mens. A dense forest of ash, beech, maple, fir, and larch covers the area. It is a country of farmers and woodcutters. It was in the midst of the villages of Laley, Aver, and Prebois that Giono situated his murder story: *Un roi sans divertissement* (A king without amusement, 1947). In the winter of 1843, after the disappearance of young Marie Chazottes and old Bergues, the villagers finally alert the *gendarmes* of Clelles. Captain Langlois and his men are dispatched to investigate a very strange case indeed. In the village, the school closed down and people dare not go out alone anymore. The presence of the police did not prevent Delphin Callas in his turn from vanishing into thin air. Apparently, he had gone out to smoke his pipe, explained his wife, but never returned. Winter set in and snow covered the lonely farms. One morning, Frédéric the woodcutter was preparing coffee when, through a kitchen window, he saw a man climb down from the large beech tree in the distance and leave. Intrigued, Frédéric went out, climbed the tree, and discovered the body of Dorothée, his neighbor, lying in a large cavity. Without losing his courage the woodcutter followed the man to the village of Chichiliane ten miles to the northwest and saw the man enter his home. Alerted, Langlois and his men set up a trap . . .

The area around Mens is called the Rebeillard in *Le chant du monde* (Song of the world, 1934): "A vast, rugged country, with white peaks like the sea; its horizons slept under mists. It consisted of hills or red earth covered with clusters of crooked pines, farming valleys, small plains with a farm or two, and villages clinging to mountain peaks like honey cakes."[27]

Giono and Bosco have often been compared, but the two authors had little contact. Giono met Bosco on a hot summer day of 1929. Their vision and techniques differ greatly. Bosco's stories develop internally as in a dream. Action is extremely slow. He once reproached Giono for his distance vis-à-vis the félibres. In an interview with Robert Ytier, Giono declared: "He (Bosco) speaks of a different Provence than mine, for Provence is made up of 'regions.' I sing the high plateaus, the mountains that look like Mount Olympus with its crown of clouds reaching the sky. I sing the hard and dry stone, the 'bancas,' the olive and almond tree. Bosco is the man of undulating hills or fertile valleys, of rich and bountiful plains. Our characters sometimes resemble one another because they are deeply rooted in the land. They are attached to it, but Bosco's land has a lot of water. My characters search for it or try to conserve it."[28]

Giono has much more in common with Pagnol, who, as we have seen, borrowed some of Giono's stories for his successful movies. But in turn Pagnol inspired Giono who, dissatisfied with Pagnol's interpretation of his stories, finally created his own film company. Pagnol helped Giono out, lending him three of his crew to shoot a movie called *Solitude* on the slopes of the Contadour. Giono and his new team shot several scenes there but never managed to finish the film. However, in 1960 Giono directed *Crésus*, in which he gave Fernandel, the Marseillais actor, the leading role. One day, Crésus, a peasant of the high plateaus, spots a bomb-like cylinder in the middle of a field. He approaches it cautiously, opens it and finds several million francs in banknotes. The film is about money and the problems that it brings. Crésus first tries to deposit the money in a bank and then decides to give it to his friends and invites them to a feast. One day the police arrive and tell him that the banknotes are fake, sent by enemies to destabilize the country's economy. The plot is Giono's and reflects his own philosophy, but the subtle humor and biting dialogue betray the influence of Pagnol.

Mountain lovers will enjoy the drive from Mens on D 66 to Corps and then on N 85 to Gap, about one hour away. A wonderful manmade lake, with swimming and boating, lies just thirty minutes away in Savines. Deep at its bottom lies the old village. Only a little chapel still emerges from the water. The building of the dam below and the flooding of the valley was a very controversial project in the 1950s and inspired Giono's film *L'eau vive* (The living water, 1958).

Farther north after Embrun and Briançon one leaves Provence and enters the Alps, a region of high peaks, sharp contrasts, and secluded valleys much like Switzerland and Austria. In 1977, Emilie Carles (1888–1979) won national recognition with her autobiography *Une soupe aux herbes sauvages* (A soup of wild herbs, 1977). Carles describes her life on her parents' farm in Val-des-Prés, ten miles north of Briançon. She tells of the hardships, the death of her mother, struck by lightning in a field, the cemetery where lay buried those who, after months of looking for employment, finally drowned or hanged themselves. But the village also had its happy times. "Veillées" usually took place in the stable. The villagers would gather around an older man or woman who would tell the stories of yore, when the wolves preyed on the lone shepherds or when the long, snowy winters forced them to stay inside for weeks. There was also the baking of the bread, an event in which all took part, for the bread was supposed to last throughout the winter, and the festival of St-Claude, during which the merrymakers drank, danced, and sang songs in their patois. Carles described the latter event with more details in *Mes rubans de la St-Claude* (My ribbons of St. Claude).

Tourist information. Gap: 12 rue Faure du Serre. Tel: 04 92 52 56 56. Fax: 04 92 52 56 57. Website: <www.ville-gap.fr>.

Briançon: Place du Temple. Tel: 04 92 21 08 50. Fax: 04 92 20 56 45. Website: <www.ot-briancon.fr>.

Where to stay and eat. In Gap. ****: *Porte Colombe*, 4 place Euzières. Tel: 04 92 51 04 13. Fax: 04 92 52 42 50. **: *Climat*, 1 mile in the direction of Sisteron. Tel: 04 92 51 57 82. *Ibis*, 25 blvd Pompidou. Tel: 04 92 53 57 57. Fax: 04 92 53 58 15. Restaurants: *Patalin*, 2 place Ladoucette. *Grangette*, 1 avenue Foch.

In Embrun. ***: *Les Bartavelles*, two miles south in the direction of Gap. AC, pool, parking. Tel: 04 92 43 20 69. Fax: 04 92 43 11 92. **: *Mairie*, place de la Mairie. AC. Tel: 04 92 43 20 65. Fax: 04 92 43 47 02. *Notre-Dame*, avenue Général Nicolas. Tel: 04 92 43 08 36. Fax: 04 92 43 58 41.

In Briançon. ***: *Vauban*, 13 avenue de Gaulle. Garage. Tel: 04 92 21 11. Fax: 04 92 20 58 20. **: *Cristol*, 6 route d'Italie. Tel: 04 92 20 20 11. Fax: 04 92 21 02 58. Restaurant: *Le Péché Gourmand*.

Sisteron

On the way down from the Hautes-Alpes a stop in Sisteron will ease the drive. The Romans settled here in 25 B.C. after defeating the Voconces (Ligurians). From the fifth to the ninth century the town fought against the Teutons and the Moors. In the Middle Ages, a castle stood on the cliff above the town. Today you can reach the citadel directly (follow the sign) in fifteen minutes, or make a detour (ten more minutes) and go through the town's picturesque labyrinth of narrow streets or *andrônes* (from the Italian *andare*, to go). The fortress stands high on a cliff above town and commands a wonderful panoramic view of the lower Alps and the Durance valley. It is an ensemble of fortifications that go back to the early Middle Ages. The tower was erected in the thirteenth century and a chapel two centuries later. In 1692, military architect Sébastien Vauban planned a large construction project, but only a well and a gunpowder store were actually built. Damaged by bombings during World War II, the tower and chapel are now restored and open to visitors.

Every summer this small town of about seven thousand inhabitants organizes *Les Nuits de la citadelle,* a theater festival started in 1928 that now includes opera, dance, classical music, and folklore. Daudet's friend Paul Arène (1843–1896) was born on the street that now bears his name. His father was a watchmaker and his mother worked as a milliner. Provençal was his native language and he learned French at the Collège des Frères in town. He was a good student and enjoyed reading Virgil and Horace. He later attended the University of Aix, where he majored in philosophy, and then spent a year in Marseille teaching. Around this time he made the acquaintance of Roumanille and Mistral, and, following his graduation in 1863, he obtained a teaching position in Vanves near Paris.

Like many young provincials, Arène was eager to discover Paris and after work he often wandered off there. He frequented avant-garde cafés such as the Café de Madrid in Montmartre and Bobino in the Latin Quarter. It was there that he met Daudet and his artist friends, Alfred Delvau and Charles Bataille. Arène soon became one of the group and shared with them a house in Clamart. But he did not forget Provence or his friends there and corresponded with Mistral and Aubanel. Besides teaching, Arène often wrote articles and reviews for *Le nain jaune* (The yellow dwarf) and *Le Figaro.* But his real passion was the theater; his first play, *Pierrot Héritier* (1865), met with some success. Encouraged, Arène gave up his teaching career and devoted his time to writing. He then worked with Daudet on *Lettres de mon moulin.* The nature and extent of his contribution have never been established with certainty. These stories first appeared in serial form in *L'événement* and *Le Figaro* under the pseudonym Marie-Gaston, in 1866. When Daudet, following his wife's advice, published them in book form in 1869, signed with his name only, Arène did not object. By then he had achieved some notoriety with his plays but especially his tales, several hundred of them.

Arène often spent his summers in Sisteron in La Cigalière, his little country house or cabanon, where, amid the olive groves and lavender,

Paul Arène, photo: Palais du Roure, Avignon

he wrote some of his best tales, including his novel *Jean-des-figues* (1868) in which he describes Sisteron under the name Canteperdrix. Toward the end of his life he started spending the winter months in Antibes; *La chèvre d'or* (The golden goat, 1889) evokes the medieval Moorish settlements there and the legend of the golden goat. Arène never married; as a young man, he had fallen in love with Anaïs Roumieux, daughter of the félibre from Beaucaire, but when he proposed, her father turned him down. Arène did not persist and suffered in silence for the rest of his life. He died in Antibes at the age of fifty-three and was buried in Sisteron under an almond tree. Mistral wrote the epitaph: "Ieu m'en vau l'amo ravido d'agué pantaïa ma vido" (I leave happy to have dreamed my life).

Tourist information. Hôtel de Ville. Tel: 04 92 61 36 50. Fax : 04 92 61 19 57. Website: <www.sisteron.com>. Email: <office-de-tourisme-sisteron@wanadoo.fr>.

What to see. The Citadel. Tel: 04 9261 27 57. *Earth and Time Museum*, 6 place du Général de Gaulle. Geology and time-measuring instruments. Tel: 04 92 61 61 30. Email: <resgeo@calvanet.fr>

Where to stay. ***: *Grand Hôtel du Cours*, place de l'Eglise. Garage. Tel: 04 92 61 04 51. Fax: 04 92 61 41 73. **: *Hôtel du Rocher*, La Baume. Tel: 04 92 61 12 50. Fax: 04 92 62 65 59. *Le Tivoli*, 21 place René Gassin. Garage. Tel: 04 92 61 15 16. Fax: 04 92 61 21 72. *Touring Napoléon*, 22 avenue de la Libération. AC, parking. Tel: 04 92 61 00 06. Fax: 04 92 61 01 19. *Les Chênes*, one mile in the direction of Gap. Pool, parking. Tel: 04 92 61 15 08. Fax: 04 92 62 16 92. *Ibis*, two miles in the direction of Gap. AC, pool, parking. Tel: 04 92 62 62 00. Fax: 04 92 62 62 10.

Where to eat. *Les Becs Fins*, 16 rue Saunerie.

Digne

Twenty-seven miles down and east on N 85 is Digne-les-Bains, or simply Digne, an ancient Roman spa and now administrative center of the Alpes-de-Haute-Provence. The town is proud of having educated Pierre Gassendi (1592–1655), one of France's leading scholars. Gassendi was actually born in Champtercier, a small village five miles west of Digne. Raised in a poor family, he showed superior intelligence and was educated in Digne and then Aix, where he studied theology. Gassendi taught philosophy in Aix (1617–23) and, later, mathematics at the Collège Royal in Paris (1645–48). He was also interested in astronomy and corresponded with the most important scientists of his time including Galileo, Kepler, Hobbes, and Pascal. He is also known for his criticism of Descartes and argued against him in the priority of the sensible world. His works were collected in six volumes and published after his death in 1658.

Pierre Magnan, photo: Jacques Sassier, Editions Denoël

But Digne is also Commissioner Laviolette's town. This quiet yet astute policeman, reader of Proust, is the product of Pierre Magnan's imagination. Magnan himself is from Manosque, where he was born in 1922. His father was an electrician. In *La biasse de mon père* he tells about his childhood there, his grandparents from whom he learned Provençal, his Aunt Louise's grocery store, and Uncle Théophile's slug juice remedy. He also recalls how his father's *biasso* or bag brought home all the different fragances of Provence, a mixture of thyme, rosemary, and particularly savory. Magnan met Giono when he was fourteen and a long friendship began. Giono lent him books, invited him to the Contadour, and introduced him to Mathilde Monnier, with whom Magnan had a long love affair. (In *Pour saluer Giono* [In remembrance of Giono, 1990] Magnan relates his friendship with the novelist and his literary apprenticeship.) Encouraged by Giono and Monnier, Magnan began writing novels of his own. Unfortunately, *Le périple d'un cachalot* (The travel of a killer whale, 1940) and *L'aube insolite* (The unusual dawn, 1943) failed to attract the public. Disappointed, Magnan stopped writing and got a job in a refrigeration company in Nice. He lived there until 1976 when, laid off, he returned to Manosque. He then took to the pen again in the detective genre and this time won applause from both critics and public.

Le sang des Atrides (The Atridae's blood, 1977) received the Prix du Quai des Orfévres. The novel introduces Commissioner Laviolette, a Provençal, born in the small village of Piegut at the western end of Savines Lake. Laviolette is an interesting breed of policeman. He is rather quiet, unlucky in love; he has cats and loves literature, particularly Proust. A series of crimes has been committed around Digne. The victims seem to have little in common except that they are all bachelors. All of them have been killed by a blow to the temple. The commissioner finds out that the murder weapon is a heavy stone cast by a slingshot. Then, he discovers the mysterious letters OR written in the snow by the third victim minutes before he died. Laviolette works in cooperation with another singular character, Judge Chabrand, a Marxist. As the plot thickens, more and more clues surface and point to a young boy. . . . Since his first success Magnan has written over a dozen novels, including several bestsellers. He now lives near Forcalquier with his wife. Like Giono's, all of his novels are set in higher Provence, Banon, Sisteron, and around Digne. Magnan particularly excels in the management of complex plots in which vengeance is often the motive. The criminal is usually a serial killer but also a local resident. The inhabitants of these harsh lands traditionally keep to themselves and mistrust the police. Fortunately, Laviolette is fluent in Provençal and well advised about the local mentality, which helps him crack the cases. The novels are always suspenseful, and the description of customs and habits of the Provençals of these rugged hills never fails to intrigue the reader. In a way, Magnan's novels reveal the dark side of the Provençals— their feuds, greed, and clannishness. *Le commissaire dans la truffière* (The commissioner in the truffle plantation, 1978) for instance, takes place in Banon, where several hippies living in an abandoned church disappear one by one. The last body was found drained of its blood. Then Laviolette discovers an old book containing secret recipes in which human blood is recommended as a good fertilizer for truffles. But inheritance problems are also involved and soon a better clue appears. The amateur of detective novels will delight in *Le secret des andrónes* (The secret of the narrow streets, 1980), set in Sisteron. There a mysterious caped man pushes his victims over cliffs or out of windows, leaving a card pinned to their chest. The investigation of these murders takes Laviolette back into the region's recent past and among the former members of the Resistance. *Le tombeau d'Hélios* (Helios's tomb, 1980) takes place near Forcalquier where several men, all members of a very secret club, have been poisoned.

Magnan's masterpiece is undoubtedly *La maison assassinée* (1984; translated into English as *The Murdered House*), a powerful novel in which violence, greed, and love are artistically woven together. Séraphin Monge, the protagonist, recently released from an orphanage, learns for the first time the tragic fate of his family. When still a newborn sleeping in a cradle he miraculously escaped the bloody massacre of his entire household. Monge swears vengeance, investigates, falls in love, and slowly unmasks the murderers. The story is poignant and the suspense is sustained throughout. Laviolette appears only at the end of the novel.

Magnan continues to pour forth novels. In his most recent one, *Le parme convient à Laviolette* (Mauve suits Laviolette, 2000), his old friend Judge Chabrand draws the commissioner from his retirement in his native village of Piegut to solve a series of strange crimes. This time the victims are pig-butchers. The assassin leaves notes on their bodies with their names and an assessment of their qualities, such as "egotistic" or "mediocre," like a woman evaluating her former lovers. Laviolette investigates, traveling up to and around Digne, and discovers that all of the victims were former members of the Resistance— but meanwhile the murderer continues to kill. Finally love proves to be a much more plausible motive, and eventually Laviolette unmasks the murderer.

Digne is also the home of Alexandra David-Néel (1868–1969), who led a fascinating life. She was born in Paris, the only child of Louis and Alexandrine David. Her father was a journalist who, for political reasons, had to move to Brussels, where Alexandra grew up. From a very early age she read Jules Verne and dreamed of faraway countries. As an adolescent she left home several times and for days in a row rambled alone, through Normandy, the Belgian coast, and Italy. She read about Asia, learned English, studied Sanskrit, joined the Theosophy Society of Paris, and finally abandoned her Protestant faith for Buddhism. In 1891, she traveled alone to Ceylon and India. Then she worked as a singer at the operas of Hanoi, Athens, and Tunis. In 1904, she married Philippe Néel, a railway engineer, but after a few years she realized that marriage was not her cup of tea, and began dreaming of traveling again. In 1911, she left her home and returned to Asia, where she stayed fifteen years.

In Asia, Néel studied the local languages, learned the sacred texts of Hinduism and Buddhism, practiced meditation with gurus, and traveled by train but also on foot all over India, Nepal, and China. She was the first westerner to enter Tibet, closed since 1792. She returned to France in 1925 with Yongden, her Tibetan adoptive son and, in 1927, she settled in Digne. It is there in a modest house baptized Samten Dzong (Fortress of Meditation) that she recorded her adventures in books such as her bestseller *Voyage d'une parisienne à Lhassa* and wrote books about Eastern religions. She attracted the media, gave lectures and interviews, and became quite famous. But Digne was a little too quiet for her and over the years she began to miss traveling. In 1937, at the age of sixty-nine, she and Yongden left for China and Tibet. This was her last trip. She returned to Digne in 1946 and spent her time writing books about her experience and knowledge of Asia. She died there at the age of 101. Her house is now a state museum. Visits are guided and free at 10:30, 2:00, 3:30 and 5:00. Tel: 04 92 31 32 38. Website: <www.alexandra-david-neel.org>.

From Digne it is possible to reach the Riviera on the Route Napoléon (N 85), very winding but picturesque. It will take you to Castellane, Grasse, and Cannes in about three hours. One interesting alternative is to take N 85 as far as Castellane and then veer right on D 952. The narrow road follows the gorges of the River Verdon to the beautiful lake of Ste-Croix and then to the very pretty village of Moustiers-Ste-Marie, where, since the seventeenth century, artisans have been making some of the finest china in Provence. From there the same D 952 will take you to the former Roman towns of Riez and

*Alexandra David-Néel, photo: Fondation Alexandra
David Néel, Digne-les-Bains*

Gréoux-les-Bains and finally to Aix-en-Provence. If you should decide instead to leave Digne via the Durance valley (N 85 to N 96) you could stop over at the tenth-century monastery of Ganagobie a couple of miles on the right past Peyruis. On this plateau covered with shrub oaks and lavender, a small community of Benedictine monks leads a life of contemplation and prayer. It is open to visitors. Tel: 04 92 68 00 04.

Digne:

Tourist information. Place du Tampinet. Tel: 04 92 36 62 62. Fax: 04 92 32 27 24. Website: <www.ot-dignelesbains.fr>.

Where to stay. ****: *Grand Paris,* 19 blvd Thiers. Tel: 04 92 31 11 15. Fax: 04 92 32 32 82. ***: *Tonic Hotel,* route des Termes. Tel: 04 92 31 20 31. Fax: 04 92 32 44 54. B&B: *Les Oliviers,* route des Fonts-Gaubert. Tel: 04 92 31 36 04.

Where to eat. Bourgogne. Origan. Brasserie de France.

Moustiers:

Tourist information. Tel: 04 92 74 67 84. Fax: 04 92 74 60 65. Website: <www.ville-moustiers-sainte-marie.fr>.

Where to stay. ***: *La Bastide,* one mile south of the village. Pool, parking. Tel: 04 92 70 47 47. Fax: 04 92 70 47 48. **: *Le Relais.* AC, parking. Tel: 04 92 74 66 10. Website: <www.provenceweb.fr/04/le-relais.htm>.

Where to eat. Les Santons. *Ferme Sainte-Cécile,* one mile in the direction of Castellane.

·

Aix-en-Provence and Environs

At the foot of Mont Ste-Victoire is Aix-en-Provence, a former Roman spa. In 124 B.C., the Romans defeated the Celts and Ligurians and settled there. Twenty-two years later Marius was victorious against the Teutons at the base of the Ste-Victoire. The Romans then lived there in peace, used the springs, and turned Aix into a spa. In the Middle Ages, the counts of Provence often resided there or in one of their castles in the surrounding countryside, and Aix was home to artists and troubadours as well. René of Anjou, the last count of Provence, author of several poems and known as "le bon roi René," has his statue on the main Cours. When he died in 1480, his nephew Charles du Maine inherited his domain but died the following year. Consequently France acquired Provence and appointed a governor there. The city had its university (founded 1409), and its population included many magistrates and lawyers. But Aix also had its writers, including poet

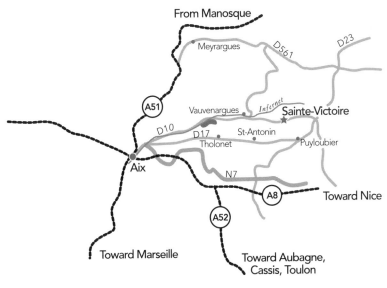

Aix-en-Provence and environs

and moralist Jean de Cabanes (1654–1717) who wrote poems such as *L'histourien sincere* and tales in the manner of Boccaccio.

Aix was then a sleepy little town. When Flaubert stopped there in 1845 on his way to Italy, he wrote in his notebook: "Aix: rien" (nothing). He had not yet met his future lover Louise Colet (1810–1876), born and raised in Aix, 20 rue de l'Opéra. Her maternal grandfather was a local notable and a friend of the revolutionary orator Mirabeau. Her father was originally from Lyons but had settled in Marseille. He soon became Gouverneur des Postes of Aix. Louise was the youngest of six children. The family divided their time between Aix and their castle of Servanes, between Mouriès and Les Baux. Louise read a lot and had a strong, independent mind. At the age of twenty, eager to leave home, she married M. Colet, a musician and professor at the conservatory, and moved to Paris. Colet had written poems since she was a young child, and her first book, *Les fleurs du Midi* (Flowers of the South, 1836), won her some recognition. Philosopher Victor Cousin, Flaubert, and then Musset were among her lovers. She held a salon in rue de Sèvres attended by a young man by the name of Alphonse

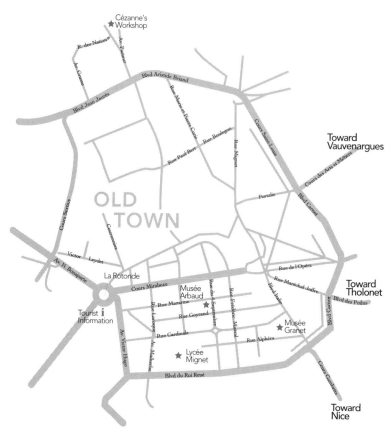

Aix-en-Provence city map

Daudet. In 1859, she traveled to Provence, and stopped in Arles. Mistral made the trip on a donkey across fields to greet her and together they went to the arenas. Colet is the author of several works on women poets, Goethe's childhood, and Italy. She probably knew Provençal, but living in Paris she chose to write in French. The Académie Française awarded her four poetry prizes. She died in Paris in March 1876 a few days after Mary d'Agoult and three months before George Sand. Gustave Courbet painted a portrait of her entitled *L'Amazone* (Metropolitan Museum of Art, New York).

Most educated Provençal writers studied in Aix. Mistral studied law and resided in Aix from November 1848 to 1851 He lived on rue Jaubert, near the Court of Justice. In 1849, he moved to rue Clémenceau and in 1850, 4 rue de la Monnaie (now Frédéric Mistral). Law was boring to him; he enjoyed Louis Méry's literature seminar on Dante much more, and he spent hours in the library reading Victor Hugo, Théophile Gautier, George Sand, and also Provençal authors such as Crousillat, Bellot, Jasmin, and Désenat. He corresponded with Roumanille, becoming more and more excited about their common project of a literary renaissance, and when he felt inspired, he jotted down poems in Provençal. Unlike his dark school years in Avignon, in Aix, Mistral enjoyed his freedom and matured rapidly. His friend Anselme Mathieu joined him there and together they visited the Ste-Victoire and the taverns of Marseille. Paul Arène and Théodore Aubanel also studied law in Aix. Marie Mauron attended the Ecole Normale (teacher training college) in Aix between 1913 and 1916. She did not like the school and was punished for reading Nietzsche. She lived in the old town where the Méjanes Library used to be and spent most of her spare time there.

When Mistral arrived in Aix for the first time, a little boy by the name of Emile Zola had been living there for five years. Zola (1840–1902) had moved there at the age of two from Paris. His father, Italian engineer Francesco Zola, was in charge of building a dam on the little Infernet River on the northern side of Ste-Victoire. In 1843, the Zolas found lodgings at rue Silvacane, in the old part of town. Mrs. Emily Zola was a Parisian, and adapting to Aix, where Provençal was still widely spoken, was not easy. To make things worse, in 1847, Francesco died. Mme Zola and her son moved to Pont-de-Béraud, about one mile north, then outside the city limits. The following year she enrolled Emile at the Pension Notre Dame for a semester. She then managed to obtain a scholarship to send him to the Collège Bourbon (now Lycée Mignet). Emile was a boarder. Life was hard; the dorms were not heated and the food was bad. His classmates made fun of his Parisian accent and things did not bode well.

Fortunately, he met Paul Cézanne, one year older and a grade above him. The two boys found out that they had many things in common, including their mothers' maiden name Aubert. They quickly became

Mont Ste-Victoire

inseparable friends and were joined by Philippe Solari and Jean-Baptistin Baille. Cézanne was a Provençal. In 1848, his father, a prosperous milliner, became a banker after the only bank in Aix went bankrupt. M. Louis Cézanne and his associate M. Cabasol, a former employee of the bank, joined forces and opened their own bank at 13 boulevard Boulégon. M. Cézanne's acute business sense made him prosperous and, in 1859, he left the Grand Cours where the family used to live and bought the estate the Jas de Bouffan ("the sheep-pen where the wind blows") on the outskirts of town.

During their holidays Zola, Cézanne, and their friends hiked up the Ste-Victoire, hunted, fished, swam in the River Arc, picnicked in lavender fields, and sat under the pine trees drinking wine and reciting and reading poems by Hugo and Musset. At this time, the forest at the foot of Ste-Victoire was wild and consisted of "barren lands, large stone fields, waste grounds, pitted here and there by abandoned quarries"[29] The Infernet gorge was dangerous and "visitors did not venture into this gloomy funnel of reddish rocks."[30] These days the scenery has not changed much except perhaps for the marked pathways. The happy moments that Zola and his friends spent there left indelible mem-

The High Country and Aix-en-Provence

Emile Zola, photo: Roger-Viollet

ories. But at home the situation worsened. Mme Zola did not get the retirement benefits from her husband's pension that she had asked for, and in 1858 she and her son returned to Paris. Zola was distressed but had no choice. He kept in touch with Cézanne, who came to visit him there quite often. His novel *L'oeuvre* is based on Cézanne's life. But Zola was not a Provençal and he remained ambivalent toward Provence. He did not support the cause of the félibres and hated Marseille, although he often spent a few days of vacation on its northern shores at l'Estaque, where Cézanne usually spent the summer.

Zola chose Aix (which he called Plassans) as the setting for *La fortune des Rougon* (1871), the first of a series of novels that portrayed the complex relationships between heredity and environment in the destiny of a Provençal family, the Rougon-Macquarts. Aix in those days was a small bourgeois town that lived without much concern for the turmoil of Paris. "Kings stealing each other's thrones, republics being made cause but a small stir in the city. When people fight in Paris, Plassans is asleep," remarks Zola.[31] At this time Aix numbered about ten thousand inhabitants. The aristocrats lived in their mansions and gardens in the south of town, the merchants and lawyers in the northeast, and the workers in the center. The distinct classes had their own habits and had little contact. Even on Sunday, Zola remembers, the bourgeois walked up and down the right side of the Cours with its stately mansions while the merchants sauntered on the left side with its shops and cafés such as Les Deux Garçons, one of Cézanne's favorite places. The town, strongly Catholic, royalist, and Provençal, was very much alive. In the middle of the nineteenth century, Aix was still surrounded by walls, which according to Zola only made it look smaller and darker than it was. Each night the gates, one in the north and one in the south, were closed and a sentinel stood watch against intruders.

Today the walls have disappeared and the town has expanded all around in the surrounding fields. Aix has approximately 120,000 inhabitants, a good third of whom are students who attend the humanities, law, and economics departments' campus of the University of Aix-Marseille. (Marseille has kept the sciences and medicine.) Despite the large student population, Aix has retained some of its aristocratic look and distinctions. Natives, or Aixois, make sure they are not confused with Marseillais and make an effort to maintain a distinctive accent, Provençal yet "with a touch of class." Culturally, Zola's days are long gone and the town can boast an active artistic life. There are more bookstores than cafés and, every July since 1948, the city organizes its own classical music and opera festival.

> Adieu mon cher Emile:
> Non, sur le flot mobile

Aussi gaiement je file
Que jadis autrefois

Quand nos bras agiles
Comme des reptiles
Sur les flots dociles
Nageaient à la fois.

Adieu, belles journées
Du vin assaisonnées!
Pêches fortunées
De poissons monstrueux!

Lorsque dans ma pêche,
A la rivière fraîche
Ma ligne revêche
N'attrapait rien d'affreux.

Goodbye, Emile:
No, on the flowing river
Happily I sail
As in the past

When our arms, agile
Like reptiles
On the docile waves
Swam together.

Goodbye, beautiful days
When wine flowed!
Wonderful fishing,
Enormous catches!

When throwing
In the clear river
My reluctant line
Did not catch much.

(Cézanne to Zola)[32]

Tracing Cézanne and Zola's footsteps in the countryside around Aix is ideal for day trips and picnics. The little road (D 10) that meanders along the Infernet among vineyards and pine forests leads to the dam that Zola's father built. Above it is a larger and more recent one from which several trails will take the experienced hiker to the top of Ste-Victoire, immortalized by Cézanne. Hiking shoes and drinking water are a must. In the Middle Ages, the mountain attracted pilgrims and monks who lived up there permanently. The chapel has been restored and the monastery turned into a refuge. On a clear day the view from the summit (ca. 3,000 feet) is breathtaking. Three miles farther on D 10 is the small village of Vauvenargues. Its castle was once the residence of the Marquis of Vauvenargues (1715–1747), philosopher and author of an *Introduction à la connaissance de l'esprit humain* (Introduction to the knowledge of the human mind) and *Caractères et dialogues* (Characters and dialogues, 1746), published anonymously. Vauvenargues was born in Aix but resided mostly in his castle. He served in the royal army but his prolonged stay there and the wars worsened his fragile health and he died in Paris at the age of thirty-two. His book attracted Voltaire's attention. In 1958, Picasso came for a visit to Vauvenargues. He fell in love with the discreet charm of the secluded village and bought the castle, where he now lies buried. It is unfortunately not open to visitors. Another favorite outing of Cézanne, Zola, and their group of friends was Tholonet, only three miles away from Aix on D 17. After 1887, Cézanne rented a room in the Château Noir there and then in Le Cabanon, a small house in the Bibemus quarry. He ate his meals in the small inn Rosa Berne, now the café-restaurant and B & B Le Cézanne (Tel: 04 42 66 91 91). But it is perhaps a couple of miles farther along D 17, on the plateau of St-Antonin, that the Ste-Victoire displays its timeless beauty. "From here the mountain, with its fantastic sail of white rocks, seems like a ghost ship in broad daylight," writes Giono in *Noé*.[33]

Tourist information. Place du Général de Gaulle. Tel: 04 42 16 11 61. Fax: 04 42 16 11 62. Email: <infos@aixenprovencetourism.com>. Website: <aixenprovencetourism.com>.

What to see. A stroll through the old town with its many shops and old fountains is a must. Two museums stand out from the crowd: *Musée Granet*, place St-Jean de Malte (Tel: 04 42 38 14 70). *Atelier Cézanne*, 9 avenue Cézanne (Email: <atelier.cezannea@wanadoo. fr>).

Where to stay. ****: *Grand Hôtel Roi René*, 24 blvd Roi René. AC, pool, garage. Tel: 04 42 37 61 00. Fax: 04 42 37 61 11. ***: *Mercure Cézanne*, 4 avenue Hugo. Tel: 04 42 26 34 73. Fax: 04 42 27 20 95. *Holiday Inn*, 5 route de Galice. Tel: 04 42 52 75 27. Fax: 04 42 52 75 28. **: *Manoir*, 8 rue Entrecasteaux. Parking. Tel: 04 42 26 27 20. Fax: 04 42 27 17 97. *Mozart*, 49 cours Gambetta. Garage. Tel: 04 42 21 62 86. Fax: 04 42 96 17 36. B&Bs: *Campagne Jeanne*, Mme Alexandrian, 670 chemin des Loups. Les Milles, three miles south of Aix. Parking. Tel: 04 42 60 83 10. Email: <martine@campagne-jeanne.com>. *La Jacquière*, Mme Thery, chemin des Mattes, Vauvenargues, three miles past the village in the direction of Jouques east on D 10 and north on D 11. Parking. Tel: 04 42 66 01 79. *La Dame d'Oc*, Mme Bosc. Vauvenargues. Parking. Tel: 04 42 66 02 36.

From Marseille to Cannes

I will see the Southern hills; I will dream; I will take my mind out of its iron cage and let it swim.

—Virginia Woolf, *Diary*

Marseille

Cassis

Bandol

Sanary-sur-Mer, Toulon

Hyères and the Iles d'Or

Le Lavandou

St-Tropez

Port-Grimaud to Cannes

Juan-les-Pins, Antibes

Cagnes-sur-Mer, St-Paul, Vence, Grasse

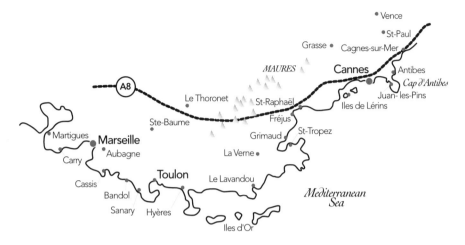

Marseille to Cannes

Marseille

"Capitalo de l'emperi dou souleù" (capital of the empire of the sun), said Mistral of Marseille. Founded in the sixth century B.C. by the Greeks from Phocaea in Asia Minor, it is the most ancient city in Provence and indeed in all of France. The location was ideal for a harbor: a large bay and a long secluded cove stretching about four hundred yards inland, sheltered from the winds by two hills. At first, relations between the Greeks and Ligurians were peaceful. An old legend relates that one day Nann, the chief of the natives, gave a banquet during which his daughter Gyptis had to choose a husband. After careful consideration and to everyone's surprise, Gyptis chose Protis, a young Greek guest. However, the chief gave his consent and the marriage was celebrated. Gyptis's dowry was the hill on which a small village Massalia, was built, with the agora, theater, and temple to the Greek goddess Artemis. The area where the Greeks settled is still referred to as Les Vieux Quartiers (the old neighborhoods). The Greeks planted vineyards and olive trees. They traded amber and copper with other colonies in Spain and tin with Brittany. They expanded and founded colonies along the coast, such as Antibes and Nice, and inland (Arles, Avignon, Glanon). In the fourth century Euthymene sailed to Senegal on the west coast of Africa, and Pytheas explored the northern lands, Scandinavia and Iceland.

Marseille remained an independent Greek polis or city-state for the next five centuries. Its culture and language were Greek. The Marseillais assisted the Romans in their second war against Carthage (154 B.C.), and in their turn the Romans helped the Marseillais fight off the

Marseille: The Old Harbor

incursions of the Celts and Ligurians. Finally the Romans settled there in 49 B.C. Between the fifth and the eighth centuries Marseille was pillaged by Germanic tribes and Arabs. The city was surrounded by walls until the end of the seventeenth century. In 1720, half its population or about fifty thousand people died in a plague epidemic. Commerce and fishing were the city's main activities, but in the eighteenth and nineteenth centuries, new industries (sugar refineries, soap factories) developed. Today the city counts approximately 800,000 inhabitants.

For centuries the sea enticed many a local Ulysses and gave the Marseillais a distinct way of life. Always caricatured as jovial, lazy, and prone to exaggeration, the inhabitants of Marseille remain deeply entrenched in their Mediterranean past. "Sian li felen de la Grèco immourtalo" (We are the children of immortal Greece), says Mistral.[1] All of its writers, including Marcel Pagnol, André Suarès, Albert Cohen, Louis Brauquier, and Jean-Claude Izzo, owe a debt to Greek literature. The city inevitably presents a sharp contrast with Paris; those visitors used to the Louvre and the Eiffel Tower complain that there is "nothing to see" in Marseille, not to mention its bad reputation for crime

Marseille: The Old Harbor

and drugs, and the fact that the French spoken there is often hard to understand.

While it is true that Marseille cannot compare with Paris for monuments and museums, its reputation for crime, acquired in the 1930s, is now wholly unjustified. But legends die hard. The remarks concerning language and the local tendency to exaggerate are nevertheless true. It is all the sun's fault, explained Daudet and Zola. The sun, indeed, plays a large role in the city's atmosphere. It slows the pace of life and forces the people to weigh their words and pronounce every single syllable of French. Another particularity of the idiom is the survival of Provençal terms. They refuse to die and disguise themselves to sound like French. Hence Provençal "pastis" (a mess) gives the verb *pastisser* (to mess up); "boulega" (to move) becomes *bouléguer* (to hurry); "barjaca" gives *barjaquer* (to chat). The problem is that young children growing up in the city have no idea that, despite their academic appearance, these words are totally incomprehensible to northern ears. These observations apply to all of Provence but are particularly true of Marseille.

But language is also the sign that more profound cultural differences exist. In the south and especially in Marseille, its southernmost outpost, Parisian logic and mentality scarcely apply. Here again it is the sun that blurs the outline of things and creates mirages. In Pagnol's famous play *Marius* (act 1, part 2) César, tired of seeing his son's incompetent bar-tending techniques, decides to teach him how to prepare a proper Mandarin-lemon-Curaçao cocktail. First, César argues that Marius's problem is that he has no notion of precise measurements, adding that the drinks Marius serves never contain the same mixture. Marius replies that this inconsistency is of little importance since customers generally order only one cocktail and, therefore, cannot compare. But César insists, arguing that cocktail preparation is an art, and proceeds to explain the recipe that has become legendary: one (very small) third of curaçao, a (slightly larger) third of lemon, a (good) third of Picon, and finally a large third of water. Marius immediately remarks that this makes, in fact, four thirds, which is mathematically impossible. Surprised by such rigorous logic from the mouth of his son, César refutes his argument, saying that it all depends on the size of the thirds. Marius, who like his father does not easily give up, tries to convince him that even a watering can does not hold more than three thirds. To which César, surpassing himself, replies: "How do you explain, then, that I managed to put four of them in this glass?"

> *César:* Tu mets d'abord un tiers de curaçao. Fais attention: un tout petit tiers. Bon. Maintenant, un tiers de citron. Un peu plus gros. Bon. Ensuite, un *bon* tiers de Picon. Regarde la couleur. Regarde comme c'est joli. Et à la fin, un *grand* tiers d'eau. Voilà.
>
> *Marius:* Et ça fait quatre tiers!
>
> *César:* Exactement. J'espère que cette foi, tu as compris.
>
> *Marius:* Dans un verre, il n'y a que trois tiers.
>
> *César:* Mais, imbécile, ça dépend de la grosseur des tiers!
>
> *Marius:* Eh non, ça ne dépend pas. Même dans un arrosoir, on ne peut mettre que trois tiers.
>
> *César:* Alors, explique-moi comment j'en ai mis quatre dans ce verre.[2]

St-Michel Festival, Marseille

Such reasoning is not surprising in Marseille, for here "Adieu" can mean both hello and goodbye, people are not "stupide" but only "fada" (literally, struck by a fairy's wand), and "fatigué" means not only tired but also ill. The police headquarters occupy the ancient palace of the bishop and are known as *L'Evêché* (diocese), and a small hill downtown is called "La Plaine." The city's numerous neighborhoods have colorful and poetic names such as La Vieille Chapelle, La Pointe Rouge, Les Quatre Saisons, La Belle de Mai, La Rose, Le Merlan (Whiting), and Le Roucas Blanc (White Rock). Finally and most important is humor,

St-Michel Festival, Marseille

which is a way of life. In fact, many argue that Marseille is not only a city but also a small country in its own right.

Marseille's most ancient poet is perhaps the troubadour Folquet (1150–1231). Folquet was a merchant of Genoan origin. He knew the Latin poets as well as the works of contemporary troubadours such as Peire Vidal and Raimbaut de Vacqueyras. In 1200, he heard the call and left his wife and two children to join the Cistercian monks of Thoronet in Provence. In 1205, he became the bishop of Toulouse and fought against the Cathars. He wrote several poems or cansos, twenty of which have survived. There were certainly many others but they have been lost. Provençal continued to be the language of communication and literature for writers such as Pierre Bellot (1783–1855), author of books of poems such as *Lou poueto cassaire* (The hunting poet). In 1841, Bellot created *Lou tambourinaïre et lou ménestrel* (The drummer and the minstrel), the first weekly magazine in French and Provençal. A few years later Joseph Désenat published *Lou bouil-abaïsso* (The bouillabaisse, 1841–46), entirely in Provençal and in verse. It too was published weekly. Gustave Bénédit (1803–1870), lyrical artist and music critic, also wrote a popular play entitled *Chichois* (1853). Fortuné Chailan (1801–1840) wrote tales and poems that he collected in one volume, *Lou gangui* (The net, 1839). Carvin was a prolific playwright, the author of several comedies such as *Meste Barna* (Master Barna, 1809) and *Mise Galineto* (Mister Galineto, 1830). When Roumanille and Mistral began their renaissance movement in 1854, Provençal literature was certainly eclipsed by the French, but it had not completely disappeared.

Many foreign writers either embarked or landed in Marseille. To Giacomo Casanova (1725–1798), who passed through the city in 1743, the boutiques and people of Marseille inevitably reminded him of his native Venice. He appreciated the quality of its cuisine and especially the *rougets* (red mullets), and then went on to discover the charms of the local ladies. In 1837, Stendhal was struck by the "surprising transparence of the air." George Sand, traveling to the island of Majorca with Chopin, complained at first about the hot sun and the people's rugged look but finally realized that the climate was healthy and the people had good hearts. On the other hand, her friend Gustave Flaubert seems to have thoroughly enjoyed his first trip to Marseille in 1840. Coming from Arles with a party of travelers, he stopped in Marseille for a few days. The sea came as a wonderful shock: "It was the following day after I woke up that I saw the Mediterranean Sea. It was still covered with the morning mist rising as if pumped up by the sun. Its blue waters spread between the gray rocks of the bay with a poised and ancient solemnity. . . . I like the Mediterranean; it has something grave and soft that reminds one of Greece, something immense and voluptuous that is reminiscent of the Orient."[3] Taking advantage of the sunny weather and the absence of wind, Flaubert went fishing with the hotel owner and his daughter. He then strolled around the residential part of town and noted that Marseille was "a nice city with large mansions that look like palaces."[4] He was pleasantly surprised by the energy of its inhabitants, going about their usual business under the scorching sun, and by their simplicity. Unlike Paris, he asserted, Marseille was a city where people could "dine without mentioning politics and drink without discussing philosophy."

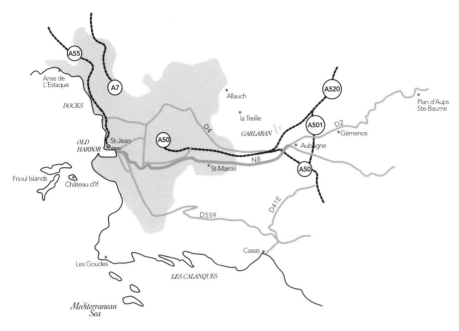

Marseille

His favorite place was, of course, the harbor *(plate 25)* with its vivid colors and myriad of travelers. It was a feast for the eyes: "Darse Street was full of sailors of all nationalities, Jews, Armenians, Greeks, all wearing their national costumes, crowding the bars, laughing with the girls, spilling wine, singing, dancing, flirting as they pleased."[5] He was indeed very far from the green pastures and gray skies of his native Normandy. No doubt he felt in another world, as the following description shows: "The sun and the fresh air of the South flow freely into its long streets. One feels something Oriental there. Walking is pleasant, and one breathes with joy. The skin opens up and absorbs the sun like a great bath of light. Marseille is now what Persia must have been in ancient times or Alexandria in the Middle Ages: a jumble, a Babel of all nations, where you can see short blond hair, big black beards, white skin striped with blue veins, the Oriental olive complexion, blue eyes, black eyes, all kinds of costumes, jackets, coats, burnoose, cloth. . . . One hears unknown languages, Slavic, Sanskrit, Persian,

Downtown Marseille

Scythians, Egyptian, all the languages, those spoken in the northern countries and those whispered in the southern lands."[6] The city fascinated him and certainly contributed to his later interest in the Orient. Flaubert went to the market and stopped in several shops, buying local pies, sandals, and an engraved cane. He then had dinner in the residential neighborhood of Prado, meandered down the Huveaune River in a small boat, and had a sunset swim in the sea.

One evening, Flaubert even attended a Provençal mystery play, usually reserved for the local population. How much he understood is difficult to say but, again, he enjoyed himself: "At the back of the stage were four or five well-dressed characters; the king with his crown, the queen, the farmer whose daughter had been kidnapped and who argued with the kidnapper while the mother grieved and tore her hair out singing a sort of complaint with numerous exclamations, like in Aeschylus's tragedies. The dialogue was lively and animated and no doubt improvised," he wrote in his notebooks.[7] On the whole, Flaubert was enchanted with his short stay in the southern city and left with regrets.

Daudet himself went to Marseille on several occasions when he traveled to North Africa and Corsica. "As far as the eye could see," he writes in *Tartarin*, "it was a jumble of masts, sails, crossing one another in all directions. Flags of all nationalities: Russian, Greek, Swedish, Tunisian, American. . . . Here and there, between the ships, a bit of sea looked like large cloth stained with oil. . . . Young sailors hailed one another in all languages. . . . On the wharf in the midst of little green and black streams oozing from the soap factories, loaded with oil and saltwort, worked a myriad of people, custom officers, agents, porters with their carriages drawn by small Corsican horses . . . pipe sellers, monkey sellers, parrot sellers . . . women selling mussels, clams . . . and sailors with baskets full of octopus."[8]

One of the few who did not care for Marseille was Emile Zola. But then again he was an Aixois, which explains his attitude. His novel *Les mystères de Marseille* (1867), written at the beginning of his career, speaks of Marseille as a city of commerce, with a natural propensity for gambling and sex. Its people were "ferocious" and greedy. However, he often spent his vacation in Estaque, then a fishing village on its northern shore, where his longtime friend Cézanne often rented a summerhouse.

Another writer who had deep roots in Marseille is Bosco, the writer of the Luberon. His grandparents had emigrated there from Italy at the end of the nineteenth century. Between 1870 and 1914, about a hundred thousand Italians, mostly from Naples and Gaete, settled in Marseille. Many of them worked as fishermen. Provençal, being closer to Italian, was easier to learn than French and the new population had little trouble communicating. The Boscos settled in the St-Jean neighborhood near the harbor. Fourteen children were born and grew up there in a three-story house. Bosco loved to come to Marseille to visit his grandparents. His favorite activity was to stroll along the wharf and watch the fishermen repair their nets and the women sell the fish. His novel *L'antiquaire* (1954) is set in Marseille.

In October 1882, Robert Louis Stevenson (1850–1894) and his wife Fanny arrived in Marseille. Like many others, he was in search of sun and warmth to help fight his tuberculosis. The Stevensons rented a house in St-Marcel on the outskirts of town, "five miles out of Marseille, in a lovely spot far lovelier than the Alps." Stevenson was pleased and described the area as "a lovely valley between hills part wooded, part white cliffs." The property was called Campagne Delfi and included a three-bedroom house, a large olive grove, and pine shrubbery. "I like the place immensely," he wrote to his mother. The house was peaceful and rustic, and close enough to transportation: "A railway station in front, two lines of omnibus to Marseille."[9] Stevenson spoke French well enough, for as an adolescent he had spent some time in Menton. He and Fanny made the most out of their stay in Marseille. They visited the downtown shops, took long walks in the surrounding hills and, above all, enjoyed the mild autumn sun. They were happy and comfortable there and his health improved. Unfortunately, early in January 1883, an epidemic of typhus broke out in the city and the Stevensons decided to leave. After a short stay in Nice, they finally settled in Hyères.

In those days, a promising young playwright was a student at the Grand Lycée (now Lycée Thiers), the city's most famous all-male school. Edmond Rostand (1868–1918), the author of *Cyrano de Bergerac*, was a Marseillais. His ancestors were originally from Orgon (where Daudet spent some of his vacations), and his family included notaries and lawyers. In 1750, Alexis Rostand left for Marseille, where he opened a linen shop. Edmond was born at 14 rue Montaux (now rue Edmond Rostand) in the same house as his maternal grandparents, the Gayets, ship owners. Young Edmond and his two younger sisters grew up in a comfortable home. His father Eugène was the president of the Caisse des Bouches du Rhône, a local bank. Rostand first attended a small private school, the Institution Thévenat, and then the Grand Lycée, like his father. The Rostands liked to entertain, and Mistral was often one of their guests. Every summer, the family would leave the heat for Luchon, a fashionable health spa in the Pyrenees. In 1884, Edmond's father

Edmond Rostand, Musée Rostand, Cambo-les-bains

decided to send his son to Paris to further his education and registered him at the Collège Stanislas. When he graduated in 1886, Rostand attended the Sorbonne and majored in law. In 1890, he married Rosemonde Gérard.

But young Edmond dreamed of becoming a poet and spent his time writing. His favorite authors were Molière, Musset, and Dumas. He achieved recognition with his play *Les Romanesques* (1894). Sarah Bernhardt was Melissande in *La princesse lointaine* (1895), based on the life of troubadour Joffroy Rudel, but the play failed. Rostand did not give up and, encouraged by Bernhardt, continued to write. Two years later, on December 1897, *Cyrano de Bergerac* triumphed at the Porte-Saint-Martin. The audience and critics alike were enthralled. Henri Bauer, writing for the *Echo de Paris*, ranked him first of the contemporary playwrights and Sarcey in *Le temps* thanked him for a return to a more national and healthy subject. The play performed almost every day for a year and half in Paris alone. Proud, courageous, but also sentimental and a dreamer, Cyrano is the embodiment of the Southern man.

In November 1915, in the middle of World War I, author Katherine Mansfield (1888–1923) arrived in Marseille. Like Stevenson before her, she was in search of sun and warmth. Mansfield was born and raised in Wellington, New Zealand, but since her college days in London she had been living in Europe. She was separated from her husband, Garnet Trowell, and was seeing John Middleton Murry, writer and reviewer of French books for the *Times*. Marseille and its cold wind must have reminded her of home, for Wellington is also known as "the windy city." The city looked "a confused and extraordinary place," but she found the port "extremely beautiful." There was indeed nothing resembling London and the contrast was stunning. "The sea is here, very clear, very blue . . . and there are high mountains covered with bright green pine trees. Tufts of rosemary grow among the rocks and a tall flower with pink bells which is very lovely," she wrote in her letters.[10] But, like many Northerners, she had not been aware that Marseille can be cold and windy and she moved eastward to Cassis.

Mansfield was a favorite writer of a twenty-two-year-old philosophy teacher by the name of Simone de Beauvoir (1908–1986) who, in the fall of 1931, arrived in Marseille to begin her teaching career at the Lycée Montgrand, the city's best girls' school. It was her first assignment; like every certified teacher in France, she was a state worker and in exchange for job security had to teach wherever the educational authorities sent her. When Beauvoir, a Parisian, received the news that she had to go to Marseille, she became depressed: Jean-Paul Sartre, the man she loved, was teaching in Le Havre (Normandy) six hundred miles away. However, she had visited Provence the spring before with a friend and had loved it. Provence was "une grande revelation," she

Simone de Beauvoir

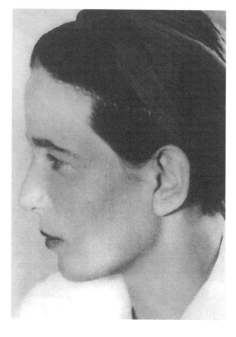

says in memoirs.[11] "I loved the dry and perfumed vegetation. . . . For the first time I slept under a mosquito net . . . for the first time in Arles I saw hedges of cypresses bent by the Mistral and I saw the olive trees' genuine color. . . . The wind was blowing on Les Baux and the fire crackled in the fireplace of La Reine Jeanne where we were the only customers" on a night that she always remembered. The memories of her trip were no doubt still fresh in her mind and gave her the courage to face Marseille where Parisians, betrayed by their accent "pointu"— or nasal and affected, according to Provençals—and their contempt for "provincials," are avoided at all cost. Beauvoir knew no one but she was sociable and courageous and decided to conquer the city.

"I remember my arrival in Marseille as a totally new turning point in my life," Beauvoir later declared.[12] As soon as she got off the train, she put her luggage in consignment, descended the stairs of the Gare St-Charles, and walked to the Canebière, the city's main thoroughfare: "Under the blue sky, sunny tiles, spaces of shade; sycamore trees in their autumn foliage; in the distance, hills and the blue sea; a clamor

From Marseille to Cannes

The rugged coast

and a smell of burnt grass rose from the city. People came and went in the middle of its dark streets."[13] She rented a room near the station to be within walking distance of her school. At work, her reception from the director and fellow teachers was rather cold, for the reasons mentioned above. But on her days off and weekends she explored the city and the surrounding countryside. "It was love at first sight," she said.[14] "I climbed all the rocky hills, strolled in all the narrow streets, breathed the tar and sea-urchin of the Old Harbor, mingled with the crowd on the Canebière, sat on the boulevard benches, in parks and in peaceful yards where the provincial smell of dead leaves overpowered the sea breeze."[15]

One of her favorite spots was the Calanques or small fjord-like coves surrounded by steep cliffs and the southernmost end of the city. On Sunday, she would get up early, hop on a bus, a brioche or a banana in her bag, and head south to Les Goudes *(plate 26)*, a little fishing village before the Calanques *(plate 27)*: "I climbed down all the Calanques, explored all the valleys, the gorges, the deep ravines. Among the dazzling rocks I walked, searching for the pathway and its arrows—blue, green, red, yellow—that led I did not know where; Sometimes I lost them, I looked for them, going in circles, beating bushes with sharp smells, scraping myself against plants still unknown to me: pines, juniper trees, oaks, yellow and white asphodels."[16]

At work, Beauvoir's liberal attitude toward the accepted mores (she had the students read Proust and Gide!) upset the students, and their parents complained to the director. The latter reprimanded Beauvoir, but she continued just the same. During the holidays, she would take the train to Paris and visit her family and Sartre, home for the vacation, or they would come down to Marseille and take her out to Isnard for a *bouillabaisse*. Together, they would visit the Fontaine-de-Vaucluse, Sainte-Baume, Aix, or Valensole. Over the months, Beauvoir finally befriended the school's English teacher and went with her to Pascal's for *loup grillé* (grilled bass) and Cassis wine, and to the movies. Beauvoir also read a lot and among her favorite authors that year were Stendhal and Katherine Mansfield. Clearly, her life there contrasted with that of the good student she had been in the preceding years. She was active, curious, and found the city exciting: "I was never bored. Marseille had always something for me to do."[17] Of course, she loved the old harbor. She sat there and "watched the fishermen standing amongst the rocks where the waves crashed."

Bold as she was, she wandered off into the less recommended areas where "women heavily made up" stood on the porches of dingy hotels. She walked up the old town and its narrow streets, climbed down the old stairways to the fish market in the rumble of the harbor. The excitement was such that back in her small room, Beauvoir jotted down ideas for a story. Reading Mansfield's letters and journal, Beauvoir traveled to Bandol in her footsteps, wandering in an olive grove and reminiscing about her impressions of the place. She identified with Mansfield, who like her was a lone woman in Provence, and thought about writing an autobiographical novel. But Marseille was too far from her loved ones and at the end of the school year Beauvoir returned to Paris. However, her experience in the southern city had been rich and left an indelible mark on her mind.

When Beauvoir arrived in Paris the play *Marius* (1929) had been a success for three consecutive years. Its author, unanimously applauded by critics, was the young Marseillais playwright Marcel Pagnol (1895–1974). Pagnol, Marseille's most famous writer, was actually born in the little town of Aubagne, "nestled on the slopes of the Huveaune Valley, crossed by a dusty road that went from Marseille to Toulon."[18] The little town, only ten miles east of Marseille, now has been almost swallowed by it. But at the turn of the nineteenth century it was quite a peaceful Provençal village. "I was born in the town of Aubagne, under the Garlaban surrounded with goats at the time of the last goat herders. Garlaban is an enormous tower of blue rocks, planted at the edge of the Plan de l'Aigle, the immense rocky plateau that looks over the green Huveaune valley," Pagnol writes in *La gloire de mon père* (My father's glory).[19]

Aubagne was also the home of Father Jean-Jacques Barthélemy (1716–1785), a classical scholar and author of *Le voyage du jeune Anacharsis en Grèce* (1788), which met with unprecedented success. It went through six editions in the next ten years and was translated into a dozen languages. The story tells the adventures of a young Scythian in Greece in the fourth century B.C. and was mainly the occasion for Barthélemy to display the extent of his scholarship. Barthélemy was elected to the French Academy, but during the Revolution he was arrested and died shortly after.

When the Pagnols lived there, Aubagne was a small town of about ten thousand people. "There were tile, brick, and pitcher factories. They stuffed blood sausages and *andouilles*."[20] But Pagnol did not get a chance to know the town, for, when he turned two, his father got transferred to Marseille, his hometown, and the family moved back there.

Marcel's father was an elementary school teacher and his mother a seamstress. The Pagnols first lived in the Saint-Loup neighborhood not too far from Aubagne, but in 1900 they moved closer to the center, rue Tivoli, and then to rue Terrusse near the little hill known as Plaine-St-Michel. By then the family included Paul and Germaine, the little sister. As a young boy, Pagnol read Hans-Christian Andersen but also Daudet, who remained a major source of influence throughout his

Marcel Pagnol, photo: Copyright Editions de Fallois

career. In 1905, he attended the Lycée Thiers, where twenty years earlier his professors had taught young Edmond Rostand. Pagnol was a good student with a keen sense of humor. Among his best school friends was Albert Cohen (1895–1981), the future novelist. One of his French professors was Emile Ripert, a poet and great admirer of Mistral and the félibres. Later, Ripert became a respected playwright. His doctoral dissertation *La Renaissance provençale* (1917) won him a position at the university. Pagnol loved writing and the theater and in 1914 founded the review *Fortunio* with his friend Jean Ballard. The review later became the famous *Cahiers du Sud* (1925–67).

In his autobiographical novels *La gloire de mon père* and *Le château de ma mère* (My mother's castle), adapted to the screen by Yves Robert in 1990, Pagnol relates how, during vacations, his family would travel to the small village of La Treille between Marseille and Aubagne. There they rented La Bastide Neuve for eighty francs a year. La Treille was "a little village situated on top of a hill, between two small valleys."[21] It was composed of a few houses with red tiled roofs and very small windows. In the center was a small place shaded by a very old blackberry tree and two acacias that "tried to outgrow the church steeple."[22] There was also a fountain "that talked to itself." The house they rented was a little past the village. It was an old farm that its owner had recently restored. On the first floor were a kitchen and dining room, and upstairs four bedrooms. It had no electricity, but a cistern attached to the house brought running water to the kitchen. This was considered a luxury not only for the time but also in these remote regions, known as "le pays de la soif" (the country of thirst), where springs were rare and water precious. Around the house was an old orchard and, not far from it, a small field where farmers tried to grow wheat and rye. The hills were covered with pines, olive trees, thyme, rosemary, sage, and savory. "You could walk for thirty kilometers and see only the small ruins of three of four medieval farms and a few sheepfolds," Pagnol claimed with some exaggeration.[23] The farm and its surrounding hills shaped Pagnol's imagination forever: "As soon as we left the village the enchantment began and a love that lasted all my life was born. Immense scenery in a semicircle arose before my eyes up to the sky: black pine woods, separated by small valleys, unfurled like waves at the foot of three rocky summits."[24]

In La Treille, the Pagnols shared the house with Uncle Jules, a jovial fellow from the Southwest who rolled his "r"s and, unlike Pagnol's father, drank wine and went to church. For Pagnol and his brother the place was paradise. The two boys discovered the local animals, insects, and the famous cicadas that he had never seen so close. They learned about plants and especially thyme. "I left the pathway and ran to touch the small leaves. A strong perfume arose like a cloud and completely surrounded me. Its smell was unknown to me, it was dark and strong and invaded my head and entered my heart," Pagnol remembers.[25] In these rugged hills, Pagnol met a little farm boy named

Lili des Bellons who taught him about hunting *bartavelles* or large partridges, rabbits, and other animals. He took him to hidden caves on secret pathways and whispered in his ears about underground springs. In the hot summer afternoons, when everybody was slumbering under the fig trees, Pagnol read James Fenimore Cooper and Gustave Aymard, Tartarin de Tarascon's favorite authors. The vacation months spent in these delightful hills left an indelible imprint on Pagnol's artistic temperament and inspired his later films.

In the meantime, as a young man Pagnol taught for a while in Tarascon, obtaining his *licence* (B.A.) in English from the University of Montpellier. Married in 1916, he continued to teach in Aix and Marseille but dreamed of going to Paris to become a writer. In 1922, he accepted a position at the Lycée Condorcet there and left Provence. Pagnol's dream came true. After a couple of promising attempts at the theater, he finally achieved success with *Topaze* (1928), a play about a dutiful but shy teacher who, forced to resign, becomes a keen businessman.

But in Paris Pagnol was nostalgic for Marseille and, encouraged by his friends, he wrote a play set in his beloved city and called *Marius*, a common local first name then. It was originally written for a Marseillais audience and was to be performed at the Alcazar, a vaudeville theater, but its director persuaded Pagnol to choose Paris instead, which entailed making a few changes in the script. Pagnol hired actor Raimu (Auguste Muraire, 1883–1946), born in Toulon, where he began his stage career as a child before working in Marseille and moving on to Paris. Orane Demazis, Pagnol's lover (he was now separated from his wife), would play Fanny. Pagnol then looked for a southern actor to take the role of Marius, but Léon Volterra, the theater manager, suggested Pierre Fresnay. Pagnol hesitated. Raimu was irate, for Fresnay was born in Alsace, but they finally accepted. Fresnay took lessons in local pronunciation. Raimu, for whom Pagnol had reserved the role of Panisse, decided instead to play César, Marius's father, and he made the right decision. *Marius* premiered at the Théâtre de Paris on March 9, 1929, and was an immense triumph. The plot is very simple: Marius works for his father César in Le Bar de la Marine on the harbor. He loves Fanny, who is also courted by Panisse, the widowed sailmaker. But since his childhood Marius dreams of sailing around the world and finally when the opportunity presents itself he takes a job on board a ship and leaves without saying goodbye.

The love story, or rather, stories—between Marius and Fanny and between Marius and his father—had rarely been treated with such truth, and Raimu's performance was so perfect that the public was enthralled. Raimu and Pagnol became inseparable. Following the success of his play *Marius*, Pagnol wrote a sequel, *Fanny* (1931). Fanny realizes she is expecting a child by Marius but finally marries Panisse. *César* (1936), the last play of the trilogy, begins with Panisse's death. Césariot meets his father, Marius, who marries Fanny. In the early 1930s, Pagnol abandoned the theater for the cinema and founded his own production company with studios in Marseille, avenue du Prado. Alexander Korda adapted *Marius* to the screen for Paramount with the same actors and Marc Allegret directed *Fanny*.

The year 1929 was a good one for Provence: it revealed two talented authors, Pagnol and Giono. After the success of Giono's novels, Pagnol decided to adapt them to the screen. He contacted the author in Manosque and explained his project. Giono found the idea interesting and agreed. Pagnol immediately set to work. His first film was *Jofroi* (1933) from Giono's short story "Jofroi de la Maussan." For the leading role Pagnol hired Vincent Scotto, a Marseillais composer. Then came *Angèle* (1934), adapted from *Un de Baumugnes* and starring Fernandel. Fernandel (1903–1970), whose real name was Fernand Contandin, was also a native of Marseille. He came from a vaudeville family and, after a few odd jobs, finally made a breakthrough in the theater there. In 1928, he left for Paris with his wife and children. Fernandel obtained some success at the Concert Mayol, played in movies such as *Le blanc et le noir* (1930) with Raimu, *On purge Bébé* (1931), directed by Jean Renoir, and *Coeur de lilas* (1931) with another young actor by the name of Jean Gabin. *Angèle* also featured Orane Demazis and a team of Provençal actors such as Charles Blavette, Henri Poupon, Rellys, and Andrex. Pagnol shot the movie in the hills near Aubagne where his team built a few stone houses for the set. Today only a few stones stand but for a long time the place was known as "le village de Pagnol." The audience and critics applauded *Angèle* and launched Fernandel's career. Pagnol hired him again in 1937 to play the part of Gédémus in *Regain*, also adapted from Giono. For his serious roles Pagnol turned to Raimu, who starred in *La femme du boulanger* (The baker's wife, 1938), from Giono's *Jean le bleu* (Blue boy). His performance won him the National Board of Review award for best actor. (Raimu died while undergoing minor surgery in the American Hospital of Neuilly in 1946. He was buried in Toulon.) The success of Pagnol's movies made Giono somewhat jealous and a quarrel arose, mostly over interpretation but also over royalties. The case had to be settled in court. Fortunately, their squabble did not last long and the two authors resumed their friendship.

Pagnol continued to produce and direct his own films. *La fille du puisatier* (The welldigger's daughter, 1941) starred Raimu and Fernandel. *Cigalon* (1935) is the story of a Provençal chef who refuses to serve customers because they do not understand his artistry. Pagnol adapted Zola's *Naïs* (1945) with Fernandel and Daudet's *Lettres de mon moulin* (1953). But his later masterpieces were unquestionably *Jean de Florette* and *Manon des sources* (Manon of the springs, 1951), poignant stories in which love, greed, and destiny are masterfully woven together in a very moving film. Pagnol made many other films but none as successful as these two. Separated from his wife, with whom he had no children, he had lived with actresses Orane Demazis, Kitty Murphy, and Josette Day, with all of whom he had children. In 1945, divorced for four years, Pagnol married a young actress by the name of Jacqueline Bouvier; they gave both their children, Frédéric and Estelle, names that evoke Mistral. From 1947 to 1951 the Pagnols lived in the principality of Monaco, on avenue des Moulins. In his later years Pagnol returned to literature with translations of Shakespeare's *A Midsummer Night's Dream* and *Hamlet* and of Virgil's *Bucolica*. He wrote his memoirs: *Le château de ma mère*, *La gloire de mon père*, and *Le temps des secrets* (The time of secrets). Back in Paris, Pagnol returned to the theater with *Judas* (1955) and *Fabien* (1956), but the plays had no connection with Provence and disappointed his audience. He died in Paris in 1974 and was buried in the small cemetery of La Treille, near his father.

If Pagnol is undoubtedly Marseille's most famous playwright and moviemaker, his friend Louis Brauquier (1900–1976) is perhaps the city's best-known poet. A student at the Lycée Thiers a few years after Pagnol, Brauquier later majored in law in Aix-en-Provence and then worked for shipping agents in Marseille. He passed the exams to become an officer of the merchant marine and sailed around the world until his retirement in 1960. Tradition has it that Brauquier was the model for Pagnol's character Marius. Brauquier's interest in literature began early. He admired the poems of Emile Sicard, editor of *Le feu*, and of Blaise Cendrars, author of *Prose du Transsibérien*. In 1918, he created the review *La coupo* (The grail) and then collaborated on *Fortunio* with Pagnol. He met d'Arbaud, Bosco, and poet Gabriel Audisio (1900–1978). He first began to write poetry in Provençal with *L'auciprès courouna de nerto* (The cypress crowned with myrtle, 1920) but then turned to French. His collection of poems *Et l'au-delà de Suez* (And beyond Suez, 1923) was awarded the Prix Catulle. He also published *Pythéas* (1931), *Liberté des mers* (Freedom of the seas, 1941), and *Feux d'épaves* (Shipwrecks' fires, 1970). In 1962, Brauquier received the Grand Prix Littéraire de Provence and in 1971 the Grand Prix de Poésie. His favorite themes were the sea and sailors and naturally he devoted several poems to Marseille, such as "Chanson de l'escale":

> Je vois s'amarrer des tartanes
> Chargées de beaux poissons d'argent;
> Victor Gelu sous les platanes,
> Parle à des nervis de Saint-Jean.
>
> Je vois des mâts et des voilures,
> Et d'éclatantes cargaisons,
> L'odeur verte des aventures
> Brûle mon sang de ses poisons.
>
> La ville est un blanc coquillage
> Bruissant de lointaines rumeurs,
> J'écoute et tous les paysages
> Me prennent ma force et mon cœur.

Des oliviers sur les collines,
Des collines grecques et nues,
La criée de la place aux Huiles,
Toutes les terres inconnues.

Je ne sais plus si je débarque
Ou si j'ai passé là vingt ans,
Si je mets le pied sur la barque,
Si j'ai couru les Océans.

I see sailings ships mooring
Laden with beautiful silver fish;
Under the sycamores Victor Gelu
Speaks to a few hoodlums of Saint-Jean.

I see masts and sails,
And wonderful cargos;
The green smell of adventures
Burns my blood of its poisons.

The city is a white shell
Rumbling with distant clamors,
I listen and all the sceneries
Take away my strength and my heart.

Olive trees on the hills,
Greek, barren hills,
The fish market at the place aux Huiles,
All the unknown lands.

I do not know whether I disembark
Or if I spent twenty years there,
If I set foot on the boat,
If I sailed around the Oceans.[26]

Victor Gelu (1806–1885), whom Brauquier mentions in his poem, wrote many popular songs. Valère Bernard (1860–1936) was primarily

Louis Brauquier, photo: Editions Table Ronde (private collection)

a painter but also the author of poems in Provençal such as *Li ballado d'aran* (The ballads of bronze, 1883) and popular novels such as *Bagatouni* (1894) and *Lei boumian* (The gypsies, 1907). The word Bagatouni comes from the Genovese dialect and refers to a poor neighborhood. Bernard applies it to Marseille's Vieux Quartier of St-Jean and, in the manner of Zola, describes the life of these poor people. In Marseille the Félibres had at their disposal several reviews such as *La sartan, L'aubo provençalo* (The Provençal dawn), *L'escolo de la mar,* and *Lou gai sabe.* Playwright Antonin Artaud (1896–1946) was born there as well as writers André Suarès (1868–1948) and Mathilde Monnier (1887–1967), a novelist. Suarès, from a Jewish family, studied at Lycée Thiers and then in Paris, where he finally settled. He devoted his life to literature, but Provence did not inspire him much and his essay *Marsiho* (Marseille) is, on the whole, very critical of his native city. He died in Paris (St-Maur) but was buried in Les Baux. Monnier came from a family of rich merchants. She studied at the Lycée Montgrand but left school at the age of fifteen to work as a seamstress. At the same time she began writing poems, short stories, and plays. She first attracted the attention of critics with a poem dedicated to Mistral and published in *Théatra*, in 1909, but success came later with novels such as *La rue courte* (The short street, 1937) and *Nans le berger* (Nans the shepherd, 1942). She wrote prolifically, including her autobiography and psychological novels. She met Giono and became Pierre Magnan's companion. She spent the later part of her life in Nice, where she died.

Today Marseille continues to inspire its younger generation. The novels of Jean-Claude Izzo (1945–2000) such as *Total Keops* (1995) and *Chourmo* (The multitude, 1996) take place in the city; so does *Les marins perdus* (The lost sailors, 1997), inspired by a true story about sailors abandoned to their fate in the harbor after the owners of their ship went bankrupt. Love and the sea are inextricably mixed and the spirit of Greek tragedians lurks, again, in the background. *Trois jours d'engatse* (Three days up the creek, 1994), by Philippe Carrese, and Michèle Courbou's *Les chapacans* (The scoundrels, 1997) are full of local color. Patrick Cauvin's successful novel *Rue des Bons-Enfants* (1990), a beautiful love story, takes place between 1922 and 1944 and recalls Pagnol's *Marius*. A good dose of Southern humor and local idioms give a picturesque touch to the dialogue. René Frégni's *Le voleur d'innocence* (The robber of innocence, 1994), largely autobiographical, takes the reader back to the Marseille of the 1950s.

Every year at the end of September Festival, folkloric groups from all over Provence and Monaco meet for the St-Michel Festival *(plates 22–24)*. After a morning parade in the streets of the 9th and 10th arrondissements, or districts, at the south end of the city, a giant aïoli lunch is served in the garden of the local town hall for all participants and spectators.

Tourist information. 4 La Canebière. Tel: 04 91 13 89 00. Fax: 04 91 13 89 20. Email: <Accueil@marseille-tourisme.com>. Website: <www.destination-marseille.com>.

What to see. Stroll along the *Vieux-Port* and through its morning fish market. A five-minute walk inland will take you to the remains

Jean-Claude Izzo, photo: Jacques Sassier, Gallimard Editions

of the Greek harbor near the shopping mall, the Centre Bourse. A small museum located inside the mall traces the city's history (Tel: 04 91 90 42 22). From the harbor a mini train will take you up to the church of *Notre-Dame-de-la-Garde*, on the hill, from which you will enjoy the best view of the city. The same mini train goes to the *Vieux Quartiers* and the *Vieille Charité*, an archeology museum (Tel: 04 91 55 50 09). Equally interesting is *Basilique St-Victor*, founded by Saint Cassien in the fifth century.

From the Old Harbor boats leave for the island of *Château d'If* (famed as the prison from which Alexandre Dumas's Count of Monte-Cristo made his escape) thirty minutes away, or the *Calanques*, a two-hour trip (Tel: 04 91 55 50 09). The Calanques are also accessible after a half-hour drive south on the coastal road to *Les Goudes*, a picturesque fishing community with unassuming restaurants. From Les Goudes it is possible to walk east to the Calanques of *Morgiou* and *Sormiou*, the only ones that have restaurants. In a cave near Morgiou in 1991, Henri Cosquer from Cassis discovered Paleolithic paintings. The entrance of the cave is under water. Hand imprints date from 27,000 B.C. and the representations of animals (horses, bulls, seals, penguins, and fish) from 17,000 B.C.

In *Aubagne*, twenty minutes from Marseille by freeway (A 60 in the direction of Toulon), the Tourist Office (Tel: 04 90 42 03 49 98. Fax: 04 42 03 83 62. Email: <ot.aubagne@visitprovence.com>) organizes day trips by bus to the village of La Treille (two and a half hours total). In the summer they are given on Wednesdays and Saturdays at 4:00 P.M.; the rest of the year they are by appointment only. Hiking day trips to the hills where Pagnol shot his movies are also available, but not in the summer. In Aubagne you can also visit the museum of the French Foreign Legion, the elite army corps founded in 1831.

The mountain of *Sainte-Baume* is accessible from Gémenos (D 2) by a small winding road (approximately forty-five minutes from Aubagne). The cave (*baumo* in Provençal) where Mary Magdalen spent thirty-three years in solitude is located in a cliff in the middle of a beautiful forest of beech and maple trees (a forty-five-minute walk). The site has been an important center of pilgrimage since the fifth century. There are a few hotels and restaurants nearby and especially in the village of Plan d'Aups, at an altitude of about 2,000 feet. (**: *Lou Pèbre d'Aï:* Pool, parking. Tel: 04 42 04 50 42. Fax: 04 42 62 55 52.)

Where to stay. ****: *Sofitel*, 36 blvd Charles Livon, on the Vieux-Port. AC, pool, garage. Tel: 04 91 15 59 00. Fax: 04 91 15 59 50. ***: *Petit Nice*, Anse de Maldormé. AC, pool, parking. Tel: 04 91 59 25 92. Fax: 04 91 59 28 08. *Mercure Beauvau*, rue Beauvau, on the Vieux-Port. AC. Tel: 04 91 5491 00. Fax: 04 91 54 15 76. *Novotel Vieux-Port*, 36 blvd Charles Livon. AC, pool, garage. Tel: 04 96 11 42 11. Fax: 04 96 11 42 20.

Where to eat. Petit Nice-Passédat, ** on the avenue Kennedy, overlooking the sea. *Miramar,* 12 quai du Port. *La Ferme,* 23 rue Sainte. *L'Epuisette,* Vallon des Auffes. *Chez Fonfon,* Vallon des Auffes. *Au Pescadou,* 19 place Castellane.

Cassis

The small fishing village of Cassis *(plate 28)* is very picturesque (take A 50 in the direction of Toulon, then exit Carnoux or Cassis). It was made famous by Mistral's *Calendau*, the epic poem in which the author also celebrates Cassis's fishermen and their customs. Mistral came several times with Daudet, who also visited here on his honeymoon in January 1867. Cassis was then a fishing village, relatively unknown except of course to a few painters and some rich English tourists. Cassis was a "vilo marino e clau de Franço" (city of the sea and key to France), said Mistral. Calendau, hero of Mistral's poem, was "un enfant de Cassis, un simple pescaïre d'anchoio" (a child of Cassis, a simple anchovy fisherman). In his poem Mistral praised the hardworking fishermen and their patient wives and boasted in passing about the quality of the local wine. In sum, Cassis was a wonderful place, and he proudly declared: "Tau qu'a vist Paris, se non a vist Cassis, póu dire: n'ai rèn vist" (He who has seen Paris and not Cassis has seen nothing), a line that every resident has memorized.

Katherine Mansfield arrived in Cassis from Marseille late in November 1915. She took a room at the hotel Firano and was ready to enjoy the next two weeks. At first she found the small village delightful. "The place abounds with charming walks," she wrote John Middleton Murry. The hotel was almost empty save for a few English people. But unfortunately the wind she was trying to escape since Marseille did not die down and the weather was still too cold for her. So after a few days she left for a warmer place: Bandol.

One of the most unexpected authors to have visited Cassis and to have thought of buying a house there was Virginia Woolf (1882–1941). How she happened to discover the little village is hard to say. She might have heard of the place from Mansfield, a frequent guest of hers in Bloomsbury. Mansfield had enjoyed *The Voyage Out* (1915) and had asked to meet her. The two women became acquainted in 1915; they admired each other's style and shared the same enthusiasm for literature. Woolf recognized Mansfield's talent early on and published her

Cassis

Prelude at Hogarth Press in 1918, but their friendship was tinged with jealousy and envy. The last time they saw each other was in 1920. In any case, by the end of March 1925, after journeying by train from Paris to Marseille, Virginia and her husband Leonard were at the Hôtel Cendrillon, "a white house, with red tiled floors capable of housing perhaps 8 people."[27] The weather was warm and trees blossomed everywhere. Everything seemed perfect. "Food delicious, harbor divine, hot; sun; vineyards, olives. . . . We sit out all the morning; go for walks; go to Marseille and Toulon, which is a lovely town, and altogether are very very happy and good and well disposed to the whole world," she wrote her sister Vanessa.[28] Since her childhood, Woolf suffered from bouts of depression. Her literary career, however, was well established at this point: the novels *The Voyage Out* and *Night and Day* (1919) had been well received by critics and the public, and she had just completed *Mrs. Dalloway* and *The Common Reader*, a collection of essays.

At the hotel, all the guests were English. "The whole hotel atmosphere provided me with many ideas: Oh so cold, indifferent, superficially polite, and exhibiting such odd relationships: as if human nature were now reduced to a kind of code."[29] After breakfast, the Woolfs would take a walk on the shore, sit on the rocks, and bask in the sun. In the afternoon they would stroll in the woods above and pick flowers. One day they walked to La Ciotat, four miles away: "It was stony, steep and very hot. We heard a great chattering birdlike noise once, and I bethought me of the frogs. The ragged tulips were out in the fields; all the fields were little angular shelves cut out of the hill, and ruled and ribbed with vines; and all red, and rosy and purple here and there with the spray of some fruit tree in bud. At La Ciotat great orange ships rose up out of the blue water of the little bay."[30] Their stay in Cassis was short but Virginia found it inspiring, and they swore to return as soon as possible.

In January 1927, Virginia's older sister, Vanessa Bell, and Duncan Grant, her lover, spent the winter in Cassis at the Villa Corsica. Vanessa Bell was a painter, like Grant, and she immediately fell in love with the bright colors and clear skies of Provence. "Vanessa established herself at Cassis discovering what madness it was to remain in England during the winter months and how admirable a place Cassis was for a painter," writes her son.[31] The Woolfs arrived in February. Virginia had just completed *To the Lighthouse* and looked forward to seeing the Provençal sun again. They stayed at the same hotel for a few days and then left for Italy. The Woolfs returned to Cassis one more time in April 1928 in their new Singer car. They stayed at Colonel Teed's Villa Fontcreuse, a mansion in the vineyards. By then Cassis had become quite popular with the English: "Cassis is becoming as notorious as Bloomsbury. Characters of the strangest sort abound," she remarked to her nephew.[32] Nevertheless the Woolfs loved the endearing place and entertained the idea of settling there. "We are thinking of buying a house here," she wrote Quentin Bell in April 1928.[33] But Cassis was far from Bloomsbury and they thought the matter over. In June 1929, Virginia and Leonard were back in Cassis for a week. Vanessa and Duncan were staying in La Bergère and the Woolfs contemplated buying La Boularde, a house a few hundred yards from it. But their lives were in London and they soon abandoned the project. In 1938, Woolf longed to join her sister, staying again in Cassis, but lacked the energy: "I should be well advised

Virginia Woolf,
photo: Roger-Viollet

Hôtel Cendrillon, Cassis

From Marseille to Cannes

to take a holiday from writing and maunder off into the vineyards at Cassis," she wrote in her diary. "But I can't: too weak minded."[34]

It was in Cassis that the idea for Woolf's novel *The Waves* (1936) was born. In May 1927, as Vanessa was writing a letter, a giant moth, "half a foot, literally," she claimed, tapped at the window. They let it in and tried to keep it alive, but the giant moth died. The incident caused Vanessa to reflect upon her maternal instincts and she concluded her letter to Virginia by saying: "I wish you could write a book about the maternal instinct." Virginia, whose maternal feelings were thwarted by her inability to have children, accepted the challenge: "Your story of the Moth so fascinates me that I am going to write a story about it. I could think of nothing else but you and the moths for hours after reading your letter. Isn't it odd, perhaps you stimulate the literary sense in me as you say I do your painting sense."[35] By June, the idea had already matured in her mind. The story was to be set "in France, near the sea; at night; a garden under the window." It was going to be a "play-poem" told as "a continuous stream, not solely of human thought, but of the ship, the night &c, all flowing together: intersected by the arrival of the bright moths. A man and a woman are to be sitting at a table talking. Or are they silent? It is to be a love story: she is finally to let the last great moth in."[36] Woolf worked on the story for several years and "the moths" eventually became *The Waves*. Cassis certainly inspired the opening page in which she so poetically describes the sea: "The sun had not yet risen. The sea was indistinguishable from the sky, except that the sea was slightly creased as if a cloth had wrinkles in it. Gradually as the sky whitened a dark line lay on the horizon dividing the sea from the sky and the grey cloth became barred with thick strokes moving, one after another, beneath the surface, following each other, pursuing each other, perpetually."[37]

Tourist information. Place Baragnon. Tel: 04 42 01 71 17. Fax: 04 42 01 28 31. Website: <www.cassis.enprovence.com>.

What to see. Musée d'Arts et Traditions Populaires. The *small* museum is open on Wed., Thurs., & Sat. from 3:30 to 6:30. Tel: 04 42

01 88 66. A boat ride to the Calanques is a must, weather permitting (Tel: 04 42 01 71 17).

Where to stay. ****: *Royal Cottage,* avenue du 11 novembre. AC, pool, parking. Tel: 04 42 01 33 34. Fax: 04 42 01 06 90. ***: *Les Roches Blanches,* route de Port-Miou. Pool, parking. Tel: 04 42 01 09 30. Fax: 04 42 01 94 23. *Les Jardins de Cassis,* avenue Favier. Pool, parking. Tel: 04 42 01 84 85. Fax: 04 42 01 32 38. *Le Jardin d'Emile,* Plage du Bestouan. AC, parking. Tel: 04 42 01 80 55. Fax: 04 42 01 80 70. **: *Cassitel,* place Clemenceau. Tel: 04 42 01 83 44. Fax: 04 42 01 96 31. *Hôtel du Golfe,* quai Barthélemy. Tel: 04 42 01 00 21. Fax: 04 42 01 92 08.

Where to eat. *La Presqu'île,* route de Port-Miou. *Le Jardin d'Emile.* *Chez Nino,* quai Barthélemy.

Bandol

Only a half-hour away on a little road (D 559) that meanders along the rocky coastline is the resort town of Bandol. Raimu came to relax in his summer home with his family and friends. He loved to wander into town to play a game of *boules* or sit at the terrace of cafés to watch the passers-by and comment on their looks in a jocular way. It is in this little town, home of one of Provence's best rosé wines, that Katherine Mansfield finally settled. She arrived in mid-December 1915 from Cassis and found a room with a view of the sea at the Hôtel Beau Rivage. "When I awoke this morning and opened the shutters and saw the dimpling sea I knew I was beginning to love this place—this South of France,"[38] she wrote Murry shortly before Christmas. The cold wind that had plagued her since Marseille had finally died down and the weather got a little warmer. Bandol looked charming and unspoiled. "There are no roads there, just little tracks and old mule paths. Parts are quite wild and overgrown then in all sorts of unexpected faery places you find a little clearing—the ground cultivated in tiny red terraces and sheltered by olive trees (full of tiny black fruit)." She occupied her days walking about, chatting with locals, reading the *Daily News* and Colette. "Yesterday I went for walk. The palm trees were magnificent—so firm and so green and standing up like stiff bouquets before the Lord. The shop people, too, are very kind," she wrote.

At the hotel, she befriended a woman from Arles who entertained her with her life story. To her great surprise, Mansfield did not seem to have any trouble understanding her and found her Provençal accent "extremely fascinating." Bandol was definitely the place she was looking for. The rugged coast and simple people most certainly reminded her of home in New Zealand. "I am very happy here. The place is so beautiful and the sun shines or it doesn't—there is the sea and the wild beautiful coast—and behind the village there are woods and mountains. Already I have so many 'secret' places—the people are awfully nice too. They are honest, one can be oneself with them."

So she found a little cottage to rent, the Villa Pauline at the angle of boulevard Clémenceau and the chemin de la Nanly. It had a small front yard and a stone verandah facing south with a view of the Mediterranean. The place was cozy and Mansfield spent her evenings reading and working on *Prelude* and *The Aloe*. During the day when the sun was high up in the sky she would stroll down to the harbor and watch the fishermen repair their nets or she would wander into town to shop. Murry finally came for a visit and took advantage of the tranquility to finish his book on Dostoyevsky. Mansfield was happy and felt healthier; she was saddened to leave Bandol in March 1916. Back in London, Provence was often on her mind and whenever she felt nostalgic about it she would read Daudet's *Lettres de mon moulin*. In fact, she liked his tale "La chèvre de Monsieur Seguin" so much that she translated it for *New Age*—her only published translation. Mansfield's biographer Anthony Alpers argues that she had identified with the small goat that after fighting with the wolf all night finally gets eaten: "It isn't possible that Katherine . . . could have fallen upon this Provençal tale, translated, and published it, without seeing herself . . . in M. Seguin's goat."[39] In her correspondence Mansfield indeed talks of Murry as the wolf. In England, her health problems grew worse, and in 1917 her doctor confirmed that she had tuberculosis and advised her to return to the French Riviera.

So, in January 1918, she was back in Bandol. But this time the situation had changed. World War I was still raging, the winter was cold, and the town was full of soldiers. Mansfield stayed at the Hôtel Beau Rivage again but war made living conditions difficult and cigarettes were especially hard to come by. She was not so happy this time, her body ached constantly, and she began to spit blood. Her stay in Bandol sparked the short story "Je ne parle pas français." Murry came for a visit in February, but in March Mansfield was back in London. In April 1918, Mansfield was finally divorced and married Murry. Today the villa in Bandol where Mansfield lived has been remodeled and is not open to visitors. However, a plaque reminds the passers-by that she once stayed there.

> *Tourist information.* Allées Vivien. Tel: 04 94 29 41 35. Fax: 04 94 32 50 39. Website: <www.bandol.org>. Email: <otbandol@ bandol. org>.

> *What to see.* A stroll in town and the harbor. A trip to the island of Bendor, ten minutes away.

> *Where to stay.* ****: *L'Ile Rousse*, blvd Louis Lumière. AC, pool, garage. Tel: 04 94 29 33 00. Fax: 04 94 29 49 49. *Delos*, on the island of Bendor. Pool. Tel: 04 94 32 22 23. Fax: 04 94 32 41 44. ***: *Le Provençal*, rue des Ecoles. Tel: 04 94 29 52 11. Fax: 04 94 29 67 57.

> *Where to eat.* La Réserve, route de Sanary.

Sanary-sur-Mer, Toulon

Three miles past Bandol is the little fishing village of Sanary-sur-Mer. In March 1930, Aldous Huxley (1894–1963) and his wife Maria bought a house and settled there. They had spent a few days in Bandol the year before, invited by D. H. Lawrence, and thought that the Provençal climate would suit them well. The house had character but needed some work, and Huxley spent the first three months redecorating and painting. It had all the commodities plus a spacious office and library downstairs where he wrote and four bedrooms upstairs. Around it was a large yard with trees where in the summer the Huxleys often slept in hammocks. They hired a maid, a gardener, and later an Italian cook. Matthew, their ten-year-old son, was in boarding school in England but usually came for a visit during his vacation. Huxley wrote in the morning and then he and Maria would go for walks or, in the summer, swim. He also painted and enjoyed gardening. At night, the Huxleys would go out, visit Sybille Bedford, their neighbor (who later became his biographer), or drive to Hyères in their red Bugatti and dine with Paul Valéry or Edith Wharton. Huxley spoke French well, for he had studied in Grenoble as a young man and his wife was Belgian. The Huxleys stayed in Sanary until 1937, but they often left for long trips to Central America, London, or Paris. The years he spent in Sanary were very productive. He worked on the edition of Lawrence's correspondence and wrote a play (*World of Light*, 1931), poems (*The Cicadas*, 1931, named after the little insect that sings in the Provençal trees during the summer), short stories (*Brief Candles*, 1931), his bestseller *Brave New World* (1932), and *Eyeless in Gaza* (1937). In 1937, the Huxleys sold their house and left Sanary for the United States.

Sanary was also the favorite place for German or Austrian artists and writers in exile during the 1930s. Fleeing the Nazi regime and its burning of books and artworks that were not German enough in spirit, many artists came to settle in Provence. Approximately five hundred Germans and Austrians sought refuge on the Riviera but more than half chose to reside in Sanary because of its climate and affordable housing. So within a couple of years, the little fishing village of about four thousand Provençals became, in the words of Ludwig Marcuse, "der Haupstadt der deutschen Exilliteratur" (the capital of German Exile Literature). Among the first exiles were Julius and Anne Marie Meier-Graefe, who arrived in 1930 and bought the Villa Banette in nearby Saint-Cyr. They helped writer René Schickelé locate a house in Sanary and he, in his turn, in 1933 assisted recent Nobel Prize winner Thomas

Mann (1875–1955) find a comfortable residence. Mann and his wife Katia arrived in May 1933. They first stayed at the Grand Hôtel in Bandol and then moved into the Villa Tranquille, decorated with taste and near the town. Mann was very worried about the situation in Germany but enjoyed his stay in Sanary. He swam and read—German newspapers, *War and Peace*, and *The Fall of the House of Usher*—and worked on *Joseph and His Brothers*. He also met with his compatriots and friends the Meier-Graefes, Emil Alphons Reinhardt, Annemarie Schwarzenbach, and Lion Feuchtwanger, who lived at the Villa Valmer. He traveled along the coast and had tea with publisher Kurt Wolff in St-Tropez. In September 1933, he left for Switzerland. When war broke out in 1939 many exiles fled to the United States. Some committed suicide; others participated in the Resistance or were interned in prisoners' camps. In 1987, a plaque with the names of the German and Austrian exiles was put up near the Tourist Office.

A little farther east is Toulon, birthplace of the actor Raimu and of Jean Aicard (1848–1921), author of poems and novels such as his famous *Maurin des Maures* (1908) that tells adventures of a sort of Provençal Robin Hood in the Maures Forest, between Toulon and Cannes. In the 1930s, Jean Cocteau and Somerset Maugham used to hang out in Toulon's numerous sailors' bars. In 1861, George Sand (1804–1876) spent four months in the Toulon neighborhood known as Tamaris, "an oasis near the sea at the foot of the mountain, among the pines." It was then the secluded place she was looking for. The place reminded her of Majorca. Her house was small but clean and cheap, and it was absolutely peaceful. There she wrote *Valvèdre* (1861) and traveled all the way to Menton and back. Back in her home in Nohant she collected her Provençal experiences in a novel that she entitled simply *Tamaris* (1862).

Tourist information. Located on the Sanary harbor. Tel: 04 94 74 01 04. Fax: 04 94 74 58 04. Website: <www.sanarysurmer.com>

Where to stay: ***: *Grand Hôtel des Bains,* avenue Estienne d'Orves. AC, parking. Tel: 04 94 74 13 47. Fax: 04 94 88 14 02. **: *Hôtel de la Tour,* 24 quai du Général de Gaulle. Parking, garage. Tel: 04 94 74 10 10. Fax: 04 94 74 69 49. *Le Marina,* 4219 ancien chemin de

Toulon, inland. Pool, parking. Tel: 04 94 29 56 48. Fax: 04 94 29 40 14. *Synaya*, 92 chemin Olive. Parking. Tel: 04 94 74 10 50. B&B: M. Bruno Castello, 646 route de Bandol. Parking, tennis, pool. Tel: 04 94 88 05 73. Fax: 04 94 88 24 13.

Where to eat: Le Relais de la Poste, La Cour des Arts, both rue Barthélémy de Don.

Hyères and the Iles d'Or

The so-called Riviera, or La Côte d'Azur, as it has been known alternatively since Stephen Liegeard's book of that title (1887), by tradition begins in Hyères. The term does not correspond to anything geographical or cultural, and Provençals do not use it, generally preferring to name specific villages or towns. The names "Côte d'Azur" and "Riviera" are used mostly by tourists, whether French or foreign. There is no clear boundary, of course, between Cassis and Cannes except perhaps that the winters become milder and the wind dies down as one moves east. What characterizes this portion of the coast is that, since the 1850s, tourism has been its main economic activity.

Hyères and the beautiful Iles d'Or, especially Porquerolles and Port-Cros, celebrated by Mistral, are an ideal stop. Leo Tolstoy and his brother Nicholas visited Hyères in 1840. In 1848, his compatriot Ivan Turgenev also spent a few days at the Hôtel d'Europe. But the little town's most famous resident was perhaps Robert Louis Stevenson, who lived there for a year and a half after brief stays in Marseille and Nice, which he fled to escape the typhoid epidemic in January 1883. He and his wife, Fanny, arrived in February 1883. They first stayed at the Hôtel des Iles d'Or but after a few days, finding Hyères to their liking, they rented a small villa called La Solitude. They were enchanted. "My house is the loveliest spot in the universe," he wrote Sidney Colvin.[40] The place was "very, very little" but it was "healthy, cheerful, close to shops, society and civilisation."

La Solitude was perched on a hill and commanded a beautiful view of the bay and the islands. On the first floor were two rooms and a kitchen, and above, four rooms, but this according to the bourgeois standards of the time was considered small. The yard was planted with roses, olive trees, aloes, figs, and marigolds. "By day this garden fades into nothing, overpowered by its surroundings and the luminous distance; but at night and when the moon is out, that garden, the harbor, the flight of stairs that mount the artificial hillock, the plumed gum-trees that hang trembling, become the very skirts of Paradise. Angels I know frequent it, and it thrills all night with the flutes of silence," he rhapsodized as if mesmerized.[41] The Stevensons also enjoyed the town and its surroundings. They took long walks and tried to meet the locals, who remained, for the most part, reserved and distant. Stevenson found the French more honest than his compatriots but thought that men were "rather indecent to women." They hired Valentine Roch, a local woman, to do the household chores and cook for them. A real bond developed between them and she remained in their service when they returned to England.

Stevenson's health slowly improved and he was able to work four to five hours a day. He had written *An Inland Voyage* (1878) and *Travels with a Donkey in the Cévennes* (1879), accounts of his trips in France, and in 1881 *Treasure Island* had appeared in serial form in *Young Folks*. At La Solitude he spent most of his time working on *Prince Otto* and *A Child's Garden of Verses*. The Stevensons might have stayed longer there but, unfortunately again, in July 1884 cholera broke out in town, and they hurriedly left for England. Later in his life as his illness worsened, Stevenson remembered his stay in Hyères as the best moments in his life.

Some time after the Stevensons' departure, French novelist Paul Bourget (1852–1935) and his wife began to spend their winters in Hyères, also at the Hôtel des Iles d'Or. It is there that he wrote *Un coeur de femme* (A woman's heart) in 1889. In 1894 the Bourgets bought a house in nearby Costebelle. It was a large mansion in a twenty-acre park of pines and cedars and included a guesthouse. Henry James visited there for a week in 1895 but felt uncomfortable. His dear friend

Edith Wharton, also frequently invited by the Bourgets, purchased her own residence, the Villa Sainte-Claire, in 1919. Wharton (1862–1937) was a Francophile and had left the United States in 1913 to settle in Paris. The house she acquired in Hyères was situated next to an old convent named Sainte-Claire-du-Vieux-Château and was not far from the Stevensons' former residence. Wharton restored it and lived there most of the year, returning on occasion to her other residence near Paris. In Sainte-Claire she wrote some of her best novels, including *The Age of Innocence* (winner of the Pulitzer Prize in 1921), *The Mother's Recompense* (1924), and *The Buccaneers* (1928). She read Proust and Colette—"one of the greatest writers of our time"—who captured the subtle aspects of female passion.[42] Wharton also entertained extensively, and among her many guests were poet Paul Valéry, painter Edouard Vuillard, and authors Sinclair Lewis, Aldous Huxley, and Kenneth Clark. Wharton and her friends often made excursions to Grasse, Cannes, and the Iles d'Or. Provence, however, is strangely absent from her novels.

The islands across from Hyères, whose name Mistral used for a collection of his poems (*Lis Isclo d'Or*), were for a long time the refuge of pirates and Moors. Saint Honorat (fourth century) lived on the island of Porquerolles for several years before he moved to the Iles de Lérins in 375. Troubadour Raimbaut d'Orange was sent to Porquerolles to repent for having written immoral verse. From 1911 to 1972, Porquerolles was the property of Joseph Fournier, a rich businessman. Port-Cros is even wilder and more secluded. To Jean Cocteau, who moored *Lancelot* there in the 1920s, the island looked as if it were "guarded by a dragon with scales like impudent little waves that spit their cold saliva at your face."[43] Cocteau and his friends stayed at the hotel. He was fascinated by the wild and lush vegetation, the perfumes of pines, and the incessant chirping of cicadas that inspired him to compare Port-Cros to "a delirious kettle."[44] The beautiful island also attracted poet Jules Supervielle (1884–1960), who came every summer between 1925 and 1939. During that time the fort of La Vigie became the summer center of the *Nouvelle revue française*, edited by Jean Paulhan (1884–1968). Marcel Arland and Henri Michaux were regular guests.

Today the islands are national parks and visitors must observe strict rules. The Ile du Levant is home to both the French navy and a nudist colony, Heliopolis.

Tourist information. Park Hotel. Tel: 04 94 01 84 50. Fax: 04 94 35 85 05.

What to see. The islands can be reached from the peninsula south of Hyères, Presqu'île de Giens (Tel: 04 94 58 95 14). The crossing takes only twenty minutes. Food and accommodation are available. Drinking water outside the villages is scarce.

Where to stay. ****: *Mercure,* 19 avenue Thomas. AC, pool, parking. Tel: 04 94 65 03 04. Fax: 04 94 35 58 20. *Mas du Langoustier,* on the island of Porquerolles. Tel: 04 94 58 30 09. Fax: 04 94 58 36 02. ***: *Le Manoir,* on the island of Port-Cros. Pool. Tel: 04 94 05 90 52. Fax: 04 94 05 90 89. *Les Pins d'Argent.* Pool, parking. Tel: 04 94 57 63 60. Fax: 04 94 38 33 65. **: *Centrotel,* 45 avenue Cawell. Garage. Tel: 04 94 01 36 36. Fax: 04 94 01 34 56.

Where to eat. Mas du Langoustier.* *Le Jardin de Bacchus,* 32 avenue Gambetta. *La Colombe.*

Le Lavandou

Some fifteen miles down the road is the small resort town of Le Lavandou. Unlike Hyères, at the beginning of the twentieth century the place was still a sleepy little fishing village of about one hundred inhabitants. It is precisely its secluded charm that attracted Willa Cather (1873–1947). She and Isabel McClung arrived there on September 10, 1902. "We came to Lavandou chiefly because we could not find anyone who had ever been here, and because in Paris people seemed never to have heard of the place."[45] There, Cather found the solitude and rustic charm she was looking for and that, to some extent, reminded her of

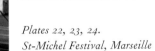

Plates 22, 23, 24.
St-Michel Festival, Marseille

Plate 25.
Marseille:
The Old Harbor

Plate 26.
Les Goudes

Plate 27.
The Calanque
of En-Vau,
photo: P. Blot

Plate 28. Cassis

Plate 29. Cannes in October

Plate 30. Nice

Plate 31. Nice Carnival

Plate 32.
Musée Matisse

Plate 33.
Villefranche-
sur-Mer

Plate 34. Cocteau's Room, Hôtel
Welcome, courtesy Mme Galbois

Plate 35. Villa Ephrussi, Cap Ferrat

Plate 36. Roquebrune: The Old Village

Plate 37.
Menton:
The Old Town

Plate 38.
Festival of Lemons, Menton

Plate 39.
Fontana Rosa

Plate 40. Sospel

Plate 41. Saorgue

her younger frontier days in Nebraska. She and McClung had at last discovered a genuine Provençal village completely unspoiled. "The coast for a hundred miles on either side of us is quite as wild as it was when he Saracens held it. It is an endless succession of pine hills that terminate in cliffs jutting over the sea. . . . Its score or so of houses are built on the narrow strip of beach between the steep hillside and the sea. They are scarcely more than huts, built of mud and stone on either side of one narrow street. There is one café, and before it is a little square of sycamore trees, where the sailors, always barefoot, with their corduroy trousers and tam-o'-shanter caps, play some primitive game of ball in the afternoon." Except for an older man who ate his lobster in silence and "drank Benedictine in sadness," the two American women were the only guests of the little hotel where they stayed for a week. It was comfortable enough by the standards of the time and they were happy to have a view "of the whole sweep of ocean." They took their meals in the long veranda, "straw-thatched and overgrown by gourd vines." The food was fresh; they ate their fill of *langouste* (lobster) accompanied by a salad made with "sea-grass dressed with the oil they get from their olives" and drank the local wine.

The weather was still warm, and Cather and McClung enjoyed walking along the shore and across the hills, where blossoms of lavender drying in the sun "mingled their fresh, salt perfume with the heavier odor of the pines." They also lingered by the small harbor and watched the fishermen's families eating on their front porch or seated under an olive tree: "figs, sea-grass salad, and drinking their sour wine and singing—always singing." One day, they made the acquaintance of two little girls and their goat and introduced themselves to some of the local notables. Then, like Daudet, they discovered their "mill." At the end of a small winding path in a pine forest, they found a little uninhabited lodge "with a red-tiled roof and a little stone porch." It was, they were told, the winter studio of a Parisian painter who was away in the capital. There, sitting or lying on the grass around the little cottage, Cather reminisced about the *Lettres de mon moulin* and daydreamed. "It is good for one's soul to sit here all the day through, wrapped in a steamer rug if the sea breeze blows strong, and do nothing for hours together but stare at this great water that seems to trail its delft-blue mantle across the world. Then, as Daudet said, one becomes a part of the foam that drifts, of the wind that blows, and of the pines that answer," Cather noted.

One day, the two women went to Cavalaire-sur-Mer on foot (eleven miles) and met a boy limping his way home and a few women knitting as they walked. "The village of Cavalaire consists of a station house and a little tavern by the roadside. The station agent lay asleep on a bench beside his door, and his old mother and wife were knitting beside him. The place is not a little like certain lonely way stations in Wyoming and Colorado." But Cather's favorite place was definitely Le Lavandou. She returned to the pine forest around the painter's lodge and lay there all day among the green fir trees and lavender, gazing at the wide blue sky. She felt she could have stayed there forever. "I do not know why a wretched little fishing village, with nothing but green pines and blue sea and a sky of porcelain, should mean more than a dozen places that I have wanted to see all my life," she wrote in her notebooks.

"Le Lavandou is wonderful and looks like the bay of Naples," said Jean Cocteau. When he and Raymond Radiguet were there in 1922, at the Hôtel de France, "the beach extended in a large crescent of soft sand, with dust of small white shells, gently beaten by a transparent water. A creek called Bataillier, seemingly tame but not really navigable, meandered in the valley among the reeds and finished its course in the middle of the bay."[46] Other temporary visitors to Le Lavandou include Tristan Tzara, Bertolt Brecht, and Henri Michaux. Nowadays Le Lavandou is no longer a small, secluded village and as a matter of fact, every summer it looks more like St-Tropez, its famous neighbor.

Tourist information. Quai G.-Péri. Tel: 04 94 00 40 50. Fax: 04 94 00 40 59. Website: <www.lelavandou.com>.

Where to stay. ****: *Auberge de la Calanque*, 62 avenue G. de Gaulle. Pool, parking. Tel: 94 94 71 05 96. Fax: 04 94 71 20 12. ***: *La Petite Bohème*, avenue F. Roosevelt. Garage. Tel: 04 94 7110 30. Fax: 04 94

64 73 92. **: *L'Escapade*, 1 chemin du Vannier. AC. Tel: 04 94 71 11 52. Fax: 04 94 71 22 14.

Where to eat. Krill, rue Patron Ravello.

St-Tropez

St-Tropez is just around the corner. In July and August this small village is invaded by thousands of tourists and show business people from all over the world. But it was not always like this. When Guy de Maupassant (1850–1893) landed there, in April 1887, on his thirty-five-foot sailboat baptized *Bel Ami* after his successful novel, St-Tropez was just another Provençal fishing village that "smelled of fish and tar, brine and the hull of boats."[47] Maupassant stayed at the hotel Bailli de Suffren and wandered through the narrow cobbled streets. Scales of sardines shone like pearls. To his imaginative mind, St-Tropez seemed inhabited by "a limping and paralyzed race of old fishermen basking in the sun . . . their faces and hands wrinkled, tanned, burnt, dried by the wind, toil, and sea foam."[48] Maupassant, who had read its history in the local library, reminded the reader that the place was "a brave small and courageous town" that fought against the Moors, the Spaniards, and the English.

Since there was little to do there, the day after his arrival, Maupassant decided to visit the Chartreuse de la Verne, a monastery in the hills behind St-Tropez where he had been years before. Early in the morning, he took a carriage and rode along the bay through the small village of Cogolin and then up to the Chartreuse. The monastery had been abandoned during the Revolution. When Maupassant arrived, "a veritable fairy-tale wood with blooming lianas, aromatic plants with powerful fragrance, and tall, magnificent trees," had grown over it.[49] The thick forest was an ideal place for hermits. A man had been living there alone for thirty years. In a wooden shack hid an elderly couple. The man was a former army officer who had fallen in love with his

Chartreuse de la Verne

colonel's daughter. They eloped and came to hide there. Maupassant paid them a visit and left full of thoughts. He then inspected the ruins of the monastery and walked back down to the buggy. A few hours later he was relaxing in his hotel. The Chartreuse has now been re-stored and in 1983 nuns returned to live there. It is accessible by road D 14 west of Grimaud (in the direction of Collobrières) and is about twenty miles from St-Tropez. The road is very winding and the trip takes about one hour by car. It is open to visitors (Tel: 04 92 08 98 63).

In 1902, Neo-Impressionist painter Paul Signac bought a place in St-Tropez. He had a small boat and often came with his friend Pierre Bonnard. St-Tropez's most famous literary resident was writer Colette (1873–1954). She first visited in 1915 during a vacation and immedi-ately succumbed to its charm. The following year, she sold her house in Brittany and bought one in St-Tropez. "I discovered it along a road feared by motorists, and behind a most common fence," she explains in *La Treille Muscate* (1932).[50] It was situated at the end of the village and sat on four acres of land: oranges, fig trees, and vineyards. The former garden had been abandoned and was overgrown with wild plants, which pleased Colette. "There is no 'garden' so I should thank destiny: there are big yellow feathers that sweep the blue sky and mimosas that sprinkle pollen with perfume," she wrote.[51] The house itself was a modest two-story construction with a red-tiled roof and a terrace covered with wisteria, oleanders, and mimosas. There were a few fir trees as well. Because of the beautiful vine that was creeping on its walls, Colette baptized her new house La Treille Muscate (The Muscat Vine) and immediately set to work with the help of a local gardener. Within a year, flowers of all sorts had grown in profusion: petunias, sunflowers, marigolds, dahlias, daffodils, zinnias, and lavender. Besides the vineyards and tangerine trees, her garden produced the best tomatoes, melons, and herbs. In the spring, the place swarmed with colorful butterflies, goldfinches, and warblers. Cocteau, a frequent guest, was ecstatic and felt as though he were in his mother's garden in Maisons-Laffitte: "I find myself in a Seine-et-Oise garden. . . . French marigolds, sweet peas, wisteria, geraniums, and the basil that casts its scent like a spell."[52] Meandering along between hedges and shaded by fig trees, a small path perfumed with thyme and wild mint secretly led to a warm sandy beach where Colette basked in the sun and contemplated the Mediterranean. "The sea continues, extends, ennobles, and adds a magic touch to this plot of land with a bright shore," she wrote.[53]

Colette was then fifty-three years old and had before her a long writing career with popular novels such as *La vagabonde* and *Chéri*. She was divorced from her first husband and separated from Henri de Jouvenel. She was a native of Burgundy but her father was a Provençal from Toulon—hence her attraction to the region. Over the years, La Treille Muscate became "home." Colette added another room, painted, and decorated the interior to her taste. Comfortably installed with her two dogs and a dozen cats, she could relax and concentrate on writing. She loved the warm sun, the dry air, and the sea. Colette also loved to entertain. During the holidays, her daughter would come for a visit. Cocteau often dropped by, dressed in a large-brimmed hat and a cape that, according to the locals, made him look like Lucifer. She also invited a group of painters including Dunoyer de Segonzac, Albert Moreau, and André Villeboeuf, who all shared a villa nearby. Segonzac

Colette, photo: Collection de Jouvenel,
Musée Colette, St-Sauveur-en-Puisaye

Colette's house, La Treille Muscate, photo: Collection
de Jouvenel, Musée Colette, St-Sauveur-en-Puisaye

From Marseille to Cannes

illustrated *La Treille Muscate* and Moreau *Naissance du jour* (Break of day, 1928).

Colette was a good cook, and for her guests she prepared *bouillabaisse, loup grillé, rascasse farcie* (stuffed scorpion fish), *riz aux favouilles* (rice with small crabs), *aïoli*, or *anchoïade* (anchovy dip) with fresh tomatoes seasoned with thyme and *pèbre d'aïl* (savory). For dessert she offered fruit fresh from her garden: melon, grapes, and tangerines. When not feasting at her generous table, she would treat her friends at Dom's in town. Colette made several trips a year to Paris for her work, but she always hurried back to St-Tropez. In 1932, she opened a beauty and perfume boutique on the harbor and often autographed her books there.

La Treille Muscate and the countryside around St-Tropez were in harmony with her sensual nature and constantly provided her with inspiration. *Naissance du jour,* for instance, reflects admirably her inner feelings for Provence. Colette loved "the old Provençal villages clinging to the crests of their hills. The ruins there are dry, wholesome, stripped of grass and green mildew, and only the geranium-ivy with its pink flowers hangs from the black gaping ear of a tower."[54] She was particularly fond of the shores, "where hemp agrimony, statice, and scabious contribute three shades of mauve, the tall flowering reed its cluster of brown edible seeds, the myrtle its white scent—white, white and bitter, prickling the tonsils, white to the point of causing nausea and ecstasy—the tamarisk its rosy mist and the bulrush its beaver-furred club."[55] During the hot summer evenings she would watch the sun gather together "the scraps of clouds evaporated by the warm sea" and twist them "into rags of fire."[56] Then, after dinner, absorbed by the "unfathomable blue of the night," she would contemplate "a worn old moon wandering along the horizon pursued by a surprisingly neat and metallic-looking little cloud, grabbing at the bitten disk as a fish grabs a floating slice of fruit."[57] Colette remains one of the few non-natives to have captured and put into words some of the poetry of Provence.

In the late 1930s, however, the situation changed. She was saddened to see her little fishing village become increasingly popular first with wealthy businessmen, who parked their Hispanos and Bugattis at the harbor next to the old fishing boats, and then with the crowds that heralded the beginning of mass tourism. St-Tropez was no longer the same peaceful place and, in 1938, she sold La Treille Muscate and left. Her house is still there but, privately owned, is not open to visitors.

Anaïs Nin visited St-Tropez in the summer of 1939, after World War II had been declared. She came to St-Tropez for a few days with her friends Zara and Rango. The place was almost deserted but the clear waters, pine trees, and warm, sandy beaches enchanted her. She and her friends sat at the terrace of Senequier and had a bouillabaisse on the beach. At night they danced and drank. Twenty years later Brigitte Bardot arrived in St-Tropez and bought La Madrague, settling there permanently. Jean-Paul Sartre and Françoise Sagan were often seen at the terrace of cafés in the 1960s. Despite its summer crowds, St-Tropez has managed to keep a great deal of its charm and its local accent.

Tourist information. Quai Jean-Jaurès. Tel: 04 94 97 45 21. Fax: 04 9497 79 08. Website: <www.nova.fr/saint-tropez>.

What to see. Walk in the small streets and harbor. The *Annonciade Museum* contains a nice collection of impressionist and post-impressionist paintings by Signac, Cross, Luce, but also by Derain, Picabia, Matisse, Braque, and Dufy (Tel: 04 94 97 04 01).

Where to stay. ****: *Byblos,* avenue Paul Signac. AC, pool, parking, garage. Tel: 04 94 56 68 00. Fax: 04 94 56 68 01. *Résidence de la Pinède,* Plage de la Bouillabaisse. AC, pool, parking. Tel: 04 94 55 91 00. Fax: 04 94 97 73 64. *La Bastide de St-Tropez,* route des Carles. AC, pool, parking. Tel: 04 94 55 82 55. Fax: 04 94 97 21 71. *La Ponche,* place du Révelin. AC, garage. Tel: 04 94 97 02 53. Fax: 04 94 97 78 61. Email: <hotel@laponche.com>. ***: *Lices,* avenue Augustin Grangeon. AC, pool, parking. Tel: 04 94 97 28 28. Fax: 04 94 97 92 01. *Hôtel Provençal,* chemin Bonnaventure. Pool, parking. Tel: 04 94 97 00 83. Fax: 04 94 97 44 37. **: *Lou Troupelen,* chemin des Vendanges. Parking. Tel: 04 94 97 44 88. Fax: 04 94 97 41 76. *Lou Cagnard,* avenue Paul Roussel. Parking. Tel: 04 94 97 04 24.

Fax: 04 94 97 09 44. B&Bs: *Campagne-Bourru,* two miles from St-Tropez, in Cogolin. Pool, parking. Tel & Fax: 04 94 54 62 21. *La Paressanne,* in Grimaud. Pool, parking. Tel: 04 94 56 83 33. Fax: 04 94 56 01 94. *Lei Souco,* in Ramatuelle, four miles south of St-Tropez on D 93. Pool, parking. Tel: 04 94 79 80 22. Fax: 04 94 79 88 27.

Where to eat. Lei Mouscardins, on the harbor. *Girelier,* quai Jean-Jaurès. *Le Petit Charron,* 6 rue Charron.

Port-Grimaud to Cannes

Farther east along the rugged coast is Port-Grimaud. Built in the 1970s in a Venetian style, the small resort deserves a stop. A couple of miles inland on D 75 is the medieval village of La Garde Freinet, beautiful little village and Arab stronghold in the ninth century. The next towns on the coast are Ste-Maxime and St-Raphaël where F. Scott Fitzgerald finished *The Great Gatsby* in the summer of 1924 and part of *Tender Is the Night* in 1929.

Cannes *(plate 29)* needs little introduction. In the late nineteenth century, wealthy English tourists came here to spend the winter. Palaces were built at a rapid pace, and the ones that still stand recall the city's glorious past. Since 1939, Cannes's most famous attraction is its film festival, which takes place in April. A walk on the beautiful Croisette along the shore early in the morning or late in the afternoon is the best introduction to Cannes. "It is only before noon that one can meet the distinguished foreigners on the Croisette . . . the young and slender women—for it is fashionable to be slim-dressed in the English fashion, walk briskly, escorted by healthy young men wearing tennis costumes. But from time to time one meets a pitiful and gaunt man shuffling along, leaning on a mother or sister. They cough and breathe with difficulty and wear shawls over their shoulders in spite of the heat. Their deep, desperate, and mean eyes watch us go by," noted Maupassant for, contrary to what doctors believed, neither Cannes nor any other town on the Riviera offered a safe haven against tuberculosis.[58]

F. Scott Fitzgerald,
photo: Roger-Viollet

On the harbor, near the Palais des Festivals, it is possible to embark for the beautiful Lérin Islands (Tel: 04 93 39 11 82). The crossing takes only twenty minutes. The excursion is ideal for a picnic. In any case bring a couple of bottles of water. There are restaurants but no accommodation. It is in Ste-Marguerite's small fort that the mysterious Man in the Iron Mask was jailed between 1687 and 1698. He was then transferred to La Bastille in Paris and died there in 1703. To this day, the identity of this masked man still eludes historians. Some believe he was Eustache Dauger, probably a French spy about whom information is lacking. The fort and the jail can be visited. There is also a small archeological museum on the premises. On the island of St-Honorat is a fourth-century monastery. Until the Revolution of 1789, a community of Benedictine monks lived there. It is now the property of Cistercians. Visitors are welcome.

Tourist information. Palais des Festivals. 1 la Croisette. Tel: 04 93 39 24 53. Fax: 04 92 99 84 23. Website: <www.cannes-on-line.com>.

What to see. Musée de La Castre (archeology). Tel: 04 93 38 55 26. The *Croisette* promenade and the *Iles de Lérins.*

Where to stay. *****: *Carlton*, 58 la Croisette. AC, garage. Tel: 04 93 06 40 06. Fax: 04 93 06 40 25. *Majestic*, 14 la Croisette. AC, pool, garage. Tel: 05 92 98 77 00. Fax: 04 93 38 97 90. *Martinez*, 73 la Croisette. AC, pool, parking. Tel: 05 92 98 73 00. Fax: 04 93 39 67 82. ****: *Noga Hilton*, 50 la Croisette. AC, pool. Tel: 04 92 99 70 00. Fax: 04 92 99 70 11. ***: *Bleu Rivage*, 61 la Croisette. AC. Tel: 04 93 94 24 25. Fax: 04 93 43 74 92. *America*, 13 rue St-Honoré. AC. Tel: 04 93 06 75 75. Fax: 04 93 68 04 58. **: *Albert I*, 68 avenue Grasse. Parking. Tel: 04 93 39 24 04. Fax: 04 93 38 83 75. *Palm Beach*, 6 place de l'Etang. Tel: 04 92 18 86 86. Fax: 04 93 43 99 49.

*Where to eat. Belle Otéro ** (Carlton). Palme d'Or ** (Martinez). Villa des Lys * (Majestic). Nea, * 11 square Mérimée. Mesclun, 16 rue St-Antoine. Félix, 63 la Croisette. Festival, 52 la Croisette.*

Juan-les-Pins, Antibes

Ten minutes east of Cannes is Juan-les-Pins. F. Scott Fitzgerald (1896–1940), his wife Zelda, and their four-year-old daughter Frances lived there from March to December 1926. Fitzgerald loved France. It was the country where his favorite writers, Ernest Hemingway and Gertrude Stein, then resided. Juan-les-Pins was also the place where his friends the Murphys had their villa. They were wealthy Americans who, like Stein and Edith Wharton, had chosen France as their country of residence. In Juan-les-Pins Fitzgerald first rented the Villa Paquita and then moved to the Villa St-Louis. Fitzgerald was then quite well off. *The Great Gatsby*, published the year before, was a great success. Dos Passos found it artistically excellent and Cocteau said that the book had enabled him to endure some very difficult moments after the suicide of his lover. In a letter in French addressed to Fitzgerald he wrote: "It is an ethereal book; the rarest thing in the world."[59] Fitzgerald was working on *Tender Is the Night* (1934). Most nights, he was out partying with his British and American friends until the wee hours of the morning. Zelda was often ill and mostly bored. Her French was not good enough to communicate with her local servants and governess and she was depressed. To occupy her time, she took dancing lessons and went to the beach with her daughter but her marriage slowly deteriorated. Fitzgerald had taken to drinking wine, which helped him overcome his shyness but turned him into an alcoholic.

Tender Is the Night is largely autobiographical and partly set on the Riviera, where Doctor Dick Diver and his schizophrenic wife Nicole have built a house, somewhere near Cannes. The Divers spend their time entertaining rich British and Americans and their wives. The atmosphere is one of lavish soirées and romance that has for its background "the diffused magic of the hot sweet South, the soft-pawed night and the ghostly wash of the Mediterranean."[60] The novel recreates the atmosphere of the Riviera in the 1920s, clinging to its past glorious days, and where a few rich foreigners with flamboyant lifestyles gambled and became involved in scandalous love affairs. One afternoon, Rosemary, the young American actress in love with Dick, hires a cab and goes to Monte Carlo: "The chauffeur, a Russian czar of the period of Ivan the Terrible, was self-appointed guide, and the resplendent names—Cannes, Nice, Monte Carlo—began to glow through their torpid camouflage whispering of old kings come here to dine or die, or rajahs tossing Buddhas' eyes to English ballerinas, or Russian princes turning the weeks into Baltic twilights in the lost caviar days." On her way back to her hotel, Rosemary pokes her head out of the window, gazes at the sea "mysteriously coloured as the agates and cornelians of childhood, as green as milk, blue as laundry water, wine dark." She catches a glimpse of the Provençals "eating outside their doors," and hears the music of "fierce mechanical pianos behind the vines and country estaminets."

Fitzgerald's description of the Mediterranean scenery is masterly and poetic, as the following passage exemplifies: "In the early morning the distant image of Cannes, the pink and cream of old fortifications, the purple Alp that bounded Italy, were cast across the water and lay quavering in the ripples and rings sent up by sea-plants through the clear shallows." There, the old stones, the sun, and the sea combined to create a highly romantic and sensual atmosphere in which Fitzgerald's characters meditate on their lives and relationships. Nicole loves to sit and dream in her garden: "Following a walk marked by an intangible mist of bloom that followed the white border stones, she came to a space overlooking the sea where there were lanterns asleep in the fig trees and a big table and wicker chairs and a great market umbrella from Siena, all gathered about an enormous pine, the biggest tree in the garden. She paused a moment, looking abstractly at a growth of nasturtiums and iris tangled at its foot, as though sprung from a care-less handful of seeds, listening to the plaints and accusations of some nursery squabble in the house. When this died away on the summer air, she walked on, between kaleidoscopic peonies massed in pink clouds, black and brown tulips and fragile mauve-stemmed roses, transparent like sugar flowers in a confectioner's window—until, as if the scherzo of color could reach no further intensity, it broke off suddenly in mid-air, and moist steps went down to a level five feet below." The Mediter-ranean landscape and its subdued, luxuriant nature contrast with the intense moral dilemmas that Fitzgerald's protagonists face.

After Juan-les-Pins is Cap d'Antibes, a beautiful peninsula with prestigious homes. In 1857, botanist Gustave Thuret created a garden with tropical plants there, and in 1870 a Grand Hôtel (now Eden Rock) was built. Russians and English aristocrats haunted the place. In the 1920s Fitzgerald, Hemingway, and Dos Passos numbered among its guests. Among other literary figures who visited the cape was Jules Verne (1828–1905), who came regularly during the winters between 1874 and 1879. He stayed at the villa of playwright Adolphe d'Ennery, with whom he worked on the stage adaptation of his novels, especially *Le tour du monde en quatre-vingts jours* (Around the world in eighty days). Early in 1886, Guy de Maupassant came there to visit his brother, who worked as a gardener at the Villa Bellevue. Maupassant rented the villa Bosquet and then moved to the Chalet des Alpes. It is during his stay in Cap d'Antibes that he wrote his novel *Pierre et Jean*. He left in April 1887.

Antibes is the home of poet Jacques Audiberti (1899–1965). He was born on rue St-Esprit three years after Paul Arène passed away at the Hôtel National. Audiberti was the only son of a local construction entrepreneur. He attended school in Antibes and at the age of fifteen sent his first collection of poems to Edmond Rostand, who congratulated him and encouraged him to write. In his room, Audiberti kept a photograph of Edmond Rostand for years. After he left high school Audiberti worked as a clerk in the local court and wrote articles for the local newspaper, *Le reveil d'Antibes*, but did not give up poetry. Like Pagnol, he dreamed of meeting with contemporary artists and writers and, in 1924, he left for Paris. There, he worked as a journalist and met the surrealists. His poems appeared in collected volumes such as *L'empire et la trappe* (The empire and silence, 1930) and *Race des hommes* (The race of men, 1937), but he also wrote novels such as *Carnage* (1942) and *La poupée* (The doll, 1956). Every summer he came back to Antibes, to which he dedicated several poems and which he evoked here and there in his works. The specialists generally agree that the local language as spoken in Antibes is at the very core of the rhythm of his poetry. His prose, exemplified by *Les tombeaux ferment mal* (The tombs do not shut well, 1963), set in Antibes and Nice, also contains many Southern expressions. Like Giono, who criticized his hometown of Manosque, Audiberti regretted seeing Antibes transformed into a holiday resort with concrete buildings and hotels, and was nostalgic for the days when Provençal was the main vernacular. "Formerly, Provençal was spoken, all over this country here. It now survives only in the skimpy skulls of a few old men who sit on the parapets of villages perched on the hills. French dealt it a hard blow, but it's being replaced, crushed, in its turn, by the language of York. You can hear the words "pullover" and "push" even in the small villages such as Aiglun."[61]

Audiberti was attached to Antibes's glorious past, when Ligurians, Greeks, and Romans lived side by side. On this beautiful blue coast where "a purple atom betrays the original redness of its terrain," the city was founded, "a transparent sapphire . . . a pagan breeding-

Jacques Audiberti in Antibes (private collection)

ground." Before the yachts invaded the old port, there were only the local fishing boats. Some with "dark red sails came from Porto-Maurizio to load clay to make pots for that miserable Italian grub."[62] At this time, hotels and casinos had not yet mushroomed everywhere and the inhabitants of Antibes lived peacefully. This was the time when "Provençal lingered a little longer, a companion of the everyday objects, sharing with them the same brown pith."[63]

Soir d'Antibes

La terre monte.
Le ciel descend.
Meure la honte,
Le crapaud dompte
Le coeur tremblant

Herbe de menthe,
Chemin, adieux,
Ile dormante,
Rien ne tourmente
L'un de nous deux.

Le char méduse
Comme la mort.
Tout nous accuse.
Ruse, âme, ruse
Vers l'autre bord.

Evening in Antibes

The earth rises
The sky goes down
Die shame
The toad tames
The trembling heart

Mint herb
Pathway, goodbyes,
Sleeping island
Nothing tortures
You or me.

The jellyfish chariot
Like death.
Everything accuses us

Feint, soul, feint
Toward the other side.

(Jacques Audiberti)[64]

Audiberti died in Paris in 1965. The following year English writer Graham Greene (1904–1991) settled in Antibes, at Résidence des Fleurs, on the harbor. Greene had deep affinities with France. A reader of François Mauriac and Georges Bernanos, he converted to Catholicism in 1926. It is in his small one-bedroom apartment that Greene wrote some of his best novels such as *Travels with My Aunt* (1969), *The Honorary Consul* (1973), and *The Human Factor* (1975). Greek novelist Nikos Kazantzakis (1883–1957), author of bestseller *Zorba the Greek*, also settled in Antibes in 1948.

Tourist information. 11 place du G. de Gaulle. Tel: 04 92 90 53 00. Fax: 04 92 90 53 01 Website: <www.antibes-juanlespins.com>.

What to see. Archeology Museum. Tel: 04 92 90 54 35. *Picasso Museum.* Tel: 04 92 90 54 20.

Where to stay. ***: *Mas Djoliba*, 29 avenue de Provence. Pool, parking. Tel: 04 93 34 02 48. Fax: 04 93 34 05 81. *Josse*, blvd James Wyllie. AC, garage. Tel: 04 93 61 47 24. Fax: 04 93 61 97 62. **: *Petit Castel*, 22 chemin des Sables. AC. Tel: 04 93 61 59 37. Fax: 04 93 67 51 28. B&B: *Le Bosquet*, 14 chemin des Sables. Pool, parking. Tel: 04 93 67 32 29 or 04 93 34 06 04.

Where to eat. Les Vieux Murs, promenade Amiral de Grasse. *Jarre*, 14 rue St-Esprit. *Oscar's*, 8 rue Rostand.

Cagnes-sur-Mer, St-Paul, Vence, Grasse

A little off the coast before Nice is Cagnes-sur-Mer, where painter Auguste Renoir (1841–1919) lived with his family from 1907 until his death. His house, Les Colettes, is now a museum (Tel: 04 93 20 61 07).

Picturesque St-Paul, a ten-minute drive inland, is one of the most visited villages in Provence. The hotel and restaurant La Colombe d'Or was a favorite of painters such as Signac, Modigliani, and Bonnard and more recently of poet Jacques Prévert, American novelist Richard Wright, singer Yves Montand, and writer Bernard Henri Levy. The Fondation Maeght nearby contains the region's best modern paintings and sculptures (Braque, Chagall, Kandinsky, Miro, Giacometti, etc. Tel: 04 93 32 81 63).

D. H. Lawrence arrived in Vence in February 1930 hoping to cure his tuberculosis. But his condition was terminal and he died there the following month. He was buried in the small cemetery.

Grasse is the city of perfumes but also of painter Fragonard (1732–1806), whose house is now a small museum. Poet Louis Bellaud de la Bellaudière (1543–1588) was born there in a family of notables. He then lived in Avignon and studied law in Aix. He is the author of several melancholy poems in Provençal collected posthumously in a book entitled *Obros et rimos provenssalos* (Provençal works and poems, 1595).

Tourist information. 2 rue Grande, St-Paul. Tel: 04 93 32 86 95. Fax: 04 93 32 60 27. Email: <artdevivre@wanadoo.fr>.

Where to stay. ****: *St-Paul*, 86 rue Grande. AC. Tel: 04 93 32 65 25. Fax: 04 93 32 52 94. *La Colombe d'Or*, place des Ormeaux. AC, pool, parking. Tel: 04 93 32 80 02. Fax: 04 93 32 77 78. B&B: *Le Mas des Serres.* Tel: 04 93 32 81 10. Fax: 04 93 32 85 43.

Where to eat. Couleur Pourpre, 7 Rempart Ouest. *St-Paul.* *

From Nice to Menton

These roads wind and wind higher and higher—one seems to drive through centuries too, the boy with the oxen who stands on the hillside with a green branch in his hand, the old women gathering twigs among the olives, . . . all these figures seem to belong to any time—And the tiny walled village with a great tree in the cobbled square. . . . It's all something one seems to have known for ever.

—Katherine Mansfield, *Letters,* ed. John Middleton Murry

Nice

Villefranche-sur-Mer, Cap Ferrat,
and Beaulieu-sur-Mer

Monaco

Roquebrune-Cap-Martin

Menton

Mountain Towns: Ste-Agnès,
Sospel, Saorge, Tende, St-Dalmas

From Nice to Menton

Nice

From 1388 to 1860 the River Var was the western boundary of the Comté de Nice, then in the hands of the kings of Savoy. The official language was Italian, but Provençal subsisted in its *Niçois* or *Nissart* form. Scholars argue that, unlike the Provençal spoken in western Provence, influenced by French, Nissart kept its archaic structures. It was, on the other hand, affected by Italian, with which it coexisted for almost five centuries, and it is not uncommon for Italians in Nice to mistake Nissart for one of their dialects.

Like Hyères and Cannes, Nice owes its economic development to the aristocrats and wealthy businessmen who left the cold winters of northern Europe and Russia for the Mediterranean shores. The practice of medicine was also instrumental in this economic boom, for doctors in the past believed that the warm climate was a sure cure for tuberculosis, the scourge of the time. Many of those who came to Nice suffered from the disease. In 1784, there were about 368 English nationals living in Nice; in 1851, there were almost as many Russians as English, and Tsar Alexander II and his wife Alexandra Feodorovna arrived in 1856. These wealthy visitors built their own mansions, churches, and cemeteries. The English presence is commemorated in the promenade des Anglais along the bay *(plate 30)*. The arrival of the train in 1864 brought even more visitors to Nice. Luxurious hotels sprang up, and a casino was built on a pier. The local economy based on fish, fruit, olive oil, and flowers was forever transformed. Peasants left their fields and worked in hotels. This boom lasted until World War I, after which the situation changed drastically. Russia was then in the hands of Communists. In

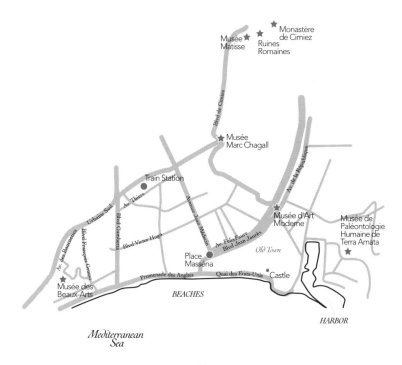

Nice

the following decades, palaces closed down one after another. With World War II the situation worsened. Although tourism flourished again in the late 1950s and is still the major industry, the visitors' average stay has been reduced to a few days.

Nice is known for its Carnival, a tradition that goes back to the thirteenth century. Every year for three weeks (mid-February) masked musicians and dancers parade on colorful floats before thousands of spectators *(plate 31)*.

Nice's climate attracted scores of writers and literary celebrities. Tobias Smollett traveled through the city in 1764. Nikolai Gogol came in 1843 and wrote part of *Dead Souls* there. Russian painter Mary Baskirchev lived as a child in the villa Acqua Viva from 1871 to 1874. Friedrich Nietzsche (1844–1900) is perhaps one of the few whose stay in Nice had a decisive inspiration on his work. He loved Provence and

From Nice to Menton

Friedrich Nietzsche, photo: copyright Hachette Livre

argued in *Ecce Homo* that genius could develop only in a hot, dry country with blue skies. In his *Fröhliche Wissenschaft*, inspired in part by the Gaya Scienza of the troubadours, he dedicated a poem to the Mistral. Nietzsche spent five consecutive winters in Nice between 1883 and 1888. He lived first at rue Segurane, near the harbor, where he felt as if he were in the suburbs of Genoa, and then at the Pension de Genève, rue Rossini. Nietzsche enjoyed the lively atmosphere of the old town, but he especially loved the sun and the luxuriant nature around him. The light, colors, and dry air all contributed to give him the energy to finish *Beyond Good and Evil*, *Human, All Too Human*, and *The Gay Science*. He attended concerts and the opera and visited the bookstores. When he was not writing, he read Baudelaire or Maupassant.

One of his favorite day trips was to Eze, a medieval village overlooking the bay of Villefranche. This place inspired the end of his

Zarathustra: "Many hidden places and villages high on the mountains around Nice have become sacred and unforgettable to me. The decisive part, called "On Old and New Tablets," was composed during a particularly difficult hike up there, from the station to the wonderful Moorish village of Eze, on a cliff."[1] The book indeed contains many echoes of the place. "I am a traveler and a climber of mountains. . . . I do not like valleys," declares Zarathustra.[2] From Eze, as from Zarathustra's island, Nietzsche could see "a bay where foreign ships liked to cast their anchors."[3] It takes approximately two hours to hike from the beach to Eze on the narrow pathway that has been baptized Sentier Nietzsche.

Mistral-Wind, du Wolken-Jäger,
Trübsal-Mörder, Himmels-Feger,
Brausender, wie lieb ich dich!
Sind wir zwei nicht eines Schosses
Erstlingsgabe, eines Loses
Vorbestimmte ewiglich?

O Mistral, cloud hunter,
Depression killer, sky-sweeper,
Howler, I love you so much!
Aren't we from the same womb
Both born and to the same fate
Forever predestined?

(Friedrich Nietzsche, from
"An die Mistral: Ein Tanzlied")[4]

Anton Chekhov, thirty-four years old and suffering from tuberculosis, arrived in Nice in October 1897. He stayed at the Pension Russe, 9 rue Gounod. Chekhov had been to Nice before, in 1894, but only briefly. This time he stayed six months. At the Pension Russe, there were about forty of his compatriots, which made socializing easier for Chekhov, who read but did not speak French. He lived on the third floor but his condition made it difficult for him to climb the stairs, so he

Anton Chekhov, photo: Roger-Viollet

soon moved down to the first floor. Chekhov loved the town. He took long walks, sat on the café terraces, attended concerts, and read newspapers. He had a hard time concentrating but managed to write three short stories. When lonely, he wrote to his friends and family in Russia. He was more interested in the Provençals than in the surrounding nature. He liked the refined tastes of the French, their courtesy and independent spirit. He interested himself in the Dreyfus affair that caused a great stir in France and admired Emile Zola's courage and moral earnestness. "France is a wonderful country with wonderful writers," he wrote.[5] Among his favorite authors was Maupassant.

When Chekhov's friend Potapenko arrived for a visit in March, they went to Monte Carlo and gambled until the wee hours. Chekhov left in April via Paris and was back in Russia in early May. He came back to the Pension Russe in December 1900. He was alone again and worked on his play *Three Sisters*. He loved the mild winter. "The roses are in bloom. . . . The weather is warm, the sun shines and the windows of my room are wide open. . . . I have the impression of being on the moon," he wrote his sister.[6] But his health did not improve and he felt weary. On January 26, Chekhov left for Italy with his friend Kovalevsky.

Jules Romain (1885–1972) taught philosophy in Nice from 1917 to 1919. He retained fond memories of the city that he evokes in *La douceur de vie* (The sweetness of life).

In 1955, Henri Bosco came to Nice to retire. He bought La Maison Rose, avenue Sainte Colette, on the residential hills of Cimiez. Bosco had chosen Nice not only because it was his mother's birthplace, but also because, in addition to the Luberon, he also loved the Mediterranean Sea. He had spent ten years in Naples at the beginning of his career and had learned to live in the shadows of Greek myths and legends. The novels he wrote in Nice, such as *Les Balesta* (1956), *L'épervier* (The hawk, 1963), and *Le récif* (The reef, 1971), reflect the importance he attached to the sea. The Boscos participated in many cultural and literary events of the city, went to church, and attended the soirées of the Alliance Française and of the mayor, Jacques Médecin. Every spring, they left for Lourmarin. In his later years, Bosco continued to read his beloved Greek and Latin authors, with a marked preference for Plotinus, Aeschylus, Theocritus, Virgil, and Tacitus. He also wrote several volumes of memoirs. He passed away in Cimiez on May 4, 1976. Mathilde Monnier and Roger Martin du Gard also retired and died in Cimiez.

Among the dozen or so authors quoted by André Compan in his *Anthologie de la littérature niçoise*,[7] Joseph-Rosalinde Rancher (1785–1843) stands out as the most famous. Born in Nice, he was educated in Marseille, after which he returned to his hometown and worked as a tax collector. He wrote poems and plays such as *La Nemaïda* (The adventures of Nem, 1823), *La mouostra raubada* (The stolen watch, 1830) *Lou*

fablié Nissart (Fables, 1832). His ideas on language and culture antici-
pated the Félibrige; Mistral read his works. In 1840, Joseph Micéa published *Grammaire Niçoise*. Among other writers working in Nissart were
Joseph Dablay (1786–1855), author of poems and *cansouns*, and François
Guisol (1803–1874), who wrote comedies and poems and founded *La
mensoneguierà* (The liar), the first review in Nissart. The theater was
particularly active with Louis Genari (1871–1952), Jules Eynaudi (1871–
1948), and Francis Gag (1900–1988).

"Non si plagnen giamai se perden pron o poù
Un mestre tout puissant nen leva tout, se voù."

Au pastre che si repauvava,
Una fëa entenduda en tau guisa parlava :
Mi mautrates touplen, beu mestre, e cada giou
Veu che creisson lu mieu doulou.
Lou sera, e lou matin mi mouses, e m'espuises,
Lou mieu manteu d'hiver m'enlèves en estieu;

Giusca dei mieu picioui crudelmen mi divises.
En soma, non hai rem de mieu.
Per mi veire ensin far la guerra
Che fauta hai mai comes soubre d'achesta terra?
L'ome es donca insensible a la rigour dei Dieu!

"Let's never complain of losing some or all
For an all-powerful master can take all away from us at will."

To the shepherd who was resting
A ewe endowed with reason thus spoke:
You do not treat me well, master, and each day
My sorrows grow.
Evening and morning you milk me and exhaust me,
In summer you shear my winter fleece
And even cruelly separate me from my children.
In sum nothing belongs to me.
To be treated in this way
What wrong have I done on this earth?
Man is insensitive and has the severity of the Gods.

(Joseph-Rosalinde Rancher, from "La Fëa e lou Pastre"
[The ewe and the shepherd])[8]

Nice's most famous contemporary writer is Louis Nucéra (1928–2000), author of several successful novels such as *Chemin de la Lanterne* (Lantern Way, 1981), *La chanson de Maria* (Maria's song, 1989), and *Le ruban rouge* (The red ribbon, 1991) in which his native city occupies a major place. Like Giono he began work in a bank; he then became a journalist in Paris. He was a good friend of singer Georges Brassens, Jean Cocteau, Joseph Kessel, and Picasso. Although he often spoke Nissart with his friends, he wrote in French. Nucéra loved the Old Town, a place that once "smelled of Parmesan cheese, fish, and barrels of warm wine." His novels describe the warm and friendly atmosphere of the place when as child he and his uncle ate *socca* at the terrace of a café. The socca is a sort of tortilla made with chickpeas and olive oil, and powdered with pepper. The whole harbor smelled like food, and

Louis Nucéra, photo:
Martinetti, Editions Grasset

even the custom officers occasionally stopped by for a bite, always carrying a rope in their belt in case they had to save the drunks who fell into the harbor. As in other coastal towns, at the beginning of the twentieth century fishermen represented a large part of the population of Nice. "The fishermen would go down to the shore at three o' clock in the morning, scrutinize the sea, and decide if they should leave to cast their nets or not. They did not trust the forecast and evaluated the weather with their eyes."[9]

According to Nucéra, unlike the Marseillais, voluble by nature, the Niçois is rather quiet. The word "Euh . . ." often serves as an answer to everything. "How are you? "Euh . . . !" This interjection sums it all up. "It sounds between *é, è,* and *eu,* a unique phonetics of which the Niçois are the only depositaries, and that encompasses all the philosophies of the world. It has several uses: answer, greeting, narration, making acquaintance, summary of male prowess, art of avoiding traps, plea, panegyric; and translates different conditions: routine, extravagance, sentence, nonchalance, chronic spleen, and torpor caused by drinking *pastis* and rosé wine."[10]

Nice is also the city where Jean-Marie Le Clézio was born in 1940 and spent his childhood: "I lived in an old house on the harbor. It looked like a Neapolitan house and was totally decrepit. Sheets were hanging on the clothes lines of all the courtyard windows."[11] His novels often evoke Nice, especially *Le procès verbal* (The verbal process, 1963).

Tourist Information. 5 promenade des Anglais. Tel: 04 92 14 48 00. Website: <www.nice-coteazur.org>. Email: <otc@nice-coeazur. org>. Also, avenue Thiers, next to the station. Tel: 04 93 87 07 07.

What to see. Chagall Museum, avenue Dr. Menard. Tel: 04 93 53 87 20. *Matisse Museum (plate 32),* 16 avenue des Arènes. Bus: 15, 17, 20, or 22. Tel: 04 93 81 08 08. *Museum of Archeology.* 106 avenue des Arènes. Tel: 04 93 81 59 57. *Museum of Modern Art,* promenade des Arts. Tel: 04 93 62 61 62.

Where to stay. ********: *Négresco,* 37 promenade des Anglais. AC, garage. Tel: 04 93 16 64 00. Fax: 93 88 35 68. Website: <www.crt-riviera.fr>. *Palais Maeternick,* 30 blvd Maeternick. AC, pool, garage. Tel: 04 92 00 72 00. Fax: 04 93 04 18 10. *******: *Novotel,* 8 Parvis de l'Europe. AC, pool, garage. Tel: 04 93 13 30 93. Fax: 04 93 13 09 04. *Grimaldi,* 25 rue Grimaldi. AC. Tel: 04 93 16 00 24. Fax: 04 93 87 00 24. ******: *Nouvel Hôtel,* 19bis blvd Victor Hugo. AC. Tel: 04 93 87 15 00. Fax: 04 93 16 00 67. *Buffa,* 56 rue de la Buffa. AC. Tel: 04 93 88 77 35. Fax: 04 93 88 83 39. *Hôtel Antares,* 5 avenue Thiers, near the station. Tel: 04 93 88 22 87. Fax: 04 93 16 11 22. *Grand Hôtel de Berne,* 1 avenue Thiers, near the station. AC, parking. Tel: 04 93 88 25 08. Fax: 04 93 88 53 64. Email: <hotel.de.berne@free.fr>. B&Bs: *Le Castel Enchanté,* St-Pierre de Féric. Pool, parking. Tel: 04 93 97 02 08. Fax: 04 93 97 13 70. *Les Nertières,* La Gaude. Pool, parking. Tel: 04 93 24 83 95. *Parc St-Donat,* La Colle-sur-Loup. Pool, parking. Tel & Fax: 04 93 32 93 41.

Where to eat. Chantecler** (Hôtel Negresco). *L'Univers Christian Plumail,** 54 blvd Jean-Jaurès. *Les Viviers,* 22 rue A. Karr. *Don Camillo,* 5 rue Ponchettes. *L'Ane Rouge,* 7 quai des Deux-Emmanuel.

Villefranche-sur-Mer, Cap Ferrat, and Beaulieu-sur-Mer

Four miles east of Nice, hidden inside a beautiful bay, is Villefranche-sur-Mer *(plate 33)*, Jean Cocteau's favorite place in Provence. Cocteau (1889–1963) had a passion for the Mediterranean Sea. It reminded him of Greece and inspired him profoundly. As a young man he had stayed in Cap Martin with his mother, in 1911, and in Cannes, in 1918. He discovered Villefranche in 1924, invited by a friend. Cocteau was then thirty-five years old and was working with Sergei Diaghilev in Monaco. Villefranche was still a small fishing village but its deep bay sheltered large military and cruise ships that could not enter the port of Nice. Like Toulon, the place was often crowded with sailors. Cocteau rented a room at the Hôtel Welcome *(plate 34)*, on the harbor. "It was a haunted hotel. It is true that we haunted it for it had no such predisposition. There was the covered street. There Vauban's walls and the barracks that at night evoke the absurd munificence of dreams. Sure, there was also Nice on the left, and Monte Carlo on the right, with their sneaky architecture. But the Hotel Welcome was simply charming and did not seem to fear anything. Its bedrooms were painted with ordinary paint. A layer of yellow covered the Italian trompe l'oeil of its façade. The bay sheltered the squadrons. The fishermen repaired the nets and slept in the sun."[12]

Away from the hustle and glamour of Monte Carlo, the hotel was simple but lively. There were English travelers, sailors, army officers and their wives, but also artists such as the dancer Isadora Duncan. The atmosphere was friendly and jovial. "We drew, invented, and visited one another's rooms. A mythology was born there with a style epitomized

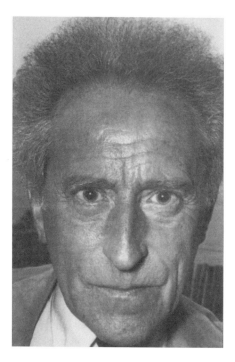

Jean Cocteau (private collection)

in *Orpheus.*"[13] Cocteau bought a small fishing boat that he named *Heurtebise,* and when he was not sailing he wrote and drew or visited his friend Paul Morand in his villa, l'Orangerie. The Hôtel Welcome felt like home. Cocteau participated it all its impromptu parties, often playing the drums in the little jazz band improvised by the sailors. "I live in a strange place . . . day and night, sailors fight and belly dance. Of the jazz band I hear only the bass drum. It is as if there was a newspaper press in the basement . . . machines clatter, nervous breakdown of women, sailors' choir," Cocteau wrote. Alcohol flowed and cigarette smoke filled the air. His opium pipe near at hand, Cocteau sat down and wrote *Orphée* (1926).

> La chambre avec balcon sans volet sur la mer
> Voit les fenêtres sur la mer,

Voile et feux naître sur la mer,
Le bal qu'on donne sur la mer.

Le balcon donne sur la mer.

La chambre avec le balcon s'envolait sur la mer.

The bedroom with balcony without shutters on the sea
Sees the windows on the sea,
Sail and lights come into being on the sea,
The ball that is in progress on the sea.

The balcony opens on the sea.

The bedroom with balcony took off on the sea.

(Jean Cocteau, from "L'Hôtel")[14]

Cocteau also visited his friends, Colette in St-Tropez, Charles and Marie-Laure de Noaïlles in Hyères. He regularly went to Nice to see Isadora Duncan, who performed there, and Igor Stravinsky, with whom he worked on *Oedipus Rex*. He was often invited to the villa La Pausa, Coco Chanel's summer residence on the heights of Roquebrune, next to Monaco. Chanel had designed the costumes for *Orphée*. But Cocteau always hurried back to Villefranche, his "workshop of dreams" where "poets of all breeds of all languages lived." They had transformed the little fishing village into "a center of fiction and inventions," he wrote in his *Portraits souvenirs*. World War II put a temporary stop to these happy times, but in the early 1950s, Cocteau came back to Villefranche, or rather this time to the peninsula of Cap Ferrat on the other side of the bay. He was then at the height of his career. His movies *L'éternel retour* (The eternal return, 1943), *Belle et la bête* (Beauty and the beast, 1945), and *Les parents terribles* (1948) had been very successful. In 1949, at a dinner party in Paris, Cocteau struck up a friendship with Francine Weisweiller, the wife of a rich industrialist who, fascinated by his talent, invited him to her villa, Santo Sospir, on Cap Ferrat. Cocteau could not resist and early in May 1950 he and his companion Edouard Dermit arrived at Santo Sospir. The magnificent house, on the water near the lighthouse, is surrounded by pines and eucalyptus trees and has a glorious view of Nice. Cocteau rapidly felt at home there. Francine was

Santo Sospir

very hospitable and her husband gave her entire freedom. She turned a room into a workshop for Cocteau and even let him paint frescos on her walls. Save for a few trips to Paris for work and to visit his mother, Cocteau spent most of the year at Santo Sospir. Francine and the two men soon became inseparable friends. They attended dinner parties together and traveled to Venice, St. Moritz, Greece, and Spain.

Cocteau had not totally abandoned his former residence in Villefranche and often walked into the Hôtel Welcome for a drink. Next to it was an old chapel that the fishermen had been using as a shed for a couple of centuries. Cocteau suggested to the local authorities that he could restore the Chapelle St-Pierre and decorate it for free. For years, the fishermen's union opposed the project but, finally, in 1957, gave their permission. Cocteau immediately set to work. For six months the poet, dressed in blue overalls hiding an impeccable white shirt and elegant necktie, worked from morning till evening. Perched on scaffolding, he used a magic lantern to project shadows on the walls that he then proceeded to paint. Cocteau told Chanel: "Villefranche shaped

From Nice to Menton

Cocteau's Chapel

my youth . . . the chapel, the exhibition room, the Soulart bookstore are the sanctuary of my mythology." The day of the opening Picasso congratulated him. In 1960, the city of Villefranche awarded him the Diplôme de Citoyen d'Honneur. Cocteau also decorated Santo Sospir, Menton's city hall, the Center of Mediterranean Studies in Cap d'Ail, and a chapel in Fréjus. Always modest about his work, Cocteau declared that he was "neither a line artist nor a painter" and referred to his murals as "writings untied and retied in a different way."[15]

Among the many guests at Santo Sospir were his longtime friend Marlene Dietrich, Greta Garbo, and writer Jean Genet. Cocteau also traveled to visit his friends. He often went to Monte Carlo, dined with Colette or Pagnol, and visited Matisse in Nice and Picasso in Vallauris. At Santo Sospir Cocteau painted, answered his numerous correspondents, and wrote *Le journal d'un inconnu* (The journal of an unknown, 1952), *Le testament d'Orphée*, and *Portraits souvenirs*. Unfortunately, all love stories have to end sometime and, in the early sixties, after ten years, his wonderful friendship with Francine came to an end. She apparently fell in love with writer Henri Viard, and Cocteau decided it was time to leave. In the summer of 1962, he and Edouard moved out and went to live in his house in Milly-la-Forêt, near Paris. He died there shortly after on October 12, 1963.

Cap Ferrat was also the residence of English writer W. Somerset Maugham (1874–1965). A frequent guest of the Hôtel Welcome, in 1928, after his divorce, Maugham bought a beautiful villa on the peninsula, only a two-minute walk from Santo Sospir. It sat on about twenty acres of palm trees and pines and had a pool. Its former owner, an ecclesiastic in the service of King Leopold II of Belgium, had spent the greatest part of his life in North Africa, so Maugham baptized it La Villa Mauresque. When Maugham settled there he was already famous and rich. Among his bestsellers were *Of Human Bondage* (1915) and *The Moon and Sixpence* (1919). Maugham was a Francophile and spoke fluent French; he was born and raised in Paris, where his father worked for the British Embassy. After his father passed away in 1884, young Maugham was sent to live with his uncle in Kent and attended King's School in Canterbury. He discovered French literature and especially

Maupassant in Hyères, where he was vacationing. On the list of his favorite French writers were also Stendhal and Balzac.

Cap Ferrat was Maugham's permanent residence, and he wrote and entertained there. He had several guest rooms and a large staff. Among the many famous literary visitors were H. G. Wells and Rudyard Kipling and, of course, Cocteau. During World War II, Maugham went to the United States and the Villa Mauresque was pillaged. Upon his return he managed to collect his furniture and restored the house. He also acquired art; according to Cocteau, on a visit to the Villa Mauresque on February 27, 1952, Maugham (who was reading *Madame Bovary* when Cocteau dropped by) told Cocteau that he had just bought two of Picasso's paintings for a very high price. Maugham traveled all over the world but always came back home to the villa, where he died in 1965. His body was cremated and his ashes were taken back to Kent.

The little resort town of Beaulieu-sur-Mer has a casino and an interesting villa to visit: Kerylos (Tel: 04 93 01 01 44), built between 1902 and 1908 as a reconstruction of an ancient Greek villa for the French archeologist Théodore Reinach. Beaulieu's *La Réserve* is one of the best combinations of four-star hotel and two-star restaurant on the coast (Tel: 04 93 01 00 01. Fax: 04 93 01 28 99. Website: <www.reservebeaulieu.com>).

Tourist information. Jardin François Binon. Villefranche. Tel: 04 93 01 73 68. Email: <ot-villefranchesurmer@rom-fr>. Website: <www.villefranche-sur-mer.com>.

What to see. On the harbor: *Chapelle St-Pierre* (Tel: 04 93 76 90 70) and the citadel with its museums (free admission).

Where to stay. ***: *Hôtel Welcome*, 1 quai Courbet. AC. Tel: 04 93 76 27 27. Fax: 04 93 76 27 66. *Flore*, avenue Princesse Grace. AC, pool, parking. Tel: 04 93 76 30 30. Fax: 04 93 76 99 99. *Versailles*, avenue Princesse Grace. AC, pool, parking. Tel: 04 93 76 52 52. Fax: 04 93 01 97 48. *La Darse*, Port de Plaisance. Parking. Tel: 04 93 01 72 54. Fax: 04 93 01 94 37. *Le Provençal*. AC, parking. Tel: 04 93 76 53 53. Fax: 04 93 76 53 54.

Beaulieu-sur-Mer

Where to eat. La Mère Germaine, quai Courbet.

St-Jean-Cap-Ferrat:

Tourist information, 59 avenue Denis-Séméria. Tel: 04 93 76 08 90. Fax: 04 93 76 16 67.

What to see. Villa Ephrussi (plate 35). Tel: 04 93 01 33 09. Email: <www.villa-ephrussi.com>. Home of Béatrice de Rothschild, Baroness Ephrussi, from 1912 to 1934. Small *Zoo* in Cap Ferrat.

Where to stay. ****: *Grand Hôtel du Cap*, at the tip of the peninsula. AC, pool, parking. Tel: 04 93 76 50 50. Fax: 04 93 76 04 52. Website: <www.grand-hotel-cap-ferrat.com>. *Hôtel Riviera*, avenue Monnet. AC, pool, parking. Tel: 04 93 76 31 00. Fax: 04 93 01 23 07. ***: *Clair Logis*, avenue Centrale. Parking. Tel: 04 93 76 04 57. Fax: 04 93 76 11 85. **: *Frégate*, rue Séméria. AC. Tel: 04 93 76 04 51. Fax: 04 93 76 14 96.

Where to eat. Grand Hôtel du Cap.* Capitaine Cook.

Monaco

A ten-minute drive away is the principality of Monaco. Monaco is not part of France but an independent state headed by the Grimaldi family since the thirteenth century. Given its situation as an enclave within French territory, Monaco developed close cultural and linguistic ties with France and Provence. In 1297, the Grimaldis, a wealthy Genoan family allied to the Pope, were forced to leave Genoa after a bitter political struggle. They settled in Monaco, a small, rocky peninsula in Provence acquired by Genoa a century earlier. In 1342, Charles Grimaldi acquired the Provençal villages of Roquebrune and Menton. Fifteen years later, Genoa invaded Monaco and Roquebrune. Rainier II sought refuge in Menton and attacked the Genoans in 1419. The latter tried again to conquer Monaco but in vain. Later, the principality became a protectorate of Spain (1523–1641) and then signed a treaty of alliance with France (1641–1793). From 1814 to 1860, Monaco was a protectorate of Sardinia and, in 1860, Roquebrune and Menton seceded and returned to France.

Until the middle of the nineteenth century, Monaco was still a secluded village. Access by land was difficult. In 1840, it took four hours for Flaubert to ride there from Nice. The little winding road was treacherous and accidents were frequent. The development of Monaco began with the arrival of the train in 1867, which reduced the trip from Nice to only forty minutes. The railway was particularly welcome because Monaco had built its own casino in 1863 and hoped to attract customers. The first years were difficult and customers rare, but after the railway finally reached the place, gamblers flocked to the casino from every part of the world. "As soon as one stepped inside, the sound of money, continuous like the waves, a deep sound, light yet dangerous, filled the ears," remembered Maupassant after gambling there one evening.[16] The new neighborhood where the casino was built was baptized Monte Carlo after Prince Charles Grimaldi. All around the casino, luxury hotels such as the Hôtel de Paris (1866) were built for the wealthy international businessmen and aristocracy. Monte Carlo rapidly developed into a fashionable resort. Charles Garnier built an opera house and Sarah Bernhardt played on its opening night in 1879. Gounod, Berlioz, and Stravinsky performed there. Diaghilev created the Ballets Russes de Monte Carlo. The restaurants hired the best chefs, including Auguste Escoffier (1846–1935). In 1910 Prince Albert I opened the Museum of Oceanography, later headed by Jacques Cousteau (from 1957 to 1988). Other events such as the automobile Rally, established in 1911, and the Grand Prix, created in 1929, further contributed to Monaco's international attraction. Nowadays, Monaco organizes numerous events including a tennis championship, fairs, and cinema and media festivals. The economic success of Monaco was such that in 1869 Prince Charles III abolished all taxes for the residents. Prince Rainier III has governed the principality since 1949. In 1956 he married American actress Grace Kelly and they had three children, Caroline, Albert, and Stéphanie. Princess Grace died in a tragic car accident in 1982.

The traditional language of Monaco or *monégasque* is an Italian dialect of the Genovese branch. However, being surrounded by Provençal, Monegasque has been influenced by Nissart, Roquebrunois, and Mentonnais from which, according to scholars, it borrowed many substantives. In the late nineteenth century, French made rapid progress in the principality and competed with Italian in the schools. At the end of the century it was the language of education, and in 1962 the Constitution declared it the official language of the principality. Unlike Provençal, Monegasque is mandatory in the schools up to the age of thirteen, after which it becomes an elective. Italian, however, is still widely spoken and Italians represent a large work force in the principality (5,000 Monegasques, 12,000 French, and 10,000 Italian residents).

Monaco's national poet is Louis Notari (1879–1961). He was born in the old town and attended St-Charles, where he probably met Apollinaire, then transferred to the Visitation (now Lycée Albert I). Notari finished his secondary education in Bordighera and attended college in Turin, majoring in civil engineering. After graduation he returned to Monaco where he created the Jardin Exotique, dedicated to desert plants (succulents). In the late 1920s, Notari and fellow members of the Com-

Monaco: the harbor

mittee for Monegasque Traditions decided it was time to write down Monegasque to record their literature. So, influenced by Mistral, Notari devised a writing system and began composing plays and poems inspired by local history such as "A Legenda de Santa Devota," in honor of the local saint. Other Monegasque writers such as Marc Curit, Louis Cani, and Joseph Sauvaigo followed in his footsteps and published their poems in the review *Rives Azur*. In 1960 Louis Frolla published his *Grammaire monégasque* and three years later his *Dictionnaire français-monégasque*.

French surrealist poet Guillaume Apollinaire (1880–1918), born in Italy, spent his childhood in Monaco. His mother, Angelica, was the daughter of Michael Apollinare Kostrowitzky, a Russian diplomat who worked for the Pope, and her mother was Italian. Wilhelm, for such was the poet's first name, and his brother were illegitimate children. The reasons for the move to Monaco are not clear but, in March 1887, Pope Leo XIII granted Monaco its own diocese and appointed Bishop Theuret to head it. Theuret, for whom Angelica had recommendations, was also the principal of the Collège St-Charles that he had founded in 1880. Priests and nuns taught classes in French, and the school counted about eighty students of many different nationalities.

Monegasque costume

From Nice to Menton

Louis Notari (private collection)

Angelica rented a two-bedroom apartment near the harbor and registered her son as a boarder. Apollinaire was a good student and stayed there until 1895 when, following financial difficulties, the school closed down. He and his brother then attended the Lycée Stanislas in Cannes and the Lycée Masséna in Nice. During her stay in the principality, Angelica changed residences several times, always in dire straits. She did not work but regularly visited the casino and the Café de Paris where on a couple of occasions the police arrested her for fights and drunken behavior. In 1899, she and her sons finally left Monaco for Aix-les-Bains. Apollinaire kept fond memories of his Monegasque days but rarely mentions the place in his poems.

Tourist information. Boulevard des Moulins. Tel: (377) 92 16 61 66. Fax: (377) 92 16 60 00. Website: <www.monaco-congres.com>. Email: <infodtc@gouv.mc>.

What to see. The small state is only two miles long and is best visited on foot or by the mini train. *Casino* (dress code and minimum age twenty-one). Prince Rainier's *Antique Car Collection* (377) 92 05 28 56. *Museum of Oceanography* (377) 93 15 36 00. *The Prince's Palace:* (377) 93 25 32 33. The changing of the guard ceremony takes place in front of the palace every day at 12:00.

Where to stay. *****: *Hôtel de Paris,* place du Casino. AC, pool, garage. Tel: (377) 92 1630 00. Fax: (377) 92 16 38 44. ****: *Hermitage,* square Beaumarchais. AC, pool, garage. Tel: (377) 92 16 40 00. Fax: 377 92 16 38 52. ***: *Alexandra,* 35 blvd Princesse Charlotte. AC. Tel: (377) 93 50 63 13. Fax: (377) 92 16 06 48. *Hôtel du Louvre,* 16 blvd des Moulins. Tel: (377) 93 50 65 25. Fax: (377) 93 30 23 68. Also more affordable are the following two-star hotels in nearby Beausoleil (France), a two-minute walk from Monte Carlo: *Hôtel Cosmopolite,* 19 blvd Leclerc. AC, parking nearby. Tel: 04 93 78 36 00. Fax: 04 93 41 84 22. *Hôtel Diana,* 17 blvd Leclerc. Parking. Tel: 04 93 78 47 58. Fax: 04 93 41 88 94. *Hôtel Olympia,* 17bis blvd Leclerc. AC, parking nearby. Tel: 04 93 78 12 70. Fax: 04 93 41 85 04.

Where to eat. *Louis XV*** (Hôtel de Paris). *Vistamar** (Hôtel Hermitage). *La Coupole** (Hôtel Mirabeau). *Bar et Boeuf,** avenue Princesse Grace. *Saint Benoit,* 10 avenue da Costa.

Roquebrune-Cap-Martin

Adjacent to Monte Carlo is the town of Roquebrune-Cap-Martin with its medieval castle and old village perched on a cliff *(plate 36).* Halfway between the village and the sea on the Grande Corniche is the Villa La Souco, which painter Simon Bussy acquired in the 1920s. He and his wife Dorothy Strachey, English woman of letters and translator of André Gide, spent the winters there. Among their guests were Gide,

Paul Valéry, Rudyard Kipling, and Martin du Gard. In 1941, they let their house to André Malraux (1901–1976), his girlfriend Josette Clotis, and their baby. Malraux had few visitors there except Jean-Paul Sartre, Simone de Beauvoir, Manès Sperber, and Oswald Spengler. He devoted his time to writing *Les noyers de l'Altenburg, Le demon de l'absolu,* and *La psychologie de l'art.* He left in November 1942.

Ireland's national poet William Butler Yeats (1865–1939) came to Roquebrune in January 1938. He and his wife first lodged at the Hôtel Carlton in Menton. Yeats was seventy-three years old and in fragile health. However, the mildness of the winter and the sunny skies appealed to him and he decided that from now on he would spend the cold months here: "The life is good for my mind and body—my life is fixed henceforth, the winter here or near here," he wrote to Edith Shackleton.[17] Between walks he corrected the proofs of his *New Poems* and worked on an essay, "On the Boiler." In March, the Yeats moved to a smaller hotel, Villa Idéal Séjour on the peninsula of Cap Martin, facing Monaco. Cap Martin was then covered with a forest of pines. In 1889, Calvin White, a British businessman, bought most of the land on Cap Martin from the town, and Danish architect Hans Tersling built the Grand Hôtel (1891) and several mansions there, including Cyrnos (1892) for French Empress Eugénie, wife of Napoleon. The Grand Hôtel soon became a favorite resort for royalty such as Elizabeth of Austria, Franz Joseph, and English kings Edward VII and Georges V, and for Italian poet Gabriele d'Annunzio and French playwright Sacha Guitry.

The hotel where Yeats stayed was small and very modest. In May he and his wife left for Ireland, but they came back the following December as promised. Yeats spoke hardly any French but he had plenty of English-speaking friends around, such as the O'Briens, at Cap d'Ail, and Lady Wellesley, in Beaulieu-sur-Mer. His health was slowly declining and he knew the end was near. He died there on January 28, 1939, as he was finishing *The Death of Cuchulain.* Two days later he was buried in the village's cemetery up on the hill, on the second terrace. Because of the war, his body could not be taken to Ireland as planned, and remained in Roquebrune until 1948, when his remains were finally returned to

Roquebrune and Menton

Sligo. There was then some doubt as to where Yeats's grave was, for during the war it had been excavated and his bones apparently put in an ossuary. The police had to investigate; medical records were brought from Ireland to help determine where his bones lay. Finally, in August 1848 the *Macha*, an Irish ship, moored at Villefranche and Yeats's bones embarked under a French military escort. The Hôtel Idéal Séjour is now a condominium residence. A plaque near the entrance door reminds passers-by that it was once the Irish poet's temporary residence. The Princess Grace Irish Library in Monaco contains a good collection of the poet's works as well as memorabilia of his stay at the small hotel.

> *Tourist information.* 218 rue Aristide Briand (in the Carnoles neighborhood, near Menton). Tel: 04 93 35 62 87. Fax: 04 93 28 57 00. Email: <officedutourisme@roquebrune-cap-martin.com>.
>
> *What to see.* The Old Village and *Castle.* Tel: 04 93 35 07 22.
>
> *Where to stay.* ****: *Vista Palace*, on the Grande Corniche. AC, pool, parking. Tel: 04 92 10 40 00. Fax: 04 93 35 18 94. Beautiful

panoramic view. *Monte Carlo Beach*, on the shore near Monte Carlo. AC, pool, parking. Tel: 40 93 28 66 66. Fax: 04 93 78 14 18. ***: *Hôtel Diodato* near the beach and the Roquebrune train station. Tel: 04 92 10 52 52. Fax: 04 92 10 52 53. In Carnoles: *Hôtel Alexandra*, beachfront. Tel: 04 93 35 65 45. Fax: 04 93 57 96 51. *Hôtel Victoria*, beachfront. Tel: 04 93 35 65 90. Fax: 04 93 28 27 02. **: *Les Deux Frères*, in the old village. Great panoramic view. Tel: 04 93 28 99 00. Fax: 04 93 28 99 10.

Where to eat. Roquebrune, *on the Basse Corniche, 100 avenue Jean-Jaurès. *Au Grand Inquisiteur, Les Deux Frères*, both in the old village. *Hippocampe*, on the eastern shore of Cap Martin.

Menton

The last city before the border is Menton *(plates 37, 38)*. "Italy begins here, one feels it in the air. Small streets with high houses, narrow and white; the carriage can barely go through. At the entrance and exit the highway is planted with oleander, cactus, and palm trees," Flaubert remarked as he traveled through town in the spring of 1845.[18] The novelist's impression was not wrong, for Menton, like Roquebrune, was then still part of the principality of Monaco. In 1717, Prince Antoine I of Monaco built a mansion in Roquebrune (Carnoles) and established his residence there. In 1848, Menton and Roquebrune seceded from Monaco and rallied to France in 1860.

Menton owes its international fame to Dr. James Henry Bennet, an English physician who, suffering from what he called "advanced pulmonary consumption," came to Menton in 1859 and the following five winters. According to Bennet, Menton's climate greatly improved his health and he was cured. In his book *Winter in the South of Europe* (1861), Bennet boasted of the merits of the lovely Mediterranean village where frost, fog, humidity, and harsh winter winds were unknown. The mild winters, he explained, allowed for a luxuriant vegetation of oranges, lemons, aloes, cactus, and small banana trees. Plenty of sunshine and dry air were good for the lungs and the kidneys, he argued convincingly: "Such a climate is perfection for all who want bracing, renovating, for the very young, the invalid middle-aged, and the very old, in whom vitality, defective or flagging, requires rousing and stimulating."[19]

But Bennet also praised Menton's social life. He described the inhabitants as "a rather handsome race, with Italian features, black hair and dark eyes,"[20] and explained that, besides their local Mentonnais idiom, they also knew Italian and French and were "exceedingly gracious and cordial to strangers."[21] Bennet's book was a bestseller and went through several editions. In his third edition (1865) he added that there was now a small British colony in Menton with a church minister, an English grocer, and a good Pension Anglaise where he was staying. He also reassured the English bourgeoisie that Menton was not a boring town: there was plenty of music, balls, and clubs. Furthermore, the countryside and the little mountain villages around it such as Gorbio and Castellar offered delightful excursions. Britons and Russians flocked to the little Provençal city. As in Nice and Cannes, several grand hotels and hospitals were built to satisfy the demand of this new clientele that included Queen Victoria and a good number of patients suffering from tuberculosis. In 1909, Menton had its casino but, unfortunately, there too World War I brought lucrative tourism to an end.

Menton had its local poets such as Marcel Firpo (1878–1973), who wrote plays, tales, poems, and songs in Mentonnais, such as *Cansù e puesie de Mentan* (1943). Firpo came from a family of stonemasons who had lived in the area for several generations. He worked for the customs office and participated actively in local politics. Firpo was a friend of Monaco's Louis Notari and helped organize the first regional festival in 1931. Another local poet was Louis Moreno, contemporary of Firpo. Son of a local wine merchant, he studied sciences at the University of Marseilles and then succeeded his father in the family business in 1929. For some time he worked with Firpo on the Committee for Local Traditions and also took an active part in politics. With Angelo Graffione he created the folkloric group *A Capelina de Mentan*, for which he composed many songs.

Menton and Roquebrune are proud of their cultural heritage. The local languages are taught in the schools as electives, and the literary and historical bilingual review *Ou païs mentounasc* is published four times a year.

A terra de Mentan nun es una pianüra
Duna verdisce u gran, duna biundisce u spigh:
Û vièie r'han strepaia ad üna rocca düra
E sempre asci car fa despü ru temp antigh.

The country of Menton is not a plain
Where wheat turns green and the sheaf gold:
Our ancestors tore it from the hard rocks
As their forefathers had done before them.

(Marcel Firpo, from "A Terra de Mentan"
[The Country of Menton])[22]

In 1863, thirteen-year-old Robert Louis Stevenson arrived in Menton with his parents for a short vacation. They stayed at Hôtel de Londres and enjoyed themselves so much that they were back the following summer. Stevenson seized the opportunity to take French lessons. He came back in 1873 with his friend Sidney Colvin, on the advice of his doctor, who had detected tuberculosis. This time he stayed several months at the Hôtel Mirabeau. During his time there his French greatly improved. He made the acquaintance of Russian ladies and read George Sand's *Consuelo*. In the spring of 1874, he returned home. A bust of American poet Henry Wadsworth Longfellow near the town hall reminds passers-by that the poet came to Menton in the 1820s. Thomas Carlyle also resided there between December 1866 and March 1867 and worked on his *Reminiscences*.

But Menton's beloved writer is undoubtedly Katherine Mansfield, who arrived in January 1920. She, husband John Middleton Murry, and her friend Ida Baker had been living in Ospedaletti, ten miles across the Italian border. But the lack of a bookstore and the anti-British feeling that prevailed among the Italians forced them to leave. Mansfield's

Katherine Mansfield, photo: Roger-Viollet

cousin Connie Beauchamp lived then in Menton with her friend Jennie
Fullerton at the Villa Flora. Beauchamp invited Mansfield, and she
gladly accepted. But, being ill with tuberculosis, she spent the first three
weeks in L'Hermitage, rue Paul Morillot, a private nursing home. She
had a room with a window opening onto a balcony. There was a lovely
garden full of tangerines, palm trees, and mimosas. Doctors came every
day for a visit. There was plenty of sunshine and that was enough to
put her in good spirits. Beauchamp owned a car and together they traveled to Monaco "to look at the poor gay world at the casino," eat ice
cream, or buy spring hats. Mansfield found the old town clean and romantic. She visited the museum of oceanography there.

Mansfield and her cousin were often the guests of Sydney Schiff, a patron of the arts who resided in Cap Martin. They even drove up the small winding road to La Turbie, "a tiny ancient Roman town, incredibly ancient," and down to Nice, a city that Mansfield found too middle-class. Menton, on the other hand, was her kind of town. "I simply love this little place *love it*."[23] Nestled between the sea and the steep mountains, perfumed by a lush vegetation, Menton was "a lovely little town" where the people were unpretentious and friendly. Mansfield was very sensitive to the beautiful nature that surrounded her, and flowers and sunshine put her in a good mood. "The sun is pure gold and a great swag of crimson roses outside my window fills the room with a sweet smell," she wrote Murry.[24]

Actually, deep in her memory, Menton reminded her of home. "Regarding the South of France I have grown to like far more than ever I did.... There is something about the rocks and stones which reminds me of New Zealand—volcanic—and the sea is really a wonderful colour. Yes I have grown to *love* it. The air in the mountains is wonderful and the pepper trees and the lemons." In contrast, London seemed a pretty dismal place to be. But although her cousin was friendly and hospitable, she and her friend had recently become Catholic and did everything in their power to convert Mansfield, which began to annoy her. Also, as an artist she felt a little out of place there and longed for her "own tribe." Menton was a lovely town, but it was neither London nor Paris and, at times, Mansfield yearned for more literary contacts. So, on April 27, she left for London.

In the summer, Beauchamp bought Isola Bella (Beautiful Island), a small villa in Garavan, Menton's residential East End, and asked Mansfield to be her new tenant. Mansfield could not resist. In September 1920, she and Ida Baker were back in Menton. Isola Bella was conveniently located near the railway station and three hundred yards from the beach. The house was on the side of a steep hill, so that the property was on two levels, with a terrace at the front of the house surrounded by a stone balustrade. There was a garden with flower beds and shrubs, shielded from the rising road by a high stone wall. Mansfield was overjoyed: "The villa is—so far—perfect. The path from the gate to the two doors has a big silver mimosa showering across it. The garden is twice as big as I imagined. One can live in it all day—"[25] The property was planted with magnolias, palm trees, tangerines, and roses. There was also a small vegetable patch, and a gardener came every Friday. The house was small but large enough for the two of them. It had a fully furnished kitchen that "gleamed with copper," a living room "with velvet covered furniture and an immense dead clock and a gilt mirror and two *very* handsome crimson vases." There was also a proper dining room, "equally charming . . . with two french windows, a 'vrai' buffet with silver teapot, coffee and milk jug which catch the flashing eye. All is delightful." Upstairs were four bedrooms. The house had no bathroom but a "large saucer bath." And, there was a telephone!

The view over the bay of Garavan was "*surpassingly* beautiful." In the west was Menton, "the Old Town, built flat against a hill, a solid wall, as it were, of shades and colours is the finest thing I've ever seen." In front of the house and as far as the eye could see spread the "deep hyacinth blue" sea with its "silver clouds floating like sails." September was wonderful. The intense summer heat had disappeared and the morning rain had brought "a thousand green spears up in every corner of the garden." In the evening, the air was filled the smell of pine and charcoal fire. What a contrast with London! Mansfield was enraptured. "Divine evening! Heavenly fair place!" she exclaimed. She did everything she could to entice Murry to come as soon as possible. "My feeling for this little house is that somehow it ought to be ours. It is, I think, a perfect house in its way and just our size."[26]

Mansfield hired Marie, a local woman, to cook and take care of the house. She appreciated Marie's culinary talents and enjoyed her simple attitude toward life. Marie was a "remarkable type . . . the kind of cook Anatole France might have."[27] She did the marketing and cooked with fresh produce every day—"veal with tomatoes, mashed potatoes, *oeufs en neige*"—and served black coffee. Besides Marie, Mansfield had little contact with the French, but she loved to chat with the gardener, who could speak about plants and flowers forever.

The childhood memories that Menton recaptured gave her inspiration. "There is a kind of whiteness in the sky over the sea. I loved

Isola Bella

such days when I was a child. I love them here. In fact, I think, Mentone must be awfully like New Zealand, but ever so much better. . . . I could be content to stay here for years. In fact, I love it as I've never loved any place but my home." The comparison with New Zealand especially evokes Karori, the small village four miles from Wellington where her family, the Beauchamps, lived. Karori was located in a small valley; it had a few farmhouses with fences, horses, hens, a blacksmith's, a wooden church, and a general store, much like Garavan then. "This little place is and always will be for me—the one and the only place. I feel. My heart beats for it as it beats for Karori," she wrote, speaking of Isola Bella. Mansfield's health improved temporarily and she was in good spirits. The little house on the hill had performed a miracle. "You will find Isola Bella in poker work on my heart," she wrote her husband.[28]

When Murry came, they drove to the village of Castellar perched on a hill behind Garavan. "We had a marvelous drive up the mountains here the other day to a very ancient small village called Castellar. These roads wind and wind higher and higher—one seems to drive through centuries too, the boy with the oxen who stands on the hillside with a green branch in his hand, the old women gathering twigs among the olives, the blind peasant with a wild violet pinned on his cap, all these figures seem to belong to any time—And the tiny walled village with a great tree in the cobbled square and the lovely girl looking out the window of flower pots in the Inn. It's all something one seems to have known for ever. I could live here for years and years. I mean away from what they call the world."[29]

Above all, Mansfield loved the French people's passion for life. "There is a kind of freedom, a sense of *living*, not enduring, not existing—but being alive!" she wrote to Murry. She did not care much for French politics but praised the exhilaration of life, which made France "a remarkable country . . . the most civilised in the world." As an artist she could not but revere a country where, according to her, people lived intensely. "I learned more about France from my servant at Mentone than anywhere. She was *pure* French, highly civilized, nervous, eager, and always *alive*, never indifferent as the English are." She also admired the French people's respect for art. "There is always the feeling that Art has its place . . . is accepted by everybody, by the servants, by the rubbish man as well as by all others as something important, necessary, to be proud of. . . . That's what makes living in France such a rest," she wrote to Dorothy Brett from Switzerland, one year after she left Menton.[30]

Comfortably installed in her house and enthusiastic about the country, Mansfield felt inspired. When she was not reading Shakespeare and

Castellar: traditional costumes

her beloved Chekhov, she wrote book reviews and short stories: "The Daughters of the Late Colonel," "The Young Girl," "The Singing Lesson," "The Stranger," "The Lady's Maid," "Poison," "Miss Brill," and "The Life of Ma Parker." However, none of her stories are set in Menton except "The Doves' Nest," which she wrote in Switzerland after she had left Menton. The characters in this story, British women living in Menton and their maid Marie—the name of Mansfield's own maid—are highly reminiscent of Mansfield's experience there. Unfortunately, in the spring of 1921 the situation turned sour. In England, Murry had been unfaithful to her on several occasions, but this time one of his mistresses, Princess Bibesco, was sending him love letters to Isola Bella. Mansfield was angered and deeply hurt. As a result, her health declined rapidly and depression set in. In February, she spent several weeks in bed and in May 1921, following her doctor's advice, she decided to leave. Mansfield and Ida finally went to Switzerland. However, her health continued to deteriorate and she died in Fontainebleau in January 1923.

Today the house still stands but is not open to visitors. Its owner is Italian and the house is closed most of the year. However, the New Zealand government bought a former tool storage room on the first floor and made it into a writing office with a desk and a few bookshelves. Every year a selected New Zealand writer comes to Menton for a couple of months and uses the room to write.

In 1922, the year after Mansfield left Menton, Spanish writer Vicente Blasco Ibanez (1867–1928) arrived there and bought Fontana Rosa *(plate 39)* in Garavan, a five-minute walk from Isola Bella. He was a successful novelist whose republican ideas had forced him into exile. After Paris, Nice, and Monaco, he finally settled on Menton because it reminded him of his native Valencia. Fontana Rosa, named for the spring that had once been in its garden, included two houses on about five acres. Its former owner was a German whose property had been confiscated after World War I. Blasco Ibanez settled there with his wife, children, personal secretary, and servants. He immediately hired workers to restore it, dig up the spring, and create gardens and a cinema. He also installed a library with several hundred books. Unlike Mansfield, Ibanez was well known at the time, and during his stay in Menton he entertained many guests and celebrities. His dream was to dedicate the house to novelists, and to that purpose he commissioned a sculptor to create busts of his favorite writers, including Balzac and Flaubert. Suffering from diabetes, he died at Fontana Rosa at the age of seventy-one. Many celebrities, including Colette, came to visit his grave and express their condolences to his widow and children. His body was later taken home to Spain. During World War II Fontana Rosa was pillaged, its library plundered, and the busts of novelists stolen. The gardens were destroyed and used as a burial ground for soldiers. Since then Fontana Rosa has been partially restored, and the gardens are open to visitors.

In the fall of 1937, Menton received a visit from Vladimir Nabokov, his wife Vera, and their five-year-old son, Dmitri. They had left the Soviet Union for Paris and had spent the summer in Cannes. The Nabokovs stayed at the pension Les Hespérides. Nabokov divided his time between writing in the morning on *Don*, going to the beach in the afternoon, playing chess, and looking for butterflies in the surrounding hills. In July 1938 the Nabokovs left for Cap d'Antibes.

Tourist information. Palais de l'Europe, near the casino. Tel: 04 92 41 76 76. Fax: 04 92 41 76 78. Website: <www.villedementon.com>. Email: <ote@villedementon.com>.

What to see. The Tourist Center organizes visits of sites such as *Fontana Rosa*, and the *Gardens of Serre de la Madone* or *Val Rahmeh*, which contain a wide variety of tropical plants and trees. There is also a tiny *Cocteau Museum* in the fort near the harbor. Tel: 04 93 35 49 71. The *Regional Archeology Museum* is also small but very interesting, and the *Palais Carnolès*, former residence of the princes of Monaco, contains a collection of paintings including Da Vinci, Valadon, Dufy, and Picabia. Admission is free.

Where to stay. ****: *Hôtel des Ambassadeurs*, 3 rue Partourneaux. AC, garage. Tel: 04 93 28 75 75. Fax: 04 93 35 62 32. ***: *Royal Westminster*, promenade du Soleil. AC. Tel: 04 93 28 69 69. Fax: 04 92 10 12 30. *Princess et Richmond*, 617 promenade du Soleil. AC. Tel: 04 93 35 80 20. Fax: 04 93 57 40 20. *L'Aiglon*, 7 avenue de la Madone. AC, pool, parking. Tel: 04 93 57 55 55. Fax: 04 93 35 92 39. *Napoléon*, 29 porte de France. AC, pool, garage. **: *Narev's Hotel*, 12 rue Loredan Larchey. AC, garage. Tel: 04 93 35 21 31. Fax: 04 93 35 21 20. *Hôtel de Londres*, 15 blvd Carnot. AC, parking. Tel: 04 93 35 74 62. Fax: 04 93 41 77 78. B&Bs: Mme Brett, 14 avenue Boyer. Tel: 04 93 28 42 49. M. Gazzano, 151 route de Castellar. Tel: 04 93 57 39 73.

Ste-Agnès: Lavender Festival

Where to eat. Le Lion d'Or, 7 rue Marins. *Le Chaudron,* 28 rue St Michel. *Au Pistou,* 9 quai Gordon Bennet. *A Braijade Meridiounale,* 66 rue Longue.

Mountain Towns: Ste-Agnès, Sospel, Saorge, Tende, St-Dalmas

Those who love the mountains can drive up to the picturesque villages of Ste-Agnès (D 22) or Sospel (D 2566), thirty minutes away, or push even further to Saorge (D 2204) and Tende (N 204), about one hour from Menton *(plates 40, 41).* There, at the foot of Mont Bégo (10,000 feet) is La Vallée des Merveilles (a good hike from St-Dalmas) and its 100,000 ancient and mysterious rock carvings (Office of the Guides: 04 93 04 77 73).

Where to stay. Sospel. B&Bs: *Villa Noelle.* Tel & Fax: 04 93 04 07 08. *Domaine du Paraïs.* Tel: 04 93 04 15 78. *Domaine Sainte Madeleine.* Pool, parking. Tel: 04 93 04 10 48.

 Tende. **: *Terminus.* Tel: 04 9 3 04 96 96. Fax: 04 93 04 96 97. *St-Martin.* Tel: 04 93 04 62 17. *: *Les Mélèzes.* Tel: 04 93 04 95 95. Fax: 04 93 04 95 96.

 St-Dalmas. **: *Le Prieuré.* Tel: 04 93 04 95 95. Fax: 04 93 04 95 96.

Menton is the last city before the Italian border and concludes our literary journey through Provence. Nice's international airport is only thirty minutes away by freeway (A 8) and Marseille's two hours. If you are going back in that direction you can stop at Thoronet Abbey on the way (A 8, exit Cannet-des-Maures). It is the oldest Cistercian abbey in Provence (1160–90), and it is there that troubadour Folquet de Marseille retreated in 1195. Closed during the Revolution of 1789, the abbey has been restored and is open to visitors (Tel: 04 94 60 43 90).

Notes

Introduction

1. René Nelli, *Troubadours et trouvères* (Paris: Hachette, 1979), 37.

Western Provence

1. "Arriver à Avignon par un beau soleil couchant d'automne, c'est une admirable chose." Suzanne Olivé-Basso, *Victor Hugo en Provence* (Avignon: Alain Barthélemy, 1985), 15.

2. Ibid., 25.

3. "Qui n'a pas vu Avignon au temps des Papes, n'a rien vu." Alphonse Daudet, *Lettres de mon moulin* (Paris: Presses Pocket, 1990), 58.

4. Frédéric Mistral, *Lis Isclo d'Or* (Marseille: Laffitte, 1908), preface.

5. "La langue provençale n'est pas morte. Les Troubadours n'ont jamais cessé d'exister." Jean-Baptiste Gaut, *Roumavagi deis Troubaires* (1853), preface.

6. Claude Mauron, *Frédéric Mistral* (Paris: Fayard, 1993), 109.

7. "On voyait des prairies lourdes d'herbes bien grasses, des haies vives d'aubépines, quelques métairies et, en été des meules d'or. De beaux peupliers au bois tendre coupaient les prairies, et souvent un mur de très vieux cyprès abritaient un champ ou une maison contre la bise." Henri Bosco, *Antonin* (Paris: Gallimard, 1980), 16.

8. "A quinze ans j'admirais déjà Mistral à l'égal d'Homère. Je n'ai rien retiré de cette admiration." Henri Bosco, "Mistral" in *Tableau de la littérature française* (Paris: Gallimard 1974), 328.

9. "L'homme m'a séduit aussitôt. L'aspect en était imposant et familier. Grand, beau, calme, une bonhomie naturelle le rendait accessible." Ibid., 329.

10. Jean Boutière, *Biographie des Troubadours* (Paris: Mercure, 1964), 441.

11. "Leur château est très beau et très magnifique. Cette maison a grand air; on y fait bonne chère et on y voit mille gens." Madame de Sévigné, *Correspondance* (Paris: Gallimard, 1978), 3:969.

12. "Mon cher cousin quelle vie!" Ibid., 1059.

13. René Char, *Commune présence* (Paris: Gallimard, 1964), 86–87.

14. Théodore Aubanel, *Li fiho d'Avignoun* (Raphèle-lès-Arles: Marcel Petit, 1980), 246.

15. Petrarch, *Lettres du Vaucluse* (Raphèle-lès-Arles: Marcel Petit, 1989), 57.

16. P. L. Ginguené, ed., *Les oeuvres amoureuses de Pétrarque* (Paris: Garnier, n.d.), 56.

17. Petrarch, *Lettres du Vaucluse*, 27.

18. Ibid., 106.

19. Frédéric Mistral, *Lis Isclo d'Or* (Marseille: Laffitte, 1980), preface.

20. Daudet, *Lettres de mon moulin*, 126.

21. Aubanel, *Li fiho d'Avignoun*.

22. Mistral, *Lis Isclo d'Or*.

23. Boutière, *Biographie des Troubadours*, 513.

24. "Un de ces jolis vins du Rhône qui font rire et qui font chanter." Alphonse Daudet, *Tartarin de Tarascon* (Paris: Livre de Poche, 1983), 16.

25. "De quarante à quarante-cinq ans, petit, gros, trapu, rougeaud . . . " Ibid., 13.

26. Mistral, *Lis Isclo d'Or*, 241.

27. Mistral, *Calendau* (Marseille: Jeanne Laffitte, 1980), 52.

28. "Cet amas poudreux de ruines, de roches sauvages, de vieux palais écussonnés, s'effritant, branlant au vent comme un nid d'aigle." Alphonse Daudet, "Histoire des Lettres" in *Lettres de mon moulin*, 200.

29. "Braves gens, maison bénie! . . . Que de fois, l'hiver, je suis venu là me reprendre à la nature, me guérir de Paris et de ses fièvres, aux saines émanations de nos petites collines provençales. J'arrivais sans prévenir, sûr de l'accueil, annoncé par la fanfare des paons, des chiens de chasse." Daudet, "Histoire des Lettres," 204.

30. "Ni pelouses, ni parterres, rien qui rappelle le jardin, la propriété close; seulement des massifs de pins dans le gris des roches, un parc naturel et sauvage, aux allées en fouillis, toutes glissantes d'aiguilles sèches." Ibid., 203.

31. "Une vieille famille provençale habitait là, il y a vingt ans, non moins originale et charmante que son logis." Ibid., 204.

32. "Je n'écris pas une ligne où vous ne puissiez retrouver l'ombre des pins de là-haut, le bruit de votre mistral et comme un écho de nos causeries cagnardines." Cited by Alain Gérard, *Le Midi de Daudet* (Aix: Edisud, 1988), 42.

33. "Une ruine ce moulin; un débris croulant de pierre, de fer et de vieilles planches, qu'on n'avait pas mis au vent depuis des années et qui gisait, les membres rompus, inutile comme un poète." Daudet, *Lettres de mon moulin*, 204.

34. "Je l'aimais pour sa détresse, son chemin perdu sous les herbes, ces petites herbes de montagne grisâtres et parfumées avec lesquelles le père Gaucher composait son élixir." Ibid., 205.

35. "Tout ce beau paysage provençal ne vit que par la lumière." Ibid., 18.

36. "Le soir, on rencontrait par les chemins le vieux meunier poussant devant lui son âne chargé de gros sacs de farine." Ibid., 29.

37. "Nous étions aux premiers jours de l'*Eglise*, aux heures ferventes et naïves, sans schismes ni rivalités." Daudet, "Histoire des Lettres," 209.

38. "J'en suis du Midi, j'en suis bien. Toute ma sensibilité d'enfant, ma source naturelle vient de là." Jean-Paul Clebert, *Les Daudet* (Paris: Presses de la Renaissance, 1988), 283.

39. "J'aurais voulu rester plus longtemps et y savourer toutes les délicatesses sans nombre du cloître de Saint Trophime." Gustave Flaubert, *Voyages* (Paris: Arléa, 1998), 52.

40. "Ces monuments romains sont comme un squelette dont les os ça et là passent à travers la terre." Ibid., 52.

41. "Les Arlésiennes sont jolies . . . c'est là ce qu'on appelle le type gréco-romain; leur taille est forte et svelte à la fois comme un fût de marbre, leur profil exquis est entouré d'une large bande de velours rouge qui leur passe sur le haut de la tête, se rattache sous leur cou et rehausse ainsi la couleur noire de leurs cheveux et fait nuance avec l'éclat de leur peau, toute chauffée de reflets de soleil." Ibid., 52.

42. Irving Stone, *Dear Theo: The Autobiography of Vincent Van Gogh* (New York: Signet, 1969); passages from the letters, in the order of their quotation, are from pages 331, 334, 336, 345, 345, 340, 388, 368, 385–86, 398, and 394.

43. "Cette merveilleuse petite ville, une des plus pittoresques de France, avec ses balcons sculptés, avec ses vieilles maisons noires aux petites portes moresques, ogivales et basses." Daudet, *Lettres de mon moulin*, 186.

44. George Kates, ed., *Willa Cather in Europe* (New York: Knopf, 1956), 168–69.

45. Ibid., 171–72.

46. Aubanel, *Li fiho d'Avignoun*, 31.

47. "Comme de la mer unie malgré ses vagues, il se dégage de cette plaine un sentiment de solitude, d'immensité, accru encore par le mistral qui souffle sans relâche, sans obstacle, et qui, de son haleine puissante, semble aplanir, agrandir le paysage." Daudet, *Lettres de mon moulin*, 186.

48. "J'aimais la nudité de la Camargue." Simone de Beauvoir, *La force de l'âge* (Paris: Gallimard, 1960), 63.

49. "Des bouquets de tamaris et de roseaux font des îlots comme sur une mer calme." Daudet, *Lettres de mon moulin*, 187.

50. Henri Bosco, *Malicroix* (Paris: Gallimard, 1948), 28–29.

51. Stone, *Dear Theo*, 355–56.

The High Country and Aix-en-Provence

1. Deirdre Bair, *Samuel Beckett* (London: Harcourt Brace Jovanovich, 1978), 282.

2. "Nous avons fait les vendanges, tiens, chez un nommé Bonnely, à Roussillon." Samuel Beckett, *En attendant Godot* (Paris: Editions de Minuit, 1952), 104.

3. "Je le lis avec un plaisir, une avidité qui ne peut se comparer à rien." Marquis de Sade, *Lettres choisies* (Paris: Pauvert, 1963), 49.

4. "J'habitais un vieux château restauré, aux immenses pièces peintes à la chaux, avec des meubles rares et anciens et toute la journée je me promenais dans une campagne de collines, d'oliviers et de cyprès les jours ruisselaient de soleil, les soirs étaient doux et les nuits pleines d'étoiles." Olivier Todd, *Albert Camus: Une vie* (Paris: Gallimard, 1996), 415.

5. Robert Ytier, *Henri Bosco: L'amour de la vie* (Lyon: Aubanel, 1996), 10.

6. Joseph Roumanille, *Li conte provençau* (Raphèle-lès-Arles: Marcel Petit, 1978), 190.

7. Claire Frédéric, *Lazarine de Manosque* (Mane: Alpes de Lumière, 1986), 29.

8. Lazarine Nègre, *Li remembranço*, quoted in Frédéric, 33.

9. "Il faisait bon chez ma mère. On chantait. Antonine sentait la prune, Louisa première la vanille. Louisa seconde mangeait des berlingots." Jean

Giono, *Jean le Bleu* (Paris: Grasset, 1932), 42. Berlingots are hard candies associated especially with Carpentras.

10. "Tout le bonheur de l'homme est dans de petites vallées." Ibid., 250.

11. "Tous les oiseaux d'hiver étaient épouvantés, et ils s'en allaient dans les collines en appelant tristement comme pour la fin du monde." Ibid., 104.

12. "J'ai vu des baleines endormies dans l'écume de collines." Giono, *Noé* (Paris: Gallimard, 1961), 64.

13. "J'aimais beaucoup la tendresse timide de son cœur forcené." Ibid., 175

14. "Son coeur est une table de multiplication. Elle se réveille la nuit et, à voix basse, elle refait le compte de ses camions." Jean Giono, *Manosque des plateaux* (Paris: Gallimard, 1986), 74.

15. "Elle pointe les prix avec son doigt . . . regarde dans la plaine et dans la colline ce qu'elle pourrait bien arracher et vendre." Ibid., 74.

16. "Un pain trop cuit. De la croûte, pas de mie." Ibid., 98.

17. "J'ai vécu toute ma vie dans ce pays généreux. Les leçons que m'ont données la vaste ondulation des collines, la vallée largement ouverte, les plateaux sans limites, le ciel si profondément arqué qu'on n'en peut pas ignorer la rondeur, sont les leçons qu'ont reçues tous les paysans de ce territoire." Giono, *Noé*, 68.

18. "Je veux qu'on sache bien que je ne suis pas dans un wagon, dans un tramway, sur les boulevards de Marseille avec un carnet à la main, en train de *copier la réalité;* que de tout de ce temps-là, au contraire, j'étais *les mains dans les poches;* qu'au fond, ce que j'écris—(même quand je me force à être très prés de la réalité)—ce n'est pas ce que je vois, mais ce que je *revois.*" Giono, 56–57.

19. "Un débris de hameau, à mi-chemin entre la plaine où ronfle la vie tumultueuse des batteuses à vapeur et le grand désert lavandier, le pays du vent, à l'ombre froide des monts de Lure." Jean Giono, *Colline* (Paris: Grasset, 1929), 9.

20. "Un bourg cendreux dissimulé dans des pierrailles et des forêts naines de chênes gris." Jean Giono, *Le hussard sur le toit* (Paris: Gallimard, 1951), 41.

21. "Répandus par petits bosquets sur des pâturages très maigres couleur de renard, sur des terres à perte de vue, ondulées sous des lavandes et des pierrailles." Ibid., 46.

22. "Collé contre le trenchant du plateau comme un petit nid de guêpes." Jean Giono, *Regain* (Paris: Grasset, 1930), 16.

23. "Un pays de coteaux, lieu de tendresses, plein de fleurs." Jean Giono, *Deux cavaliers de l'orage* (Paris: Gallimard, 1965), 47.

24. "C'est, entre deux flancs de montagnes, un petit bourg paisible, sans bruit. Le mot qu'on y prononce le plus souvent c'est: soleil. On prend le soleil. On va prendre le soleil. Venez prendre le soleil. Il est allé prendre le soleil. Il ne fait pas soleil. Il va faire soleil. Il me tarde qu'il fasse soleil. Voilà la soleil, je vais prendre le soleil. Ainsi de suite. C'est le plus gros bruit." Jean Giono, *Les âmes fortes* (Paris: Gallimard, 1950), 141.

25. "Avant qu'un commerçant ait fait un tour sur lui-même, tu tuerais un âne à coups de figues. Les sucres d'orge fondent dans les vitrines." Ibid.

26. Frederick Goldin, *Lyrics of the Troubadours and Trouvères* (New York: Doubleday, 1973), 187.

27. "C'était un large pays tout charrué et houleux comme la mer; ses horizons dormaient sous des brumes. Il était fait de collines forestières en terres rouges sous des bosquets de pins tordus, des vals à labours, des plainettes avec une ferme ou deux, des villages collés au sommet des rochers comme des gâteaux de miel." Jean Giono, *Le chant du monde* (Paris: Gallimard, 1934), 28.

28. "Il parle d'une autre Provence que la mienne car cette terre est faite de 'pays'. Je chante les hauts plateaux, les montagnes qui ressemblent à l'Olympe avec la couronne de nuages qui touche au ciel. Je chante la pierre dure et sèche, les 'bancas', l'olivier et l'amandier. Bosco, c'est l'homme des collines ondoyantes, des piémonts fertiles, des plaines riches et grasses. Nos personnages se ressemblent parfois car ils ont des origines terriennes profondes. Ils sont enracinés, mais chez lui il y a beaucoup d'eau. Les miens la cherchent ou l économisent." Ytier, *Henri Bosco*, 57.

29. "Des landes incultes, de vastes champs de cailloux, des terrains vagues creusés de loin en loin par des carrières abandonnées." Emile Zola, *Les mystères de Marseille* (Paris: Casterman, 1978), 34.

30. "A cette époque les précipices de Jaumegarde gardaient encore toute leur sinistre horreur et les promeneurs ne s'aventuraient guère dans cet entonnoir funèbre de rochers rougeâtres." Ibid., 34.

31. "Que des rois se volent un trône ou que des républiques se fondent, la ville s'agite à peine. On dort à Plassans, quand on se bat à Paris." Emile Zola, *La fortune des Rougon* (Paris: Presses Pocket, 1999), 101.

32. John Rewald, ed., *Cézanne:Corrrespondance* (Paris, Grasset, 1978), 18.

33. "D'ici la montagne avec sa fantastique voilure de rochers blancs, est comme un vaisseau-fantôme de plein jour." Giono, *Noé*, 151.

1. Frédéric Mistral, *Lis Isclo d'Or* (Marseille: Laffitte Reprints, 1980), 106.

2. Marcel Pagnol, *Marius* (Paris: de Fallois, 1988), 28.

3. "C'est le lendemain, en me réveillant, que j'ai aperçu la Méditerranée, toute couverte encore des vapeurs du matin qui montaient pompées par le soleil; ses eaux azurées étaient étendues entre les parois grises des rochers de la baie avec un calme et une solennité antique. . . . J'aime bien la Méditerranée, elle a quelque chose de grave et de tendre qui fait penser à la Grèce, quelque chose d'immense et de voluptueux qui fait penser à l'Orient." Flaubert, *Voyages* (Paris: Arléa, 1988), 52.

4. "Marseille est une jolie ville, bâtie de grandes maisons qui ont l'air de palais." Ibid., 54.

5. "La Rue de la Darse étaient pleine de marins de toutes les nations, juifs, arméniens, grecs tous en costume national, encombrant les cabarets, riant avec les filles, renversant des pots de vin, chantant, dansant, faisant l'amour à leur aise." Ibid., 53.

6. "Le soleil, le grand air du Midi entrent librement dans ses longues rues; on y sent je ne sais quoi d'oriental, on y marche à l'aise, on respire content, la peau se dilate et hume le soleil comme un grand bain de lumière. Marseille est maintenant ce que devait être la Perse dans l'antiquité, Alexandrie au moyen âge: un capharnaum, une babel de toutes les nations, où l'on voit des cheveux blonds, ras, de grandes barbes noires, la peau blanche rayée de veines bleues, le teint olivâtre de l'Asie, des yeux bleus, des regards noirs, tous les costumes, la veste, le manteau, le drap, la toile. . . . Vous entendez parler des langues inconnues, le slave, le sanscrit, persan, le scythe, l'égyptien, tous les idiomes, ceux qu'on parle au pays des neiges, ceux qu'on soupire dans les terres du Sud." Ibid., 54.

7. "Sur une estrade au fond se tenaient quatre à cinq personnages richement vêtus; il y avait le roi avec sa couronne, la reine, un paysan à qui on avait enlevé sa fille et qui se disputait avec le ravisseur pendant que la mère désolée et s'arrachant les cheveux chantait une espèce de complainte avec des exclamations nombreuses comme dans les tragédies d'Eschyle." Ibid.

8. "C'était à perte de vue un fouillis de mâts, de vergues, se croisant dans tous le sens. Pavillons de tous les pays, russes, grecs, suédois, tunisiens, américains. . . . De temps en temps, entre les navires, un morceau de mer, comme une grande moire tachée d'huile . . . des mousses qui s'appelaient dans toutes

les langues. . . . Sur le quai, au milieu des ruisseaux qui venaient des savon-neries, verts, épais, noirâtres, chargés d'huile et de soude, tout un peuple de douaniers, de commissionnaires, de portefaix avec leur bogheys attelés de pe-tits chevaux corses . . . des marchands de pipes, des marchands de singes, de perroquets . . . Des vendeuses de moules de clovisses . . . des matelots passant avec des pots de goudron, des marmites fumantes, de grands paniers pleins de poulpes." Alphonse Daudet, *Tartarin de Tarascon* (Paris: Livre de Poche 1983), 60–61.

9. Sidney Colvin, ed., *The Letters of Robert Louis Stevenson* (London: Methuen, 1880–87), 2:91, 92.

10. Vincent O'Sullivan and Margaret Scott, eds., *The Collected Letters of Katherine Mansfield* (Oxford: Oxford University Press, 1984), 1:200.

11. Simone de Beauvoir, *La force de l'âge* (Paris: Gallimard, 1960), 63.

12. "Je me rappelle mon arrivée à Marseille comme si elle avait marqué dans mon histoire un tournant absolument neuf." Ibid., 93.

13. "Sous le ciel bleu, des tuiles ensoleillées, des trous d'ombre, des pla-tanes couleur d'automne; au loin des collines et le bleu de la mer; une rumeur montait de la ville avec une odeur d'herbes brûlées et des gens allaient, ve-naient au creux des rues noires." Ibid., 93.

14. "J'eus le coup de foudre." Ibid., 94.

15. "Je grimpai sur toutes ses rocailles, je rôdai dans toutes ses ruelles, je respirai le goudron et les oursins du Vieux-Port, je me mêlai aux foules de la Canebière, je m'assis dans des allées, dans des jardins, sur des cours paisibles où la provinciale odeur des feuilles mortes étouffait celle du vent marin." Ibid.

16. "Je descendis dans toutes les calanques, j'explorai les vallées, les gorges, les défilés. Parmi les pierres aveuglantes où ne s'indiquait pas le moin-dre sentier j'allais, épiant les flèches—bleues, vertes, rouges, jaunes—qui me conduisaient je ne savais où; parfois je les perdais, je les cherchais, tournant en rond, battant les buissons aux arômes aigus, m'écorchant à des plantes encore neuves pour moi: les cistes résineux, les genévriers, les chênes verts, les as-phodèles jaunes et blancs." Ibid., 95.

17. "Jamais je ne m'ennuyai: Marseille ne s'épuisait pas." Ibid., 105.

18. "Nichée sur les coteaux de la vallée de l'Huveaune, et traversée par la route poudreuse qui allait de Marseille à Toulon." Marcel Pagnol, *La gloire de mon père* (Paris: de Fallois, 1988), 21.

19. "Je suis né dans la ville d'Aubagne, sous le Garlaban couronné de chèvres, au temps des derniers chevriers. Garlaban, c'est une énorme tour de

roches bleues, plantée au bord du Plan de l'Aigle, cet immense plateau rocheux qui domine la verte vallée de l'Huveaune." Ibid., 11.

20. "On y cuisait des tuiles, des briques et des cruches, on y bourrait de boudins et des andouilles." Ibid., 21.

21. "Un petit village, planté en haut d'une colline, entre deux vallons." Ibid., 82.

22. "Partis à la rencontre du soleil, ils essayaient de dépasser le clocher." Ibid., 85.

23. "La Bastide Neuve était la dernière bâtisse, au seuil du désert, et l'on pouvait marcher pendant trente kilomètres sans rencontrer que les ruines basses de trois ou quatre fermes du moyen âge, et quelques bergeries abandonnées." Ibid., 102.

24. "Nous sortîmes du village: alors commença la féerie et je sentis naître un amour qui devait durer toute ma vie. Un immense paysage en demicercle montait devant moi jusqu'au ciel: de noires pinèdes, séparées par des vallons, allaient mourir comme des vagues au pied de trois sommets rocheux." Ibid., 87.

25. "Je quittais le chemin, je courus toucher les petites feuilles. Un parfum puissant s'éleva comme un nuage, et m'enveloppa tout entier. C'était une odeur inconnue, une odeur sombre et soutenue, qui s'épanouit dans ma tête et pénétra mon coeur." Ibid., 91.

26. Louis Brauquier, *Je connais des îles lointaines: Poésies complètes* (Paris: Table Ronde, 1994), 102.

27. Anne Olivier Bell, ed., *The Diary of Virginia Woolf* (Harmondsworth: Penguin, 1982), 3:8.

28. Nigel Nicholson, ed., *A Change of Perspective: The Letters of Virginia Woolf* (London: Hogarth Press, 1977), 3:176.

29. Anne Olivier Bell, *Diary of Virginia Woolf*, 3:8.

30. Ibid.

31. Quentin Bell, *Virginia Woolf: A Biography* (New York: Harcourt Brace Jovanovich, 1972), 124.

32. Nicholson, *Letters of Virginia Woolf*, 3:481.

33. Ibid., 480.

34. Anne Olivier Bell, *Diary of Virginia Woolf*, 5:18

35. Quentin Bell, *Virginia Woolf*, 126.

36. Anne Olivier Bell, *Diary of Virginia Woolf*, 3:139.

37. Virginia Woolf, *The Waves* (London: Hogarth Press, 1943), 5.

38. O' Sullivan, *Collected Letters of Katherine Mansfield;* passages quoted are from 1:220, 223, and 238.

39. Anthony Alpers, *The Life of Katherine Mansfield* (New York: Viking, 1980), 284.

40. Colvin, *Letters of Robert Louis Stevenson,* 2:144.

41. Ibid.

42. R. W. B. Lewis, *Edith Wharton: A Biography* (New York: Harper & Row, 1975), 520.

43. "[G]ardé par un dragon aux écailles de petites vagues insolentes qui vous crachent une salive froide à la figure." Hugues de La Touche, *Sur les pas de Jean Cocteau* (Nice: Rom, 1998), 81.

44. "Une bouilloire en délire." Ibid., 82.

45. George Kates, ed., *Willa Cather in Europe* (New York: Knopf, 1956); passages quoted are from pages 154–59 and 161.

46. "Le Lavandou est une merveille. . . . Il ressemble à la baie de Naples . . . la plage se prolongeait en un large croissant de sable fin, composé d'une poussière de petits coquillages blancs, que venait battre doucement une eau transparente. Un ruisseau nommé Bataillier, bien qu'il semblât à la fois paisible et peu navigable, serpentait dans la vallée parmi les cannes et venait se jeter au milieu de la baie." De La Touche, 66–67.

47. "On y sent la pêche et le goudron qui flambe, la saumure et la coque des barques." Guy de Maupassant, *Sur l'eau* (Paris: Encre, 1979), 113.

48. "Le peuple boiteux et paralysé des vieux marins qui se chauffe au soleil sur les bancs de Pierre . . . leurs visages et leurs mains sont ridés, tannés, brunis, séchés par les vents, les fatigues, les embruns." Ibid.

49. "Un bois de contes de fées, de lianes fleuries, de plantes aromatiques aux odeurs puissantes et de grands arbres magnifiques." Ibid., 136.

50. "Je l'ai trouvée au bord d'une route que craignent les automobiles, et derrière la plus banale grille." Colette, *La Treille Muscate* (Paris: Lubineau, 1955), 9.

51. "Il n'y a pas de 'jardin' remercions le hasard: il y a les grands plumages jaunes qui balaient l'azur, les mimosas d'où pleut le pollen avec le parfum." Ibid., 15.

52. "Je me retrouve dans un jardin de Seine et Oise . . . les oeillets d'inde, les glycines, les géraniums et le basilic qui jette son odeur comme un sort." De La Touche, *Sur les pas de Jean Cocteau,* 59.

53. "La mer, continue, prolonge, ennoblit, enchante cette parcelle d'un lumineux rivage." Colette, *La Treille Muscate,* 11.

54. "J'aime les vieux villages provençaux qui épousent la pointe de leurs collines. La ruine y est sèche, saine, dépouillée d'herbe et de moisissure verte, et seul le géranium-lierre fleuri de rose pend à la noire oreille béante d'une tour." Colette, *Naissance du jour* (Paris: Flammarion, 1966), 233. Translation as *Break of Day* by Enid McLeod (New York: Noonday Press, 1993), 130.

55. "L'étroit marais où l'eupatoire, la statice, la scabieuse apportent trois nuances de mauve, le grand jonc fleuri sa grappe de graines brunes comestibles, le myrte sa blanche odeur, blanche, blanche, amère, qui heurte les amygdales, blanche à provoquer la nausée et l'extase—le tamaris son brouillard rose, le roseau sa massue à fourrure de castor." Colette, *Naissance du jour*, 119; *Break of Day*, 51.

56. "Le peu de nues qu'évapore la mer chaude, les entraîne au bas du ciel, les embrase et les tord en chiffons de feu." Colette, *Naissance du jour*, 116; *Break of Day*, 49.

57. "Une vieille lune usée se promène dans le bas du ciel, poursuivie par un petit nuage surprenant de netteté, de consistance métallique, agrippé au disque entamé comme un poisson à une tranche de fruit flottante." Colette, *Naissance du jour*, 137; *Break of Day*, 64.

58. "C'est seulement avant midi qu'on rencontre sur la Croisette tous les nobles étrangers . . . Les femmes jeunes et sveltes,—il est de bon goût d'être maigre—vêtues à l'anglaise, vont d'un pas rapide, escortées par de jeunes hommes alertes en tenue de lawn-tennis. Mais de temps en temps, on rencontre un pauvre être décharné qui se traîne d'un pas accablé, appuyé au bras d'une mère, d'un frère ou d'une sœur. Ils toussent et halètent ces misérables, enveloppés de châles malgré la chaleur, et nous regardent passer avec des yeux profonds, désespérés et méchants." Maupassant, *Sur l'eau*, 48.

59. F. Scott Fitzgerald, *Lettres à Zelda* (Paris: Gallimard, 1985), 123.

60. F. Scott Fitzgerald, *Tender Is the Night* (Harmondsworth: Penguin, 1995); passages from the novel, in the order of their quotation, are from pages 105, 81, 65, and 94–95.

61. "Toute cette contrée, naguère, l'imprégnait la langue d'oc. Elle ne végète plus que sous quelques crânes étriqués de vieillards au parapet des villages qui dominent les étendues. Le français l'a sonnée. Vous trouvez du *pullover* et *push* jusque dans des patelins comme Aiglun." Jacques Audiberti, *Les tombeaux ferment mal* (Paris: Gallimard, 1963), 25.

62. "Des tartans à voile rouge foncé qui venaient de Porto-Maurizio charger de la terre à marmites pour les misérables tambouilles italiennes." Ibid., 14.

63. "Alors le provençal vivait encore un peu, solidaire des objets habituels, partageant avec eux le même suc brun." Ibid.

64. Michel Giroud, *Audiberti* (Paris: Seghers, 1973), 159. First published in *Vive Guitare*, a collection of poems (Paris: Laffort, 1946).

From Nice to Menton

1. "Viele verborgne Flecke und Höhen aus der Landschaft Nizzas sind mir durch unvergeßliche Augenblicke geweiht; jene entscheidende Partie, welche den Titel Von alten und neuen Tafeln trägt, wurde im beschwerlichsten Aufsteigen von der Station zu dem wunderbaren maurischen Felsenneste Eza gedichtet." Friedrich Nietzsche, *Ecce Homo* (Frankfurt: Insel Verlag, 1979), 108.

2. "Ich bin ein Wanderer und ein Bergsteiger . . . ich liebe die Ebenen nicht." Friedrich Nietzsche, *Also sprach Zarathustra* (Paris: Aubier Flammarion, 1969), 2:11.

3. "Eine gute Reede, an der auch fremde Schiffe gern vor Anker gingen." Ibid.

4. Friedrich Nietzsche, *Die fröhliche Wissenschaft* (Frankfurt: Insel Verlag, 1982), 294.

5. Henri Troyat, *Tchekhov* (Paris: Flammarion, 1984), 243.

6. Ibid., 301.

7. André Compan, *Anthologie de la littérature niçoise* (Toulon: Astrado, 1971).

8. Joseph-Rosalinde Rancher, *Lou fablié nissart* (Nice: Lou Sourgentin, 1985), 94.

9. "Les pêcheurs descendaient sur le rivage à 3 heures du matin. Ils examinaient la mer et décidaient ou non de partir ou non pour la première pose des filets. Ils ne se fiaient pas à la météo: le temps se contrôle au coup d'œil." Louis Nucéra, *Chemin de la Lanterne* (Paris: Grasset, 1981), 175.

10. "Le son est intermédiaire entre le *é* le *è*, le *eu*—phonétique à part dont les Niçois sont dépositaires—contient toutes les philosophies de l'univers. Il a de multiples usages: réponse, salut, narration, manière de lier connaissance, résumé de mâles épopées, art d'éventer les pièges, plaidoyer, panégyrique; traduit divers états d'âme: routine, extravagance, jugement, je-m'enfichisme, spleen chronique, torpeur née du pastis et du rosé." Ibid., 117.

11. "J'habitais cette vieille maison sur le port, un peu napolitaine, com-

plètement décrépie avec des draps qui séchaient à toutes les fenêtres de la cour." Gérard de Cortanze, *Le Clézio: Vérités et légendes* (Paris: Editions du Chêne, 1999), 52.

12. "Un hôtel hanté fut l'Hôtel Welcome à Villefranche. Il est vrai que nous le hantâmes, car rien ne l'y prédisposait. Il y avait bien la rue couverte. Il y avait bien les remparts de Vauban et la caserne qui, le soir, évoque les absurdes magnificences du rêve. Il y avait bien, à gauche Nice à droite Monte-Carlo, et leurs architectures sournoises. Mais l'Hôtel Welcome était simplement charmant et paraissait n'avoir rien à craindre. On avait passé une couche de peinture jaune sur les trompe-l'oeil à l'italienne de sa façade. Le golfe abritait les escadres. Les pêcheurs réparaient les filets et dormaient au soleil." Jean Cocteau, *La difficulté d'être* (Monaco: Editions du Rocher, 1983), 83.

13. "On dessina, on inventa, on se visita de chambre en chambre. Il naissait une mythologie dont *Orphée* résume le style." Ibid., 84.

14. Hugues de La Touche, *Sur les pas de Jean Cocteau* (Nice: Rom, 1998), 49.

15. "Je ne suis ni dessinateur ni peintre. Mes dessins sont de l'écriture dénouée et renouée autrement." Jean Cocteau, *Le passé défini* (Paris: Gallimard, 1983), 1: 23.

16. "Un bruit d'argent, continu comme celui des flots, un bruit profond, léger, redoutable, emplit l'oreille dès l'entrée." Guy de Maupassant, *Sur l'eau* (Paris: Encre, 1979), 151.

17. Joseph Hone, *W. B. Yeats* (Penguin, 1962), 469.

18. "L'Italie commence, on le sent dans l'air. Petites rues à hautes maisons blanches, étroites; à peine si la voiture y peut passer. Avant d'arriver et en sortant, la grande route est plantée de lauriers-roses, cactus et palmiers." Flaubert, *Voyages* (Paris: Arléa, 1998), 102.

19. James Henry Bennet, *Winter in the South of Europe*, 3rd ed. (London: n p., 1865) 124.

20. Ibid., 169.

21. Ibid., 172.

22. Marcel Firpo, *Cansù e puesie de Mentan* (Bordighera, 1943).

23. Vincent O'Sullivan and Margaret Scott, eds., *The Collected Letters of Katherine Mansfield* (Oxford: Clarendon Press, 1993), 3:277.

24. Ibid., 280.

25. John Middleton Murry, ed., *The Letters of Katherine Mansfield* (Hamburg: Albatros, 1934), 260.

26. Ibid., 261, 266, 267, 264.
27. Ibid., 264.
28. Ibid., 277, 287.
29. Ibid., 295.
30. Ibid., 369.

Index of Names

Page references in italic type denote illustrations; *84f* and *180f* refer to color plates contained in the color sections following pages 84 and 180, respectively.